THE
SENECANS

THE
SENECANS

Four Men and Margaret Thatcher

PETER STOTHARD

OVERLOOK DUCKWORTH
NEW YORK • LONDON

This edition first published in hardcover in the United States and the United Kingdom in 2016 by Overlook Duckworth, Peter Mayer Publishers, Inc.

NEW YORK
141 Wooster Street
New York, NY 10012
www.overlookpress.com
For bulk and special sales, please contact sales@overlookny.com,
or write us at the above address

LONDON
30 Calvin Street
London E1 6NW
info@duckworth-publishers.co.uk
www.ducknet.co.uk

PICTURE CREDITS: Page ix and 221 © News UK & © Press Association; p1 © Tarker/Bridgeman Art Library; p4 © Peter Stothard; p7 © Peter Brookes/News UK; p9 © Matthew Richardson/Alamy; p15 © Press Association; p29 © The Spectator; p37 © Marcus Cyron/Creative Commons; p41 © Peter Stothard; p45 and 269 © The Estate of Beryl Bainbridge; p47 © Rex Features; p49 © Hazel O'Leary; p63 © Peter Stothard; p73 © Sally Soames; p79 © Peter Stothard; p89 © Sue Foll; p93 © News UK; p99 © News UK; p115 © Sue Foll; p125 © News UK; p131 © Peter Stothard; p139 © Peter Stothard; p155 © Richard Willson/News UK; p167 © Peter Stothard; p177 © News UK; p189 © Wellcome Collection; p197 © Peter Stothard; p248 © Peter Brookes/News UK; p255 © Hazel O'Leary; p265 © Shutterstock; p269 © The Estate of Beryl Bainbridge; p272 © Peter Stothard; p274 © Alamy; p277 © Estate of Zsuzsi Roboz/Messum's

Cataloging-in-Publication Data is available from the Library of Congress

Book design and typeformatting by Bernard Schleifer
Manufactured in the United States of America
ISBN US: 978-1-4683-1342-0
ISBN UK: 978-0-7156-5137-7

FIRST EDITION
2 4 6 8 10 9 7 5 3 1

To Cordoba

Contents

FOUR MEN AND MARGARET THATCHER

David Hart (1944-2011): educated at Eton College; film-producer; property developer; political adviser; arms industry lobbyist; farmer; playwright; novelist

Frank Johnson (1943-2006): educated at Shoreditch Secondary Modern; journalist for the *Sunday Express*, *Daily Telegraph* and *The Times*; parliamentary sketch-writer; editor of *The Spectator* (1995-99)

Sir Ronald Millar (1919-98): educated at Charterhouse and King's College, Cambridge; actor; playwright; writer of musicals; Hollywood screenwriter; speechwriter

Margaret Thatcher (1925-2013): educated at Kesteven and Grantham Girls School and Somerville College, Oxford; research chemist; barrister; politician; British Prime Minister (1979-90)

Lord (Woodrow) Wyatt (1918-97): educated at Eastbourne College and Worcester College, Oxford; Labour politician; Conservative newspaper commentator; businessman; playwright; political adviser; diarist

September 2014

Quintus Metellus Pius was so anxious for his deeds to be praised that he consulted poets from Cordoba – even though their Latin came with a foreign accent

—CICERO *In defence of Archias,* 62 BC

Puente Romano, Cordoba

5.9.14

Believe me. I was serious twelve years ago when I said that I was going to stop writing about politicians, stop forever the laptop key in my head that predicts a T into Thatcher, an M into Major, a B into Blair. I made a promise to myself when I stopped being the Editor of *The Times*. I promised to go back to what I did before I was a journalist at all, back two thousand years to books and cities of books, to Naples, Alexandria and here, beside a Roman bridge over slow, brown water, in Roman Spain. There seemed no reason that Margaret T, her heirs and successors, would ever trouble me again. Twenty-five years with them was enough.

I meant it too when I said I was never going to write one of those 'memoirs of the print trade' that I have occasionally enjoyed. Last week by the River Thames, when I left Thomas More Square for the last time and came here to Cordoba, there were lives like mine all over my floor. Turn right out of the lifts on Tower Three, Level Six: turn ten yards along the carpet tiles, and there you would have found them, pages and pages of Born, Learnt, First Break, First onto Fleet Street, scoops, scrapes, prizes, always more success than failure, often successes that would have been even greater if some greater betrayal had not occurred.

Last week all these books, the kind I always said I would not write, were waiting for packers to take them to the Oxfam shop nearest to London Bridge. This week *Dogs and Lampposts*, by my fellow editor, Richard Stott, and dozens of others, by friends and the not so friendly, are safely under charitable supervision, looking for good new homes.

So no, my life is now different. I edit the *Times Literary Supplement*, the *TLS*, a very different kind of paper. Over four decades I have been a critic, reporter, a writer of opinions, an editor, and now I am almost a student again. When I arrived yesterday at this café table by the Guadalquivir river, my aim was to finish a book which stars an ancient Roman, a writer who was born in Cordoba around the time when BC turned to AD. Lucius Annaeus Seneca was his name, sometimes Seneca the Younger because his father too lived and wrote here and lived off the profits of olives as everyone here always has.

Why Seneca? He wrote books which were important to me both when I was a journalist and before. He was a politician who wrote plays, or a playwright who played politics (people still argue which came first), or maybe he was even more important as a philosopher. Cordoba has been a city of words and power for longer than anywhere west of Rome, one of the earliest homes for poets paid to make virtues more renowned, a first base for flatterers with foreign accents.

Seneca was the heir to a family business of writing and politics here, the writing of speeches for farmers and financiers in this hottest, driest part of Spain and also in Rome where the younger Seneca grew up to be himself one of the richest and most powerful men in the world. He became a prime minister (not yet in capitals) at the court of the Emperor Nero, possibly the richest great writer ever to have earned a fee.

So Seneca is much on my mind, his arguments, Stoic arguments as they are known, small questions about cold water, travel and alcohol as well as the big questions, how to survive in dangerous times, how to live a good life in even the worst of times. I found him first when I was young in the

1960s and secondly when Margaret Thatcher was in power almost 2,000 years after his death.

I have brought to his birthplace a story which also stars four courtiers of the Thatcher age. That is my aim, a portrait of lesser characters who can sometimes shed light on the greater. Their names are enough for now: David Hart, Ronald Millar, Woodrow Wyatt and Frank Johnson. All served Margaret Thatcher in different ways.

This is an account of plotting and principles. It comes from an age which in Downing Street and surrounding streets was both a Reading and a Believing Age. So much was different then.

What I need to do here in Cordoba is to read again what I have written and see what I want anyone else to read. This is a book that has come into being in a curious way. Five months ago I had no fixed plan for *The Senecans*, not for this year, maybe for next year, as I've said in many past years. What made me begin was a strange encounter with my own past.

But in order to write this book I had to break some of those earlier promises about putting politics behind me. Accept, please, that I did not break them lightly. Five months ago I did not set out to recall stories of these men around Margaret Thatcher. Remembering is hard work. Answering someone else's questions is not what I wanted to do.

Even less did I intend anything like that other kind of memoir, the Editor's career, the ideal obituary, the *apologia pro sua vita* as Seneca would have seen it. There is much in *The Senecans* that a writer of his own newspaper life, anxious to grasp some twig of posterity, might sensibly have omitted. Editing is my profession but it seems too late for much self-censorship now.

What I did was to answer the questions of a peculiarly persistent interviewer, a woman who I would at most times have seen briefly or not at all, a writer herself, a diligent researcher at what was for her a fortuitous time, months when my mood was to remember rather than forget.

Miss R was not my first interviewer with research in mind. This was not the first time that a writer about Margaret Thatcher asked me to help. I saw things that others did not. Newspaper editors see many things. But this year, this time, was different. Miss R disturbed me from the start and somehow I was ready to be disturbed.

Each night, I wrote down what she said and what I said in return. It is she who set the terms in April, posed the questions till August, waited for the answers and, only last week, did I understand why.

April 2014

*Almost nothing is more disgraceful than not know-
ing how to give or to receive benefits. If benefits are
badly placed, they are badly acknowledged, and, when
we complain of their not being reciprocated, it is too
late. When we are about to lend money, we are careful to inquire into our debtor; but our benefits we give,
or rather throw, away*
— SENECA *On Giving and Getting*

Thomas More Square, London, E1

2.4.14

'When did you first see Mrs Thatcher?'

Miss Robbins is the speaker's name. She holds the letter that I sent her. She screws it into a ball in her hand. She snaps out her question and seems set to snap again, unsettled, perhaps, by the wreckage around her feet, the tottering boxes and tumbling paper piles.

There is unsettlement all around. I am about to be moved from the north bank to the south bank of the River Thames. Only for another five months will I be here.

She stops, unscrews my letter, flattens it between her hands and stares down at the address.

'Thomas More Square?'

She voices the question mark as taxi drivers do. A square? This is East London where there are no squares of the shape you see in Euclid or the West End. TMS (as we call it) is a tall glass tower, with concrete slabs and a sandwich shop on one side, a road to a housing estate on another and two lower towers completing a shape I cannot name.

We are together looking down at Wapping, the north bank of the Thames that was so notorious a battleground of the Thatcher years. If we push out the boundaries until we find some sort of imaginable square there is first the Highway, the Ratcliff Highway as it used to be called in the days of Jack the Ripper, the press gangs for Nelson's navy and the marches against Oswald Mosley's blackshirts. Opposite the crawling Highway of lorries runs the empty, broader river, slow brown in a briefly straight line from Tower Bridge.

In the view through the window in front of me is a press gang of a different kind, a former home of four great newspapers, red brick and glass, fiercely fought for when I arrived there in 1986. Beyond and further in front, if our minds travel far enough, are Essex and the North Sea. Behind me is the slab of stone that gives our address its name, the place where England's once greatest writer and reader of Latin was executed by an axe-man in the summer of 1535.

'Thomas More Square?' Miss R has a list and a chart and asks the question again.

'I have not been up here long', I say. For much, much longer I was down there.' I point to the abandoned offices of *The Times*, the newspaper through which I first met Margaret Thatcher and which I edited for more than a decade.

'Who was Thomas More?' She juts out her jaw as though to say that she has just temporarily forgotten.

'He hardly matters if you are interested in Margaret Thatcher', I reply.

'Tell me anyway', she says, kicking aside a pile of old books as though clearing a seat in a bar. I offer to find her a chair. She chooses a pile of modern political novels instead.

'Thomas More', I respond, 'was a great man of Latin. He used many of the texts you are trampling on now. But he got his gong in history for being bloody-minded, for burning people who disagreed with him and failing to recognise Henry VIII's second wife. He lost his head for that.'

She stares straight at me, then down again at my letter to her and beneath it her own letter to me.

'I know where you are. I know why you are here and where you are going. You know what I want to talk about. When did you first see Margaret Thatcher?'

I wonder if I should ask her to leave. I have other things to do. She is irritating me already. The office seems suddenly hot behind its sixth-floor sheets of glass. Temperature controls, like other controls, are failing as our last months here pass by.

It was last June when she wrote to me first, with questions for her thesis on 'The Thatcher Court', questions about the lesser courtiers whom she knew I knew, the 'Rosencrantzes and Guildensterns', as she put it, not the Hamlets. Although she wrote a persuasive letter, I was not persuaded at first, only when she wrote again last week. By then I was surrounded by so many relics of her chosen time, so many boxes for the removal men. I was staring for the last time at so many places where those courtiers once came. It seemed wrong to say no.

That may have been a misjudgement. She has cropped

hair, a bit of a bolshie look, as we used to say, white shoes and a small recording machine.

'When did I first see Mrs Thatcher?' Her eyes are a protest: does he have to repeat every question? Her hands crush our letters back into a ball. She leans forward and looks hard.

'It was February 1985', I reply, 'a few weeks before my 34th birthday. I was a junior editor on the staff of *The Times*. We had an Editor's lunch, one of those occasions where politicians can be questioned in conditions of fake friendliness.'

Despite her manner I am trying to be helpful and friendly myself. I don't know how much she understands.

'An Editor's lunch is a chance for quiet exchanges of favours, a story on a rival, a request for understanding about an upcoming problem, deals so quiet that many of those present may not even know they are being made.'

She nods. That is something she thinks she does understand.

'Margaret did not behave well. It was one of her "remembering the Brighton Bomb" days, or so one of my knowing colleagues said. Or she had just "spoken to poor Cecil Parkinson": that was another explanation.'

I point outwards, to the ground outside, to the gatehouse that was once a fort.

'We had not quite arrived at Wapping then but we were on our way. The battles down below between police and strikers, men and horses, newspaper unions and managers, had not yet happened. We soon won't even be able to see the battlefield. We are leaving soon', I add unnecessarily.

Miss R stands up from her literary perch and shifts her small weight from left foot to right. She waves me to go on.

'Margaret was certainly not at her kindest that day. No, we did not discuss murder or adultery, nothing as embarrassing as that. We did not mention the IRA attempt to assassinate her during the Tory Party Conference at Brighton five months before, nor "Cecil's lovechild resignation" during the same conference the previous year. But a lunching journalist in those days could prosper mightily by pretending to understand the Prime Minister's moods. Maybe my knowing colleague was right.'

'What did you talk about?'

'Her enemies mostly, the people whom she thought should be our own enemies too. No one who worked for a university or the BBC would have overheard us without anxiety.' I mention those enemies in particular because I am trying to tease Miss R who herself is some sort of historian, part of 'a project'. That is what she claimed in her letter. But she has a toughness that comes from somewhere very different from here. She is not easily teased.

I am answering the question that I think she has asked. I remember many details of that Thatcher lunch. It was the first of its kind for me. I was new then to the game that Miss R now wants to replay.

She said in her letter that she wanted details. I give her details. 'The Prime Minister was tugging at her necklace, twisting the clasp to hide the pearl that was stained. She was wearing brown and gold, a dress that could have smothered a small child or curtained a bay window. Britain's first female Prime Minister wore an acidic scent which, if it were a wine, would have been corked, but as a perfume was the spirit of Christmases long past. She looked and spoke like a vinegary sponge.'

'How did you respond?'

'There were about eight hosts around the table, the Editor of *The Times* at that time (his name was Charles Douglas-Home), and the heads of our main departments. Sycophancy or silence were the only choices on the menu. Most of my colleagues chose the sycophancy. As the most junior I like to think that I picked the silence but I cannot be sure. Once her enemies had been dispatched, the ingratitude of friends occupied much of the time between the Marks & Spencer melon balls and the mints.'

She checks that the numbers are changing on her machine as once reporters used to check the whirring of tape.

'The knowing colleague whispered that the melon balls were the same as those we had endured a few weeks before with the Irish Taoiseach, Garret FitzGerald. Mrs Thatcher heard only the word FitzGerald and frowned. She liked neither him nor the pale green fruits and changed the subject.'

'"What shall I say when I address a Joint Session of Congress in Washington next week?", the Prime Minister asked.'

'"Tell them that you are the same exciting and radical woman that they fell in love with when you were first elected five years ago", said the lizard on my left, a man whose fragrance was as fresh as the Prime Minister's was not. This was the Business Editor, Kenneth Fleet.'

'Mr Fleet was a man of the smoothest confidence, my first departmental boss. Before I arrived in newspapers I had never met anyone like him. He lost his way only when he starred in advertisements for Prudential Insurance.'

Miss R does not laugh. Her face has turned away. She looks out towards the faraway sea – away from the site of Thomas More's execution on Tower Hill, down along the cobbled dockland street, up to the East London sky to the tower blocks and churches. She looks back at me across the crowded office carpet, the boxes awaiting the removal men, this floor-scape today like an architectural model of the buildings outside.

Her eyes say that this is not what she wants to hear but that she will hear a bit more anyway. I recognise that look. I remember looking that way when I first asked questions for a living myself, asking questions that some superior wanted to be answered. Sometimes an interviewer has to set a subject free. Sometimes we profit from answers to questions that we have not asked. Most often we are too impatient.

'Listen to me again', she says, more sharply than an interviewer should. 'Seeing Margaret Thatcher doesn't mean meeting her, having lunch with her, talking to her at a party or doing whatever else you did later.' She speaks as though to a child or a suspect in a murder investigation.

She wants us to get to the menu selections and sycophancy in due time. She wants to get to her four courtiers, one by one. What she wants to know first is something from long before that lunch, something very simple: when did I first see Mrs Thatcher 'in the flesh?'

She pauses. We both pause. The words 'flesh' and 'Mrs Thatcher' seem somehow ill matched.

'Even if it was only the flesh of her face', she continues as though correcting her own vocabulary.

'Fine.' I will tell her. She is pressing me for stories. I understand that. It can be a thankless task.

More melon-ball memories from 1985 would have made better stories. The single conversation that I had alone with Mrs Thatcher that day was about Anthony Berry, son of the sometime owner of the *Sunday Times*, her Deputy Chief Whip and one of those who died at Brighton in that bombing where she was the one intended to die. It was she who raised his name.

I may have been the last man to see Sir Anthony alive, our paths crossing on the stairs at the Grand Hotel after the Party Conference after-parties, his steps directed upwards after walking his dogs by the sea, mine downwards and out into the hotel next door. In the next thirty years I hardly ever saw Margaret Thatcher again when she did not mention this dead heir to a newspaper dynasty.

Sir Anthony was not her own sort of Conservative. He was a privileged part of the party coalition she had to keep together if she could. He was in Brighton that night only by accident, only because someone more important had to stay behind in London to fight the Miners' strike, the conflict that, in the year before the battles of Wapping, was the biggest item on her inventory of industrial unrest.

Bombing of Grand Hotel, Brighton, 1984

Nor was he well known. He was hardly known to me at all, nothing beyond a smile across a room of wine glasses, Tory Treasurer Alistair McAlpine's glasses that night of the bomb, one bathtub of champagne bottles and another hiding the explosives. Margaret connected us because she had heard me describe the dogs on the stairs. It was a connection she liked to make.

Miss R looks down again at her recorder. 'We need to start much further back than the Brighton Bomb.'

She wants me to make her story easy, one thing after another she says. I don't see how my first mere sighting of Mrs Thatcher is a significant story at all. And I am good at spotting a story.

I will answer her anyway. Miss R is aiming to be a historian and in the job I do now at the *Times Literary Supplement* we respect historians. We don't tell them what they should ask and how they should write. Recognising small details that seem unimportant is what great historians do best, journalists too. Bits and pieces can be something or nothing. Every day there are facts that die before darkness.

Before I can follow her direction she suddenly changes it. She says that she is from Essex as though that were suddenly relevant. I say that I was once from Essex too. She points to her white shoes with her first smile, a reminder of once popular jokes about 'Essex girls', not the kind I have so far expected her to make. She draws her feet back to the sides of her book pile. She begins her questions again, impatient, Impatience on a Monument you might say.

There is not yet a pattern here. Apart from her claim to profession, I know only how she looks and seems, contained, clawed, mostly careful. Her hair is clipped tight. She is five shelves high when she is standing, maybe about five foot six. I guess that she is about thirty years old but I can do no more than guess. I have checked by Google and there is no trace to guide me. She has not written a book before, or not under the name that she has given.

We stare out away and past one another. I share her appreciation of the view from this sixth-floor window. I look out on it myself as much as I can. Below me sits my landscape of three decades, the places where I used to write about politics, edit *The Times*, walk, talk and plot with political people, all of the names on Miss R's list. Now I merely look down on those rooms and roads from this temporary home in a neighbouring tower, from 3 Thomas More Square down on to the gatehouse, to old black bricks, new pink doors and bicycles, and soon I will not even be as close to my past as that.

So yes, I tell her what she wants to know. When did I first see Mrs Thatcher? 'It was August 1979 in London, four months after she became Prime Minister, five years before she escaped assassination at Brighton, six years before the sycophants' lunch. It was only a year after my life as a journalist had begun.'

I point down river. 'I was in Greenwich, South London, not near to the usual Thatcher haunts, not Chelsea, not Westminster, not anywhere I ever heard Margaret say a fond word about, at least not while she was in power, not until, after three election victories, they forced her to resign.'

'They? Who were they?'

'Most of them were Tories who never wanted her at all except as a winner of votes they could not win themselves.'

I am wondering if I need to go through her triumphs into Downing Street one by one, 1979, 1983, 1987. Miss R must know these few unassailable facts.

The first win was after Labour's Winter of Discontent when striking trade unionists let trash pile in the streets and the dead go unburied. The second came after the Falklands War and the third when while winning she lost too much, too many of her friends and something of her mind. Beside crumpled letters and a recording machine Miss R has a calendar of the decade on a spreadsheet, the kind our accountants keep.

'Finally "they" got her out, forced her to pretend that she wanted a Barratt Home instead, Dulwich not Greenwich, I think, not that she stayed there long. Dulwich? There it is. South and east and down away over there somewhere across the river. As if they could ever get her to spend her time pottering about in Dulwich – or West Harwich, East Greenwich, any of the wiches not far from here beneath the clouds blowing today towards us.'

'Why were you in Greenwich that night?'

'I was there to write about a play. I was a part-time critic at the time and the play was called *The Undertaking*. Its writer was an actor called Trevor Baxter. Its theme was the way that people want to be remembered when they are dead, the very different ways from those that will be chosen by their relatives, lovers and friends.'

'A little way offstage was a tomb in which the powerful paid handsomely to lie in the uniforms of their lifetime's passions, their dressing-up clothes not their business suits, a financier in a ballet frock, a general in the loving arms of his batmen, an eminent scientist trussed like a chicken. It was a good story. I remember it now as a good play too but I did not say so at the time. I was a young critic. I thought I should be critical.'

'Margaret was a new story then but no one thought she would be remembered so much now. No one shouted at her in 1979. The "Poll Tax" was still a 600-year-old error made by Richard II. Not many loved or even hated her. She was new. She was a woman. She was not Ted Heath, the sexless sailor whom, to his unforgiving horror, she had succeeded. There was a wall on stage and, behind it, an orchestra rehearsing a new symphony to celebrate the soul of the European Economic Community, the "soul that is Love".'

I see a smile. Miss R is perhaps at last hearing what she wants to hear. She sits back on her pile of books, novels at the top, lives of Romans and Tory ministers underneath, and finds that there is a bookcase for her shoulders not far behind. Her feet slide forward. She looks as though she is about to be photographed for a magazine. She almost laughs.

'Was that the time', she asks solemnly, 'when the EEC was beginning to become something less Economic and more Community, when Britain still had its "British disease"?'

'Yes, exactly. I don't think I ever enjoyed myself more.'

She adjusts a second electronic device, the pad on which she makes her notes. She straightens her back, a struggle when on a frail support of print. She is speaking as though from a script to a lecture hall of students. I begin to explain but she puts her finger to her lips. That EEC and strikes question, she silently says, is hardly a question at all, not one I need to answer.

So I continue with my answer to the first question, the one she is so insistent on, with what I remember from the day on which I first saw 'that woman' as she would become, the woman who afterwards would hover high and low over the buildings down there on the ground. I am looking again out towards Greenwich. The theatre was somewhere under one of those incoming clouds, perhaps beneath that bit of pale blue sky, the bit by the bend of the river.

The Undertaking was a play of scenes designed to shock. A Tory lady was looking forward to the "black meat" of "a bulging brute" whom she might enjoy on a trip to Africa, the kind of language that was just still permissible in 1979 as long as the character was a Conservative. Inside the tomb, alongside the grand-passionate and perverted dead, was the dream-delivering undertaker himself, dressed to ape both Leopold II of Belgium and Lenin.'

'There was also a duplicitous Foreign Office mandarin. To Mrs Thatcher all FO men were "mandarins", never a term of endearment from that day till the day she died. There was a young girl, apparently buried alive, an old woman newly risen from her grave, and much talk of memory, law and order, more than two hours of it with only the briefest interval.'

'I was there that night with the man who is first on your research list. Perhaps you know that already?'

'It was David Hart, political adviser, wealthy fantasist himself and then a very new friend to me, who, soon after the play was over, pointed out Britain's first female Prime Minister in the back of a low black car. She had just returned from a holiday in Scotland, David told me knowingly. She did not look relaxed but then she hardly ever did, he said. She was dressed in a coat that may have been a dress, with a scarf that scoured her neck as she turned her head, waving to my friend through the grey glass window, or so he said.'

Miss R stands up from her books. 'I will be back on the next day but one', she promises.

4.4.14

The next day but one has now arrived. Miss R has not yet come and it is almost evening.

Maybe I have already missed her. Earlier this morning there was an office outing to the funeral of one of my *Times*

THE SENECANS

Literary Supplement colleagues, Richard Brain, by name and nature, our foremost stylist in grammar as in dress, whose choice for burial, if he had the chance to make it, would have been a pink cravat and a blue pencil.

Instead of waiting for my interviewer I was waiting for mourners in a monastic relic of the City, remembering little, merely learning that every Charterhouse brother (no sisters allowed) has a number signifying his seniority; and that every death there, and they are very regular, means promotion for those lower down the ladder.

Even on a non-funereal Friday the *TLS* is quiet at this late afternoon time. It is no trouble for me to be waiting here beside the grey sky, in the same position as yesterday, where I sit most days, writing about the political excesses of two thousand years ago, editing book reviews, and, most important now, separating rubbish from relics for the removal company. Distinguishing between the two is not easy and I have avoided it for decades. Everything that Miss R saw on Wednesday is still here though it will not be here for long.

A single 'when did I first' question will not be enough. I know already that she wants to ask about others who linked me and Margaret Thatcher, other questions about Mr Hart and the courtiers I came to call the Senecans. 'When did you first see Mrs Thatcher?' is only one of these questions.

I sense that she will keep our appointment and there seems to be no reason not to see her again. I am flattered that a historian would want to see me – or ask when and what I have seen. It is a long time since I have played a part in anything ever likely to be history.

Her first means of arrival should maybe have alarmed me more than it did. She appeared in this office, six floors in the sky, suddenly and without warning, an unusual feat in a modern tower where there are no corridors, few walls and even those are walls of glass. As I will tell Miss R if she asks me, David Hart, her subject and my friend, liked to arrive at his own parties that way. He used secret passages, doors without handles, opened by his touch on a spring, a butler's lift too, as I recall, adapted so that a single stout host could be among his guests without ever welcoming them.

Miss R wrote in her letter that she wanted to know as much as she could about David Hart, his power and pretensions, his games, his dogs, his pleasure when the young people drank wine that was older than themselves. He seems to be the man at the Thatcher court whom she has studied the most. Then there are the older men, Sir Ronald Millar and Lord Wyatt, rewarded by titles for their labours, and the dark, comic journalist Frank Johnson too, a cast of gilded ghosts who used to strut on the Wapping stage.

I am not sure why she has picked precisely this cast. To me they are united in many ways, most peculiarly by our Latin lessons in a shabby Wapping pub, shared studies of grammar and Seneca, a secret that sometimes surprised even ourselves. Maybe she has somehow learnt about these lessons.

She is a researcher and determined. That much is certain. How did she get in here? She could have been a terrorist, an affronted author, an unpublished poet, a publicist. She could have been someone I offended while editing *The Times*, a supporter perhaps of the England football manager (Hoddle, yes, that was his name) whom I forced from his job because of an interview in which he professed some primitive form of Buddhism. For years I was abused by friends of Glenn Hoddle. It is easy to give offence as a newspaper editor, necessary I would say.

I tried not to seem surprised to see her, successfully I think. She had our letters but there was no call from Security, no summons to meet her from the lift. Perhaps she came with someone else. This place is not what it was. Surprises happen more often. We are moving very soon. Our boxes are packed. No one cares as much as they once did.

So, when finally she arrives tonight I am not expecting her. I have my back to my desk, my eyes towards East London and the sea and, when I turn back to work, she is simply there. She stands on the thin grey carpet and starts to speak, snapping and smiling by turns. It seems churlish not to return the smiles.

In fact, I am genuinely pleased to see her. Normally I try to avoid the phrase 'in fact', even to think it. In matters of English usage I prefer to follow Frank Johnson's advice, the example of a master stylist, a poor politician but a masterly satirist of politicians, my Latin pupil, the quietest of those four men whom Miss R has mentioned without saying why.

All of them were writers, Sir Ronald of speeches and West End musicals, Lord Wyatt of newspaper columns and diaries, Mr Hart of novels and pamphlets, opinions in *The Times* if he got the chance, and 'plays of ideas' performed at his own expense. That much they most certainly had in common. Sir Ronald was the most successful of them, made famous and rich by *Robert and Elizabeth*, *Abelard and Heloise*, and adaptations of political novels by C.P. Snow. The most frustrated was Mr Hart.

Frank Johnson was the strictest of critics. Inter alia (Frank came to love his Latin) he advised all newspaper writers against 'in fact', also against 'genuinely', 'recently' and 'famous'. This time I am ignoring him.

In fact, Miss R and I become a bit more familiar as we talk, like pet and new pet-owner, not sure of our roles but already sensing something of each other's insecurities, businesslike but well beyond the smiles of mere business. This time we do not talk for long. We don't go back to her questions. In fact, she leaves almost as soon as she arrives. We do not kiss cheeks but we do shake hands, only a little awkwardly, as men who know each other do, those of us who are not sure whether we should be shaking hands or smiling on regardless, smiling as though an old conversation has never ceased.

To shake or not to shake? That is a choice I often pondered in my younger days. I hardly ever used to make it correctly. My parents were from the anxious East Midlands, Nottingham lace and Nottingham coal. They brought me up in an Essex community of engineers, of controlled politeness, constrained, without any general confidence, with rules but without a rule for every situation I would later meet.

It is hard to lose the manners of youth. All four of Miss R's men, the ones she has chosen, used occasionally to chastise me for failures in etiquette, the massively wealthy Mr Hart most of all. Sir Ronald, the would-be wealthy Lord Wyatt and the literary Mr Johnson saw Mr Hart's own manners as often lacking too.

This evening the crowded office floor does not help. To say goodbye we stretch towards each other like children using stepping-stones to cross a pond. Her thumb is a hook in my hand.

So I am left to myself. I see already that this is going to be a story about me and four men and Margaret Thatcher. Maybe we will go a bit beyond her and into the times of her successors, to John Major and to Tony Blair. She was like a bright sun, hard to see directly, and she cast a long shadow. Throughout her public life her courtiers were like mirrors, each reflecting different aspects of her character, each one worth looking into by those who would understand her.

THE SENECANS

My story will be of how she exchanged and sometimes failed to exchange her favours. Or, at least, I am happy to make that the story. Miss R will be the one asking the questions. I am merely the interviewee, ready to start in August, 1979, if she wants to start that far back, my last month of ignorance of courtly life.

In that humid summer, five years after ceasing to be an Oxford student, I still wanted to be a classicist of some kind, a writer about Greece and Rome. I knew about the ancient Senecans, colonial lords of Roman Cordoba. I knew nothing much of modern power. I knew a little about Thomas More. I knew only one character even remotely like David Hart – and he was a fictional tycoon called Trimalchio, a creation of satire by one of Seneca's own fellow courtiers in the age of Nero, a generous host who terrorised his guests with the theatre of food.

Sir Ronald, who was a classicist himself before he sailed to Hollywood, also knew about the billionaire butt of Petronius's *Satyricon*, the arriviste who serves fish swimming in sauce like the sea, birds flying from the body of roast beasts, offal that looks like shit. Ronnie thought the comparison to David Hart somewhat unkind. He had never seen David piss into a silver pot and wipe his hands on the hair of the nearest servant. I needed greater experience of modern life.

David was not like Petronius's monster. Nor, however, Sir Ronald had to admit, was he quite unlike him either. I was keen on Latin novels then. There are not many of them to read. Gaius Petronius was one of the first comic novelists (his grander fans included D. H. Lawrence and T. S. Eliot) and he wrote about food, drink, flattery, death and defecation. He was Nero's 'arbiter of taste', pet prose-master and eventual victim. Or, at least, some scholars think that he was.

Some think that there was more than one Petronius. Gaius may not have been the name of either. There is always uncertainty in distant history, almost always too in the kind that is close.

As for Sir Ronald, I saw him as more like Lucius Annaeus Seneca himself. Cordoba's greatest son much occupied my head at this time. He was less crazy than Petronius, less playful, long-winded but more useful. Thomas More was one of many who prized the practical advice of Nero's speechwriter and tutor, the playwright paid to put the best words forward at all times, to make his master as little hated as was possible. Ronnie's speeches (let me name him as she did, 'dear Ronnie') were invaluable to Margaret Thatcher.

If these memories seem a little detached, that would be a very fair comment about me at the end of the 1970s. I much preferred the first centuries BC and AD to all other centuries particularly my own. Ronnie was right. There was much of the now that I did not know and had not seen. I afterwards became more a part of modernity but am slipping back again now.

By 1979, when Margaret Thatcher and I coincided after *The Undertaking*, I had tried various jobs, from BBC Radio in Leeds to advertising chocolate. I spent as much of my time as possible in front of a stage. I wrote theatre reviews for a magazine that no longer exists. I was twenty-eight years old. I had a new job at the *Sunday Times* and a part-time role, at £5 per script, reading plays for the National Theatre, newly opened on the South Bank of the Thames amid a pious promise that every text submitted by the public would be considered for glory.

Alongside the politics and the Latin, spilling out today from a soon-to-be-sealed box on my floor, are some of the play-titles from that time, invoice letters with NT in red capitals, *Stations Upon The Pilgrimage Of The Werewolf* (by Dai Vaughan), *On The Knowledge* (by Dai Vaughan), *Krieg Ist Ein Traum or A Waltz* (by someone who may not be Dai Vaughan but whose name has faded over the years).

Each £5 fee is accompanied by a cross note from a woman in the script department deploring what a waste of effort this all was. *Princess Ascending?* We think not. *The Alternative?* If only. *Go Down, Mr Pugh? Bete Noire? The Fuhrer Is Coming?* Not if he had to read stuff like this.

The Undertaking, a new play by a man better known for acting in the television series, *Doctor Who*, was one of many I reviewed that year. The Lenin-and-Leopold-like undertaker notes that all investigation is stopped into a 'national scandal' when 'unstoppable procedures' reveal 'just who is involved'. If Miss R were a newspaper interviewer looking for cheap points, she could say that I already had the next phase of my life in mind, the search for corruption and cover-up, the things that journalists like to find. But Miss R is not writing for a newspaper.

In the Autumn of 1979 that 'next phase' had barely begun. I had just spent eighteen months as a restless young man working lazily in an oil company office and with time to spend on writing short pieces about politics and poking them anonymously through the doors of magazines. Crossing the Thames at night to offices like this one where I am sitting now, waiting to see if an editor might bite on my morsel: that was my weekly thrill.

One of these offerings, on some now incomprehensible controversy of the day, had attracted enough attention to get me offers of full-time jobs in journalism. That was how I joined the *Sunday Times* as a business and political reporter – at the much-improved salary of £7,500 per year.

A printed contract for my first 'proper job', carbon-copied

in the manner of the time, is on my floor too, beside my 'scoop' about Industrial Democracy in the now defunct *New Society*. Miss R can see both if she wants to. She can check the numbers from before the time that she was born. I can never remember numbers. This is maybe the only joy of moving, the easy reminders of lost details.

So August 27th, the date clear from a clipping here from *Plays and Players*, was, in fact, one of the last days of my old life. I was at a theatre in faraway Greenwich, with a brief to see a two-act play that began, as I recall it, with a European symphony and ended with a woman famed most for her part in a vermouth commercial being raped by a skeleton. And that was certainly the night that I first saw Margaret Thatcher. I am sure that she did not see me.

8.4.14

On this day last year Lady Thatcher died, aged eighty seven, mildly demented, demeaned, in my view and the views of many, by a title that she did not need and need never have taken. I was in hospital at the time. I hardly noticed that death elsewhere. I did not mourn it.

To judge from the flickering grey images on a high-mounted TV the only thing she had ever done in her three transforming terms as Prime Minister was to take back the Falkland Islands in 1982, the year before her second election victory. There were sailors and soldiers everywhere. To hear the news commentaries she might have been being buried with two crossed batons and a wreath of oak leaves. The funeral would have perfectly suited any Field Marshal anywhere. Argentine or British? It would hardly have made a difference.

SPECIAL COMMEMORATIVE SECTION: THATCHER IN THE SPECTATOR
Ferdinand Mount • Auberon Waugh • Charles Moore • Alexander Chancellor

13 APRIL 2013 | £3.50   WWW.SPECTATOR.CO.UK | EST. 1828

THE SPECTATOR

Margaret Thatcher, 1925-2013

Charles Powell • Andrew Roberts • Cecil Parkinson
Barry Humphries • John Simpson • Matthew Parris
Steve Hilton • Bruce Anderson • Rod Liddle

So instead I am mourning her here now. Most of those with whom I watched her rise and fall are dead too. Miss R's four chosen men are all gone. So much that reminds me of them is also about to die, directly in front of my eyes, brick by brick, pane by broken pane, a demolition in which more than matter will descend as dust. Not only are the newspapers now leaving Thomas More Square, but the original 'Wapping' that is down below me, the one that only the oldest among us knew, is about to be destroyed. And only a few now will mourn that.

The first time that I saw this Wapping was a month before the street battles of 1986, the year before her third election victory, the days of the greatest secrecy I had ever known, days of enforced silence, the stress of everyone. Charles Douglas-Home, the Editor at the melon-balls lunch, was dead. His successor, Charles Wilson, and a driver called Jo brought me down here in a black-windowed car.

The distance was short. At 1 pm I was at the Gray's Inn Road offices where my job as a Thatcher-watcher had begun. At 1.15 pm I was shown the future and how it would work, computers without print-workers, print machinery with ten men instead of a hundred, the ramps down which lorries played the part of trains, the gatehouse and walls that would protect us until the enemies of change became used to it.

As a man of new hopes for employment I hoped very much that the future was going to work. My first job after the security of Shell UK had lasted only three months. By January 1979 the *Sunday Times* and its daily sister were 'shut down' in one of the many so-called, sweetly called, 'industrial disputes' that propelled Mrs Thatcher to power. It had felt quite possible that they would never open up again.

The papers did reopen and struggled on. The new Conservative Prime Minister promised to cure the British sickness without killing the British patient but the treatment was slow. All power to her – or so it seemed to me, and to most of those who managed the newspapers, including the new editor of *The Times* in 1986, a Scot like his predecessor but less ideological, an ex-marine, a giver and demander of fierce loyalty, irascible and well suited to an almost military campaign.

All battles between trade unions and employers were political then. Strikes were the subject about which political writers wrote. There are hundreds of newspaper cuttings on this floor to remind me, once pasted in order, now yellow and free.

Almost no one keeps cuttings any more. They have websites. The only record is electronic. But in the 1980s we all had 'cuttings books', marbled ledgers of our productivity, stiff pages which the editor could count if our value for money was in doubt. The requirement for stories was not high. Newspapers were small and staffs were huge until the 'Wapping Revolution'. But even in the early 1980s it was useful to have one's name in the paper from time to time. The order to visit the managing editor and bring your cuttings book was a headmasterly summons demanding attention and sticky paste.

I have never thrown mine away. They are all here now, filled with gaps but still a record of what I used to do. For several weeks in 1980, from Doncaster to Dagenham, I seem to have done nothing but count the days 'lost to strike action'. The results cover four full pages, a blurring record from a time when newspaper offices too were just small parts of factories and not, like Thomas More Square, suitable for a City bank.

In another week I interviewed 'the man who puts the words in Mrs Thatcher's mouth'. That was how I first met Ronald Millar, not yet Ronnie or Sir Ronald, playwright, speechwriter, soon to be my closest friend among the courtiers on Miss R's list.

Miss R is right to want to understand the role of these lesser men. Yes, all Mrs Thatcher's courtiers were men. Each gave her a different form of comfort. Thus they were means of seeing her when other means were closed, their minds flexible when hers had to be fixed. Sometimes eccentric, always expendable, they gave as well as took. When I was first writing about her I needed these exchanges. I saw her in person, 'in the flesh', hardly at all.

That very first 'editorial lunch', after I had moved from

the *Sunday Times* to *The Times* in 1981, was a rarity. That was why the level of sycophancy was so high. There was less close association between Prime Minister and journalists than became common later. A lunch was an 'event'. For her it was almost a stage performance. In one of the paper piles on the floor there is a detailed note of it that I can use if Miss R wants a detailed answer. I am beginning to hope that she does.

There will be records here (and elsewhere?) of when the Senecans met and what we learnt, how we laughed together about the knifing of friends, of enemies too, how we rejoiced in falls and failures. We loved undue expectations and unjust deserts. We loved the whole business of news-papers, a love that remains.

We had so many rows – beginning with why the Argentines were able to invade the Falklands, arguments less reprised at her death than the Goose Green glory of the Islands' recap-ture. We had harsh words about the sinking of an enemy ship called the *Belgrano*, about the 'disgraceful' *Times* role in the affair of Cecil Parkinson's mistress, the transmigration of footballer's souls, and the struggles about whether a helicop-ter company called Westland should be sold to Europeans whom no one had ever heard of or to Americans who were equally obscure. But little anger lasted beyond a day, the unit of time that on a newspaper is everything.

It was during that so-called 'Westland crisis' (everyone knew the phrase in 1986) that *The Times* and its sisters moved down below to the place that became 'Fortress Wapping' or simply 'Wapping', taking the name of a whole riverside address to itself, to a new print plant of brick and steel where no member of a print union would ever tread. It was a brutal process of change, all of it happening within the view from this window. There was violence, there was a death. The roads shook with the rage of lorry-drivers and those attempting to stop them. The result was to be a new newspaper era.

Wapping, like Westland, was both an industrial dispute within a single company and a conflict of visions, Europeans or Americans, Thatcher or the paternalism that had predominated before. My notebooks of the time are mostly of minutiae, some of it hard now even to understand, reports of acts by unremembered names. But some names remain, some acts by Miss R's chosen names. I will answer her as best I can. I saw some things here that others did not see. I have stayed much longer than most. I have looked at events through more lenses. Perhaps I can claim some sense of proportion – or, if merely another distortion, at least one that is different.

When I first drove through that gatehouse down below, seven years after that theatrical night out in Greenwich, six years after the 'shut-down' and sullen reopening, my job was still to write about the Thatcher court, Margaret, her enemies and friends. I acquired other positions too, writing rhetoric and opinions, editing the rhetoric and opinions of others. In 1992, after John Major won his only election as Prime Minister, I became Editor of *The Times* with new ties to Miss R's four men, ties that lasted till they died.

I dealt with some mad men of my time. Many are not on Miss R's list but easily might have been. David was neither the maddest nor the most important but he fascinated me from the start. He was also the first to identify that I might be as useful to him as he was to me. Classics is a good training for understanding a court, a constant reminder of madness and mutual dependency. It was useful that I always kept some part of my mind in antiquity just as I had done as an Essex boy, as an adolescent at Oxford, and as and whenever

I could. Latin became a shared language at Wapping for a while.

Today, as I'm getting ready to leave here, not quite thirty years on, I am lucky. I can be an open classicist again. I have 'come out', as it were. Much of my 'day job' at the *TLS* is to read and write about Greeks and Romans and those, like the Thomas More of our square, who brought classical languages to England.

For more than a decade I have been back in the books where I began. When I wrote in 2010 about my near-death from a rare form of cancer it was in a book about the Spartacus slave war. When I wrote in 2012 about the fatal cancer of my oldest Essex friend it was in a book about Cleopatra. The approach of any death intensifies memory.

Every day I edit the *TLS*. I concentrate on the classics as much as I can. I spend time with Romans, politicians, philosophers and poets, with the men and women who study them, with those who are sometimes like them now. It has been an easy adjustment of emphasis, hardly more than that. Wondering what to say to Miss R at first made remembering harder, her restlessness, her petulance, what seems to be a peculiar sense of entitlement. I am now beginning to remember much more. In its final weeks this place is becoming more of a spur than any person alone could be.

Soon our great brick 'plant', the dull red squatter outside my sixth-floor Wapping window, will itself be dead, the one over which so many fought so hard in the Thatcher high days. Even when the fighting was over, Fortress Wapping remained its name. It is soon about to be razed and replaced by flats that will have other gentler names, or so the developers hope.

I can tell the kind of people that the new owners want, the men and women on the posters, men with laptops, women holding hands with women holding phones, the young with £2-5 million to spend, not, I suspect, Miss R. I am beginning to miss that plant already, unlovely and unloved as it always was when it was alive. Its walls have not fallen yet but the time must be close.

There are the ghosts here not just of the people who came, who worked here, who lobbied and plotted, but also of the players who brought us here, who set the scene. Margaret Thatcher never came to Wapping herself but she so often seemed to be here. She seems to be here now. No. I must not get beyond what I saw.

Here on the emptying shelves I have a note of most of what she and I ever talked about, most of the times that we met, fewer quotes of her exact words than a historian would like, more usually the gist of what she said. I have notes of her rages and notes, as long as I can find them, about the men who tried to calm her – with flattery, gossip and theatre trips.

I must not make assumptions. I need to prepare myself. Miss R has already asked questions about the towers in the landscape, old Wapping blocks of flats built to house the men and women bombed out of the slums by Hitler. She seemed disappointed that I knew so little, the names of a few pubs on the ground, nothing in the sky apart from some heavy Hawksmoor churches, even those names being a bit blurred, a George in the East and a St Anne's being less distinct than I would have liked.

Her displeasure came not, I think, because she cared about churches or concrete but because I might have been damaging myself as a witness to what she does care about. Mine are more bookish times now. Miss R is not concerned about the controversies of my new life. She cares about what happened in recent history, always the most forgotten kind.

10.4.14

When Miss R arrives today she is most pleased by her own notebook, smug I would say but don't. This is not a new electronic device. She holds it so that I can see the printed name, with a stamp from Foyles bookshop, SENECA, its cover page orange and the next page lemon, both colours faintly silvered. The printed letters of the name are blue-black, the colour of her nail varnish. SENECA belongs to one of the bookseller's SCHOOLS OF THOUGHT.

I make no comment. I don't know whether she is prodding or mocking. Eventually she pushes it across my desk. There are few of her own words in it yet. Most of the pages are still blank. But the publisher's words are succinct: 'Seneca (c. 4BC–65AD) wanted to keep his integrity and flourish in treacherous times. He directed political reforms while trying to keep Nero, the most volatile of emperors, under control'.

'Is that fair?', she asks.

'Yes', I reply, 'fair as far as it goes.' I cannot keep back that always irritating 'as far as it goes', favourite of those who dislike issues of long study reduced to a single word.

'I want to talk about your Senecans. Were they "trying to control"?'

'Not in every case. David preferred Margaret Thatcher when she was out of control. Seneca was the first political speechwriter. That was his main attraction to Ronnie. A writer is often in a position to control the ruler for whom he writes.'

She raises a pale plucked eyebrow. 'Seneca is also praised in the notebook for his insight that "immediate pleasure is an unreliable guide to living a good life". True?'

Seneca and Socrates

'That is certainly what Seneca said', I reply. 'He used to write it often and in many ways. Margaret Thatcher instinctively agreed with him. She was a Stoic in that and many respects. She thought that too many of her predecessors had indulged the public love of immediate pleasure. The Senecans, of course, like all good courtiers, liked to find respectable support for every view that she held.'

Miss R continues to read aloud. She speaks at a higher pitch and volume than our office space requires, as though these were slogans to be etched on the glass walls.

'"Seneca was interested in making money but knew that it couldn't guarantee security. He hardened himself against the natural fear of losing what he had by regular bouts of voluntary frugal living". Is that true too?'

'That is how Seneca wanted people in the future to see him. But the three points are not quite the same.'

'So first: making money?'

'By owning silver mines and lending at high interest. Yes, he did like to make money although taking money was easier and left him more time to think.'

'And natural fear?'

'The natural was good. Anything that he deemed natural was the virtuous thing.'

'Voluntary frugal living?'

'His chest heaved every day of his life. His throat was a cave of coughs. His stomach ached at the slightest provocation. He made wine on an industrial scale but drank in moderation – or that is what he claimed. He enjoyed sex and cold baths whenever and with whomever he liked. Does that count as frugality or not?'

Miss R frowns. She closes the book. Her purchase from Foyles may not explain everything about Seneca. It misses the tough, practical thinking about politics, the contrariness, the appeal to first principles that were so prized at Margaret Thatcher's court and so missed after she had gone. It misses the mechanics of exchanging favours, the problems of giving benefits to all when all will not deserve them. It misses much that was to become important to all of the four men on her list.

The publisher of SCHOOLS OF THOUGHT does, however, explain one big thing about Seneca. The teacher's son from Cordoba wanted to help. He wanted to be a help to himself. Miss R reads aloud in her glass-etching voice again.

'"He encourages us to be tough with ourselves so that we can cope with life and make the most of bad circumstances. Dampening hope or preparing for adversity liberates your energies".'

I have nothing to say about the liberation of energies. But this self-help Seneca from Foyles is, quite correctly, a man who intended to do good.

'Virtuous intention was important to him. He aimed high while recognising that he might never match the best of men.'

'Seneca did not become Emperor of Rome himself', I add, 'despite being the candidate of virtue in some men's minds.

He thought anger was the greatest evil. A man had to stay cold and calm, a ruler most cold and calm of all.'

'Passion was not a part of sound reasoning but its most pernicious enemy. He never had the chance to test his thoughts on the biggest political stage. A hundred years later his successor Stoic in your plastic packet, Marcus Aurelius, did succeed, the so-called "last of the Good Emperors".'

She takes her notebook back, complains about the confusion in my office and leaves the room. Five minutes later I see her walking out the back way eastwards towards the plant that is about to fall, down the road beside the rum store to the end. I watch her until she turns left towards the pale, purple columns of The Old Rose, the pub, long closed now, where the Senecans used once to study Stoicism and learn their verbs.

18.4.14

Cranes are arriving like dinosaurs for breakfast in a swamp, a rain-swept convention of diggers and dumper trucks. This is a scene with few people and much machinery, just like the world that is departing. The Wapping print-production lines, so dramatic when I saw them first, were bright blue. The colour for demolition is yellow.

When Miss R arrives she has no raincoat. Perhaps she has a friend here who drives her into the basement where the service lift begins, where security is not so strict. She sweeps back my half-formed question and joins me at the window. We watch the show.

Does she enjoy this sort of meeting? It is hard yet to say. Doubtless she is talking to dozens of people. I hardly look fit for a big part in her history. She writes down some of what I say, but not enthusiastically, merely with a dogged purpose, like a student seeing an examination answer through the verbiage of a lecture. Sometimes I must have something she needs.

I want to help her if I can. I am not sure why. Because a few facts ought not to be forgotten? Because I am flattered to be asked?

Maybe I would be more persuasive if I were better dressed, wearing one of my old blue suits chalked with a thin stripe, made by the only tailor I have ever had, a maker of fox-hunting kit in York whom I met by chance and kept by habit.

From the evidence today of the packed box on my floor marked 'Peter's photographs', those suits did not fit my body well. The jackets were double-breasted, at least double. The trousers were equally full, held by yellow braces I cannot imagine wearing now. But they were the uniform for being heard then.

Those suits long ago went to moths and Oxfam. When I saw Miss R last week I was wearing the same grey-pink cotton jacket that I am wearing today, bought a decade ago in Rome when I was a thin man, and some pumice-grey trousers, creased from their time in the back of my desk drawer beside shoe polish and sugar cubes.

The instruction from on high in the company is that all

desks must be emptied within three months. In September I am going to the Roman city in Spain where Lucius Annaeus Seneca was born. Before I go to Cordoba, everything of mine must be out of here. I need to take special care of the contents of the case closest to me, David Hart's Renaissance erotica (photocopies only), his *Sons and Lovers* (David Lawrence was his favourite alias), Ronnie Millar's Roman tragedies (all by Seneca), three Booker Prize-winners, one of them a bribe from Woodrow Wyatt, and various black novels by Beryl Bainbridge, who never won the Booker Prize but was all the more loved for that by Woodrow.

Beneath these are various relics of my own in Latin, Greek and what the memoir-writing politicians of my own time claim is English. Every day this Spring is a removals day although nothing yet has been removed. I have enjoyed this *TLS* office, the last of dozens where I have made newspapers, my very last it seems, before the absolute new era of 'open-plan'. My past is filed here in a solid form.

As well as paper of every age and colour there is a small brass grinding pot which my mother used to call 'the middle thing' when I was a Chelmsford child on our armament-makers' estate, a blue school cap with my senior school's motto, *Incipe*, an injunction to Begin!, an Oxford tie from a time no one wore a tie, two cracked pillboxes, one showing a whiskered Victorian with a copy of *The Times*, the other a Roman empress spreading her legs on a throne. Miss R strokes the school cap and ignores Messalina. There are files of letters, brown ink pages tied with rusting wire, a thousand books at least, novels, histories, memoirs of every kind including mine.

Miss R today is less like a historian's assistant, more like a mother in a teenager's bedroom, intolerant of the filing on the floor. She trips. She swears. There is no place to put her mid-heeled shoes, not white this time but two-tone blue with a bow, right foot and left foot eventually secure but further apart than she would have liked, small stacks of Latin staring up in between. She is coming to resent the boxes that are waiting to be taped and moved, all twelve of them. I know the number because I watch her write it down, XII, as though denoting a Roman poem or a Pope.

She stands rather than risk the seat of books. She turns down the offer of a chair from the main office outside. She leans against a cabinet. She slides on a slippery plastic file. Only while she settles do I properly note what she is wearing, the blue skirt ruffled shorter over her left thigh than the right, the white plastic bangle on her wrist. Her shoulders are wider than would be normally seen today in Thomas More Square, power-dressed as we used to say in the 80s, dressed in period for her research as I am tempted to say now.

It seems more important today for her to be near the

window than to be comfortable. Together we admire the cranes. I ask her again if she wants a chair. There is room for another behind my desk if I disturb a small part of my soon-to-be travelling museum. But the remains from my fifty years as student, reporter and editor do not have to defend their ground. Instead she takes two halting steps and scans again the line of sky, the cloud-clinging concrete blocks, the slate and marble churches, the bricks of what were once the London Docks, the red-brick cube of the plant and the black-brick cylinder beside it for *The Times*.

'You must be sorry to be leaving here', she says, looking again at the boxes as though to check once more that she has counted them correctly. 'We can both see so much of what we need to talk about.'

May

*It is fourteen years since I joined your campaign
and eight years since you became Emperor; in that
time you have piled such honour and wealth upon
me that nothing is missing for my happiness except
moderation in its enjoyment*

—SENECA's resignation attempt,
reported by Tacitus

9.5.14

When I left Thomas More Square last night it was almost midnight, a common departure time for a reporter or an Editor of *The Times*, less so for an Editor of the *TLS*. A searchlight was hanging in the sky, drawing circles on the ground, hung from a helicopter, I presumed, although behind the Level Six glass I could not hear it. A bright metallic pool of light made an ice-rink of the gatehouse car park for the old plant, the ground immediately below. Slowly the beam found the long, low line of brick behind, the dockland Rum Store that once housed *The Times*, suddenly gold instead of black.

Then the light hit the red cube built for the *Sun* and the *News of the World*, for the managers, the lawyers, the accountants, the print machines themselves, six stories high and newly spot-lit as though for a conjuror's trick. Finally it traced a bright white line between The Old Rose on the Highway and the river before sweeping on again to the steeples and tower blocks beyond. A manhunt? A preparation for a visiting president?

This morning there is only hard, horizontal rain against the warehouse opposite the plant gates, low cloud propelled by wind around the large white letters, A, B and C, that are stencilled on the black-painted brick. This windowless break against the storm carries the name of Thomas Telford, a Victorian master of brick. The next wall celebrates a Mr Breezer. Neither of these names was visible last night, nor in 1986 even during the day. So much was obscured then.

There is also a deep pit down below me that was not there

in 1986, not there yesterday either, newly dug by a yellow
machine behind the gate, just inside the gate that last night
was an ice-rink of light, where the battles of Wapping were
fought and where the destruction of the main building will
soon begin. The straight-cut sides of what will perhaps be a
pond are some six-feet wide and twelve-feet long.

This was only one part of the battlefield, not a part of
great significance at the time. The pit is simply in the part
that I can now see from my window, something that I can
show Miss R if she asks.

When the newspapers first arrived this was the eastern
corner of the car park, though not a place where any sane man
or woman would park a car. Wapping was a genuine battlefield, not a metaphorical one, not a football match. The only

metaphors were the ones written by the journalists inside, the same tired phrases day after day as Frank Johnson complained. When the Socialist Workers came among the pickets, or when the police came among the International Marxists, this pit was where the missiles were thrown and thrown away.

So a battle with weapons? Yes. Bitter and brutal? Yes, sometimes it was both. The print union leaders knew that if newspapers could be made without their members at Wapping, their power would be over in Fleet Street and everywhere. And so it proved.

'But how bitter and brutal?' That is the first question from Miss R this morning who arrives with a copy of the *Daily Mirror* and the *London Review of Books*, both competitors from the Left to the papers of Thomas More Square. 'Was it as bad as the battlers on both sides made out? Missiles? How many and how often? Weren't you exaggerating as newspaper people do?'

'Well, yes, probably more weapons were thrown away than thrown. That was what David Hart used to insist, always with sadness. David was a devout fighter in the Thatcher army. He wanted the battles to be as bitter and brutal as possible.'

'Why? What did he want?' She wrenches the subject from politics to people. I am coming to expect this now.

'Where did David come from? Where did the rest of the court come from?'

'Certainly not all from the same place.' She makes a note.

'I wondered often about David. I occasionally asked him. There was an official story – about a Jewish banker's family, some trouble with a gardener's daughter at Eton, a little film production, a larger bankruptcy, a life of property speculation, military procurement and the mind. And there was a story of a different kind of intelligence, Mossad and the CIA and even sometimes our own.'

'When did you see him first?' Miss R's second question today is one of her stock questions.

'In David's case the time of seeing and meeting were, in fact, the same.'

'When?'

'It was a year before the night at the Greenwich Theatre. He had first written me a note while I was still at Shell and pushing stories through magazine doorways. He was curiously well informed. I should have seen the oddity in that. He found me when I barely knew where I was myself. He asked me to lunch and I accepted.'

'What did he look like then?' Miss R asks without waiting to hear any more.

David Hart

'Well, he had a head that I most certainly did not want to be hit by.'

She looks quizzically.

'Yes, I know that this is a bad sentence; Frank advised against ending any sentence with a preposition; so did the late Richard Brain of the *TLS* and so does the style guide of *The Times*. But 'hit by', positioned for emphasis, purposefully out of its proper position in the way that Latin allows, suits a memory of David's head very well.'

'I first saw him as a reflection, an image in the wood of a dining room table, in a house where he could throw walnuts into the gardens of Buckingham Palace. I was late and he was already sitting with his back to a mahogany door, black hair cropped short, broad neck bound in a red napkin, talking to his butler, looking like some prosperous communist propagandist, the kind imagined by novelists when Marxism was in its youth.'

'I sat down next to him (there were only two chairs) and he thrust his head towards me, the bristles on his brow almost on the bridge of my nose. He began with paintings by Walter Sickert, bought by his father, he said, who had beaten Lord Beaverbrook for them, none costing more than £200, one of them connected in some way to the Camden Town murder of 1907. He affected surprise that I had not heard of this great news event of its time, the throat-slitting of a prostitute, a Jack-the-Ripper story but from west not east.'

'I nodded with minimum commitment. His Sickerts seemed a well trodden path of conversation, the first of many such paths as I came to discover. David liked best what was familiar to him but exotic to others. He moved on to D. H. Lawrence (perhaps he thought this would give a better impression) and about belief belonging to "the blood" not the "fribbling intervention of mind" (which merely made me think he was mad). Then came the subject of traitors and "tagging" and how, if he did not trace and track down the subversives in the political departments of the press – "not excluding *The Times*" – the chances of Margaret Thatcher coming to power were even less than conventional wisdom decreed.'

'I smiled at him. I was merely a reader of *The Times* back then. Lunch for the two of us was a pyramid of roast birds and bright vegetables. It seemed impossible to me that a quail or an artichoke or quince could be removed without the structure's collapse. But a shaven-headed boy filled our plates and nothing fell. David had a silver toothpick and a thin grey dog that he said was a lurcher.'

'After this first time we remained friends till his death in January 2011. When I was powerful he was a pest. When he was a friend in need he was also a pest. But he was a very special pest and I was fond of him.'

'He was physically strong, recognisably so in rooms where most were writers, well able to lift an enemy or a bale of hay until in the last decade of his life he was gradually wasted by disease and could barely lift an eyebrow.'

'As a narrator of the truth he was frail, a fuzzy presenter of his own past even as he was a very precise observer of the present that we came to share. So I am sure that he was right about where the Wapping missiles went. Many of the throwers at that part of the line were clerical workers and journalists. There must be many a reminder in that pit of sharpened iron and glass, some of it hurled in anger, most discarded in fear.'

'David pretended much of his knowledge but he did understand dissent. Unless it was his own he was against it. He made a speciality of finding Margaret Thatcher's enemies. He came to know her through one of her favourite think tanks, the Centre for Policy Studies. He befriended its most radical members. He was resilient to failure, sending to her short speeches and thoughts for speeches, accepting that lesser, closer courtiers would keep them from her until from time to time he broke through.'

'When I first wrote about politics this softly moustachioed Mr Hart was the most belligerent, bull-headed, most vehement, viscerally political man I had then met. I had not seen such raging certainty for twenty years.'

Miss R lowers her head towards her notes, murmuring a query without looking at me.

'That first man of certainty was the right-wing Essex father of my left-wing Essex girlfriend or, to be strictly honest, the girl I most wanted to be my friend. He need not be part of your story. He and David, for all their shared frustrations with the world, could never possibly have met.'

She pushes her pen into her paper, pulls it back and points for me to go on.

'David believed most of all in battling an enemy to the end', I tell her, returning to the former field of conflict in front of our eyes.

'Thus Wapping was something of a disappointment to him. Except on Saturday nights when the pickets' enemies, police horses mostly, felt the force of ball-bearings and darts, this was a mostly peaceful show. No newspaper worker, he would wistfully complain, wanted to be caught with an object that might be interpreted as a Molotov cocktail. It was much safer to toss a Coke bottle over the low part of the car park wall, where the pit has now appeared, than to risk its association with someone else's cottonbud fuses or four-star fuel'.

'A Molotov, said David as though he had known the inventor personally, was much more appropriate as a talking point at Wapping than as a protest weapon. Despite sharing the same streets as the battles against the blackshirts of the 1930s and the dock-owners of the 1960s – or with the Thatcher government elsewhere over the coal mines – ours was fundamentally a war about print. It was a war for talkers. Many among the pickets could have passed a Part One degree course in Molotov Studies. Few, David suspected, had ever thrown one.'

'The chief risk for the printers was of misinterpretation. The Metropolitan Police, or "Maggie's army" as the pickets jeered, might easily confuse a trade unionist who wanted his hereditary job back with an armed man seeking Socialism. That was a real risk. Mr Hart was just one of those keen to misinterpret the picketers if they could. He used to send in articles for publication in *The Times*, perfectly typed in 22-point Times New Roman on handmade paper, exposing communists in the newsrooms of other newspapers.'

'Back in 1984, in the high days of the Right after Margaret Thatcher's second election victory, he turned the Miners' strike into an ideological war. He has received due credit (and disgust) for that.'

Miss R interrupts coldly. 'Yes, there is going to be a play called *Wonderland* about him.'

'Is there? I don't know.'

She looks pleased.

'In 1986 he wanted Wapping to be like the coal mines. If a picket could be demonised as a petrol-bomber he or she would be. But David always knew when he was struggling. He loved life's extremes. He was sometimes a fool. In his shorts and flat cap he often looked like a fool. But *Wonderland* would be the wrong word. He was not a deluded fool.'

'There were varieties of extremists on both sides of our battlefield. David was on the side of 'freedom to print'. He always wanted the word 'freedom' in his causes. The other side fought for the freedom of trade unions, manipulating language from the other edge of politics, anarchists who played arsonist at night, those who saw newspapers as full of capitalist lies that only print-unions should profit from printing.'

'What do you mean?'

'Well, it was very profitable for the unions to have monopoly rights to print the very articles they deemed politically unacceptable.'

She taps her feet in impatience.

'Hereditary monopoly rights were a fact for many print-workers, jobs handed down the generations. Yes, it was unpleasant to pass the picket lines. But many who abused us for entering the 'Great Wapping Lie Factory' were like any other heirs to a good thing. Yes, they scratched our cars and called us "scabs" but they were prosperous protesters, enjoying their anger, and did not want anyone to think otherwise for very long.'

'Pickets came and went for the shortest shifts before resuming their work as teachers, taxidrivers or minders of other newspapers' machinery. David Hart was not the only temporary attender on the line, not the only demo-tourist who, twenty eight years ago, was standing on the ground below us.'

'And as I remember now, it was David's plan that I too should find a black leather jacket and woollen hat and pretend to be a protester for a while. He thought it was feeble to be so close to a historic event and not to get in among it.'

'During the Miners' strike he had got "snow on his boots" and learned directly what was being said and done 'on the street'. That was when he adopted his David Lawrence name as suitable for the Nottinghamshire coalfields. He had travelled hundreds of miles and thought it ridiculous that I wouldn't venture out a hundred feet.'

'I refused at first. In 1986 I was Charles Wilson's deputy, in charge of leaders and opinion and much else. I had a lot to lose from the misrepresentation of such a mission. If it were so important, why was David Hart himself only so occasionally among the pickets? He was too well known now, he

said, thinly attempting to convey sadness as well as pride. I
didn't want to be a spy, I argued. He replied that I wouldn't
be spying, I would be seeing.'

'I gave way and on one Thursday night in June I was down
there in jacket and hat. Thursdays were always quiet. The
protesters were saving their strength for the weekend, lobbing
only the sporadic bottle of green glass, Fantas and 7Ups, all
of them probably already excavated now from the pit down
below, historical evidence of a kind though unlikely to have
been recognised as such by the excavators.'

'I was sure I was being watched. I looked around nervously
for anyone whom I knew or who might know me. I was
so nervous that I hallucinated almost everyone I had ever
known, from Left and Right, friends and enemies of my
father, my first girlfriend, my first would-be girlfriend, Latin
teachers, fellow journalists from Oxford and the BBC.
Afterwards I don't recall telling anyone, certainly not Frank
Johnson who thought that David was absolutely mad, that I
was too influenced by his madness and our idea of what we
called history almost wholly deceptive.'

Frank preferred only the grandest historical themes and
Wapping, he said, 'would never be one of those'.

12.5.14
Today the pit has gone. There is only a small pile of bricks,
stones and demonstrators' rubble on what before the weekend was the short side of a possible pond. Perhaps the developers have already buried what they wanted to bury, or
unburied it, or tested for pollution or pollutants, or done
the minimum required to prove that there are no remains of
earlier settlement here, no shackles of Napoleon's prisoners

of war, no Tudor tokens or relics of the Roman trade in dogs. Whatever they have done they have done it quickly.

13.5.14

Don't think I spend all of my time staring at diggers and dumpers. I read book reviews, I edit pages. Yesterday afternoon I was a mile away from here on Fleet Street at a Memorial Service, remembering a man who never passed through those old Wapping gates, one of my very first newspaper bosses, an editor from the old *Sunday Times* who stayed outside when the time came for the then new age.

Ron Hall, an opera-loving mathematician, a master of headlines and Greek wine, worked for Harold Evans, the revered editor who gave me my first newspaper job. Those who praised Ron bemoaned what happened here in 1986. We sang rousing hymns and remembered what newspapers were like two revolutions ago.

These were the journalists, judged then and since as the greatest of their kind, scourges of political scandal, the kind whom Woodrow Wyatt, flatterer of the powerful, and Frank Johnson, comic master of parliament, liked least, the kind whose influence on me and *The Times* they disliked even more. In some ways I wish that Frank and Woodrow had been there. We could have had more of the conversations we used to have about what journalism was for. But they would not have been there even if they were alive.

From a polished pew I watched grey re-enactments of my earliest days as a journalist in our pre-Wapping home, young meteors now old, men and women with the same ways of mocking, sniping and sniffing, softer in some cases but not in all. In the latecomer's seats I thought I saw Miss V, my oldest friend, that girl who never quite became a girlfriend, daughter of that first man of the Right I ever knew. I could not be sure.

It was quite possible that she might have been there. Those journalist giants of their age were the first who knew me outside of Essex and Oxford also to know Miss V, a regular visitor to our disputatious newspapers, supporting the trade union side as she had always done when we were young.

16.5.14

On a rainless afternoon the outlines of the pit below are visible again. Beside them is the yellow JCB which dug and returned the earth. Seen from up here, the rectangle has returned, the proof of how aerial archaeology works, by the watching of clay dry. The light is so bright that the two lines of fir trees between the fence and the former hole are of sharply different colours, the one of them lit pale and melon green, the other shadowed like deep forest.

I will miss everything about this view when we are finally removed to our next new home. No one again will ever see it as it is now. The eastern sky of churches and tower blocks, will remain. But the sometime home of the *Sun* newspaper, the *News of the World*, the *Sunday Times* and *The Times* has today started to fall. The days of dust and preparation are over. The 'plant' has begun its collapse to the ground, mingling thin white dust with the air and thistledown of Spring.

18.5.14

Miss R arrives early this morning. She goes straight to the white chair I have brought in from outside and puts her red cap down beside it. The piles for the removal men do not worry her now. She separates her own piles, notes the plastic match between her seat and her wristband, picks up a book, flicks through some papers, looks at some photographs of me in fat men's suits.

'When did you first hear of Seneca?'

It is as though she is talking about Thatcher, Millar or Hart. She asks her standard question. She checks the piles of books and notes, the spilling brown-inked letters, the variously labelled Seneca files.

Is the man from Cordoba on her list? I am ever more used to answering her now. She seems to know some of my answers before I give them. But then she is a researcher. She has done research.

'I first heard of Seneca on the same day that I first saw him.'

She lowers her chin like a satisfied teacher.

'I saw him when I was still a child. He was made of wood but no less frightening to an eleven-year-old for that.'

'Go on.'

'Are you sure?'

'Yes, I'm sure. We have time. I want it all.'

I look out of the window. I point down the river, calling out a catalogue of place names, listing dots on the map before the Thames becomes the sea, the Wapping Canal, Isle of Dogs and Millennium Dome, Tilbury, Grangemouth, Southend, a twist to the north to Walton-on-the-Naze, a place of bungalows, breakwaters, bingo, beaded net curtains and balsa wood.

'I'll begin with the balsa.'

Miss R sits back. Everything that happens in this story began in Walton, the seaside town that throughout my Essex childhood was neither Clacton (rough with dodgem rides and slot machines) nor Frinton (too posh, not even a pub) and thus the place that my parents might comfortably take me. Without my experience in Walton I might not have experienced Wapping or Cordoba at all.

'So yes, in 1962, the year when I first saw Seneca beside the sea, it was the wood called balsa that began it all, the soft, pale wood that grows like weed in South America but to me was the precious material of models, of aircraft, boats and castles. Anyone then could make a car, an abbey, a jet plane, a place of inquisition from balsa. Mr V, the father of my twelve-year-old friend V did exactly that, although he did not show all of his work to her, only to me.'

'This V was the girl with whom I was then trying to spend most of my time. Because V was her name I knew her parents by the same initial. She wore pale skirts above pale knees, wide belts and a necklace with a single agate stone. If I had been more free I would have followed her like a dutiful dog. As a dutiful schoolboy I tried to follow her as best I could.'

'It was a wet Sunday in May, a day like today, pebble-dash dampened by warm rain, old ladies on their way to the Odeon, inky clouds over the nasal peninsula that gives the town its name. East London is part of the east of England, the part where I was born but do not live now. On the east side is where this story stays.'

'Seneca was, as I saw him first, as real as any of the players in my story when they were alive, even more equal now. In his same first scene in the same pale room behind the same covered windows, like every horror-comic hero from a childhood, Seneca has stayed the same.'

She picks up a pile of letters and sifts them through her hands.

'So this is how it was and still is. My wooden Seneca is a Roman in his early sixties, about the same age as I am now, though heavier in the face than the self whom you have come to see, sun-blasted, dark-eyed, shocked, a frightened man who is used to frightening others, a rich man who wants to be less rich, suddenly much less rich, an artist who has prospered by giving political advice but who no longer expects either to prosper or to advise.'

'On the face of this Seneca there is damp and cold in every crevice, fear visible in the wrinkles that run like waste-pipes, right and left, on each side to where his hair grows high above his ears, hidden in the rolls below his chin, only imaginable within his phlegm-filled throat, a man in a crisp white toga that is quickly becoming creased, a man asking a favour while fighting for his life.'

'Despite the passage of half a century this balsa scene in a library in a model palace is as solid in my mind as is Dockland brick on the ground. The walls are made of boxes the size of matchsticks. There is a tiny chest of overflowing scrolls. The balsa Seneca himself is barely more than a curved stick; with him is a shorter, stout-stomached man, the Emperor Nero. The man who first showed me this creation added parts of speech and speeches to give his human figures life. Without those words I would have known nothing. A knife on balsa, however sharp or subtly used, does not show terror or pride.'

'In every book about Seneca (and there are dozens of them here about to be boxed and moved, hundreds more in more learned places) the writer explains that the family Annaei came originally from Spain, that the father was a teacher of speechwriting, that the eldest son earned a bit-part in the Acts of the Apostles, a nephew in the history of epic poems but that the middle son became the star, the power-broking artist who swayed the fate of an empire.'

'Those history books were not, however, what brought Seneca and me to our first time together. I was too young for them in 1962. It was Mr V, leaning over the table on which he never ate, who explained to me why the tutor of Nero's childhood, the writer of his speeches, the calmer of his whims, the profiteer from his policies, was at this moment at the most perilous point of his life, standing (as in my memory he still stands) beside a balsa couch, his heavy-lidded eyes dipped down, waiting for a signal from the reclining young tyrant that he might speak. That was when I first heard Seneca's name, not a very flamboyant name, not a Spartacus or a Cleopatra, a name that nonetheless, like those others, stayed.'

Miss R turns and traces a circle with her hand.

'Seneca and Nero are together and alone, unusual positions for an emperor and a victim. Nero is not on a throne and that too is a concession to his former teacher who, when permitted, can look directly at the thick neck, thin lips and light grey eyes of the man to whom he once taught the arts of persuasion.'

'What exactly is going on?', she asks.

'In 62 AD or 1962?'

'Both', she barks.

'In 62 AD. Seneca has for thirteen years been the closest man at Nero's side. It is eight years since, as a boy of seventeen, Seneca's pupil succeeded to the throne of Rome.'

'During this time there have been ominous changes. Seneca's job as tutor came from Nero's mother, Agrippina, whom Nero has just murdered. Seneca's power has been assisted by a head of the palace guard who has just died from an infection in his throat.'

'In his eighth year of absolute power Nero wants to be an artist more than a statesman – and the presence of a political adviser who writes plays and philosophy is an irritant, a reminder of a rival. The Emperor, his hair yellowing, his legs thinning, has come to prefer more ruthless flatterers. Seneca wants permission to retire. He has no family in Rome except his wife. There was a son but he has long ago died.'

'Seneca wants escape, nothing more than escape. Will Nero

let him go? Will he thank him? Will he have him killed? Will he watch him be killed? Those questions invite the damp and the cold even though the afternoon is hot.'

'So what was the point in 1962?'

'That retiring from a political court is as hard as arriving in it. That was the first political lesson I ever heard. V's father whispered it into my eleven-year-old ear that day behind the net curtains of his bungalow by the sea, twisting his knife towards a fleshy lump of wood. Neither Hitler nor Stalin liked men to retire of their own free will. No more did Claudius or Nero.'

'This Mr V became my teacher as well as seaside puppet-master. The balsa Seneca thanks the balsa Nero for the opportunities that have made him rich and offers to return that wealth (or most of it) to the place from which it came. He recalls his humble origins in Cordoba, in distant Spain and pleads to be able himself to return to where he began. This is the right time, he says. To do and acquire more would offend the laws of due proportion.'

'Nero listens. He screws his eyes. He gives the look of an old friend and the answer of an executioner. His face is hard to read, just as Seneca taught him to make it. He turns his old tutor's arguments back on him, just as he once learnt to do, just as his mother once wanted him to learn to do.'

'Nero does not need to prove a case only to take his tutor's case apart. He speaks of his own youth and Seneca's useful age, his continuing desire to be warned when he is on slippery paths, the inevitable incomprehension that will surely occur if Seneca suddenly disappears. The careless or unkind might even allege that Nero has frightened him away – and that might be a damaging charge to the Emperor, surely an outcome that Seneca does not wish.'

'The conversation ends. The skin from Seneca's cheeks collapses over his ears. The lines across his chin are like the thin spokes of a wheel. The face, like the man, is lessened by the loss of imperial light. Nero can return to writing, to his new wife of whom his mother disapproved while she was alive, and to dressing men and women in pitch-dipped gowns and burning them in his gardens. Seneca can bathe and change his own sweated clothes. His career does not abruptly end. For a short time it is allowed to fade away.'

Miss R walks to the window and takes a deep breath as though it were open, as though she were about to speak herself. Is she surprised? What was she expecting? This is not a story I have ever told before.

'Was seeing Seneca like that a shock?'

'Not entirely. On the way to Walton V indicated in her own indirect way that all might not be quite as I expected. On that grey 60s Sunday, while we waited for the green-and-yellow bus, she warned me both of her father's ways with Roman history and his record of rages. But I did not understand what she meant. In 1962 I was eleven years old and my knowledge of Rome and rage were equally small.'

'That was when Mr V had only recently left the semi-detached house, almost identical to the one attached to my own father's work, on the Essex clay of the Rothmans Marconi estate. V's parents were deemed "separated", a rare, cold word in that place and time. V was a year older than me but many years wiser. When she told me to tread carefully with her dad it did not

seem important. I listened. I loved to hear her speak. But I lacked experience as well as knowledge of what she was saying.'

'"Sheltered' is how my childhood would now be termed. Anger was as alien as extravagance. My primary school teachers would bluster from time to time but not at me, and not at V either when she was in the same class at the same school the year before. My own father, Max, a recent escaper to Essex from the Nottinghamshire coal-lands, was the mildest of men, even milder than the gentlest teachers in our gentle Rothmans estate where men designed military machinery.'

'V's father was a laboratory technician. He made hard steel models of military radars during the day and soft wooden models of almost anything else by night, nights that for the past few months he had been spending some thirty miles away by the sea, in the town that Daniel Defoe called Walton Under the Nase, a more accurate name, I have always thought, for a place permanently tumbling into the sea. Mrs V (as I always knew her) had ejected him from the family home. I did not know how or why.'

'It was rare for V to agree to see me on a Sunday but, when her job was to visit her estranged father, she found me useful. My reward was to spend bumpy hours looking at her legs in her weekend-shorter skirt. The price was to be in Walton at 1 o'clock on that October day, sitting at the high end of a steeply sloping sofa, waiting too long for lunch, admiring wooden walls and pillars in the window of a bungalow glowering at the sea.'

'I was nervous because, as on the two previous days I visited Mr V, I was not supposed to be there. My mother, the prouder of my parents, an escaper from the city of Nottingham itself rather than its surrounding "sticks", disapproved of the laboratory technician and his daughter. Our Rothmans estate was home to engineers and mathematicians from all over the country, each of them chosen for their part in making radars for the postwar safety of the West. With no common roots, ours was a world of hastily defined social distinctions – and for us in the lower middle of the range of classes, those who were a fraction lower down were deemed much the most dangerous.'

'All the children of the military engineers learnt their letters and numbers, mostly numbers, in the same classrooms of Rothmans school, a single-storey block of bricks. But outside school I was supposed to face slightly up the social ladder rather than slightly down. Laboratory technicians like Mr V were a little lesser than electrical engineers like Max Stothard and it was better, my mother said, that I stayed away from where they lived, either as man and wife together or, yet worse, apart.'

'The Seneca scene occurred on the third visit by V and me to Walton. We were late. The back seat of the bus had spent more than an hour on the roadside, the peculiar indicator then to other buses that it was over-heated, under-dieseled or in some other sort of distress. When we finally reached the right street, V asked if I minded going on alone while she found a shop and bought some sort of peace offering on behalf of her mother.'

'I walked up the crazy-paved path through a lawn of artificial grass, the door opened, and Mr V smiled at me like a white mouse and pulled me in. He said nothing. He shuffled me beyond his hall of small wooden model toys, past the cloakroom in which he had built a precisely scaled model of our estate (I could see my house and its own plastic grass: I could see the house that once had been his), and into the front room where there was just one large model – of Roman pillars, pilasters, porticoes, peristyles and ponds. Behind thick curtains, a double row of net that gave a dirty, salt-stained light, modesty even by the standards of Essex in 1962, was a peculiar imagining of an imperial past.'

'V and her father were alike in many ways, both blond and pale-clothed, pale-faced too, puffy around the arms, like the cream chewy toffees that the travelling sweetshop brought us, like the balsa itself which in this house, unpainted and unvarnished, filled every visible space. He was a blotting-paper man, she a sheet of chalk, a neatly matching pair except that, after half an hour, still only one of them was there. V had not returned. There was only one of the V family visible on that May afternoon, in cream slacks, short-sleeved cricket sweater and an almost colourless aertex shirt.'

'I waited for him to speak. On the first of my previous visits he had asked me about my senior school plans, just as a kindly neighbour should do, querying what subjects I was most looking forward to. Latin, French, Physics? Not Physics. On the second occasion he asked why I thought that the Rothmans estate had been designed in the way so clearly shown in his model. Why were there larger detached houses by the school and smaller ones, joined to one another in twos, threes and fours further away? Ours were both part of the middle but not in the same part of the middle.'

'What was meant by middle class? Did I see myself on the Right or on the Left? At some time soon I might have to choose. On the first visit we ate egg sandwiches on the sofa of his kitchen, its walls as luridly coloured in red and yellow as his front room was white. There was a green parrot in a gilt cage. I told him that I was looking forward to Latin because a teacher had already introduced me to it and because my grandfather had left me a Latin book.'

'The second time, while V was slowly making tea, he told me that the estate was a sign of order, a structure of people as well as bricks. Order was a necessity. His voice was barely audible and I did not then understand even what little I could hear. I was dutifully waiting only for the explosion that V said would one time surely come. When we left for the bus stop an hour later, I was still waiting. As we left I suggested to V that she had exaggerated her father's rages, a jibe that cost me excommunication for the whole, long journey home.'

'Only on the third visit did I hear the wooden Seneca plead for his life.'

19.5.14

Miss R left hurriedly last time. She had to take a call. Her visit today seems similarly to be interrupted. She arrives noisily and adds a suitcase to the patterns on the floor. This time she prefers not to sit. She arches her back against the wall, a position permanently poised for a strike.

I am 'not being helpful enough'. Her mother is buzzing her phone. Her mother is a nuisance. I am a nuisance too. She wants to get back to her assignment. She has a new list of questions.

I look at her as though to protest. But I have begun this. I will go on with it. I am a bit surprised at my own patience but these are strange days, useless for any work of my own, not till I get to Cordoba.

I could have answered many more of the questions if David Hart had not developed Primary Lateral Sclerosis, his rare form of Motor Neurone Disease, and ended his life, unable to speak or walk or make any more than the most limited use of his voluntary muscles.

David was one of those who knew about 'the letter', the three sheets of paper on Mrs Thatcher's table, the one directly outside the door to her Downing Street flat, where her closest confidantes could leave the most private things. He knew about 'the interview', too, or rather the side of it that I at *The Times* did not know.

'Tell me about this letter – and about "the interview", the interview "given by the Rt Hon Margaret Thatcher FRS MP to *The Times* on Monday 24 March 1986". She speaks in quotation marks, reading from her list.

I cannot tell her much. David claimed to know everything about both. I can tell her merely that 'the letter' was important for the brutality of the attack on its beleaguered recipient and her deep hurt in response. There was hurt from 'the interview' too.

Miss R is right to be interested. Personal harm is at the heart of politics. So very few people ever knew about her hurts. David knew because Ronnie Millar told him. But I never got to ask Ronnie enough about it before he died, or to ask David before he became weak and voiceless, typing a little but mostly only medical queries, asking how Stephen Hawking's condition was so slightly and significantly different from his own, googling with a single finger joint, sucking Chateau Lafite, his favourite, through a straw. Nothing can bring back answers to questions never posed.

The kind of history happening outside my window today is so much clearer. This is land beside the Thames outside the Roman city walls that I walk past every day, land for traders, sailors, stevedores, soldiers, criminals, their guards and the desperately poor. White flakes fall thickly now on the ground around the disused gates, exposing other pits of past construction. Barrows appear below car parks.

Plastic sheets protect the walls that are to be kept, the old brick walls, fifty-three courses of grey and gold that were here before the newspapers came. Only the red brick plant itself is set for immediate collapse. That will soon be history in the more usual modern sense, neither the uncovering nor questioning of evidence but the newly obliterated 'you're so history' kind.

It is amazing for me to see this. Hardly anyone else at 3 Thomas More Square seems to find it so but hardly anyone else here now was in Wapping when it mattered. There are hundreds of newspaper-makers above and below me in this office tower and everyone wants as fast as possible to get away. The fall has begun. Even on ground so often refilled over two thousand years this is an event.

20.5.14

I am expecting more questions about Margaret and the letter but instead she wants to know yet more about the V family.

'They were so different from my own', I say.

'Really?'

'The difference was not in every way. My father and Mr V looked quite alike. Mr V was somehow whiter because he was blond but Max Stothard was pale too, sharply so, where his hair stood against his skin. Maybe all adults looked the same then.'

'My father had escaped a secretive family of Nottinghamshire Methodists to take a degree in Physics. Mr V had taught himself. They did not like each other but that was not a serious thing. Any casual observer would have seen interlocking cogs in Britain's military machine for making radars.'

'The big difference between them was the place of argument in life. In 1962 the Vs introduced me not only to politics, which eventually brought me to Margaret Thatcher and my Senecans, but to books of all kinds. The box room at the top of their stairs, the room that in our house was reserved for me and our suitcases, was their one place without balsa.'

'Instead, they kept there the condensed versions of every sort of book from Marx to Miss Marple, Gibbon to Gertrude Stein, Kingsley Amis and Kingsley Martin, crime novels, classics from French and Russian, "Readers Digests" mostly, "Campbell's" as Mrs V called them, stories without the added water, just like the soup.'

'These books made V something of a polymath as a young girl. She could sound as though she had read almost everything. It was always dangerous to have an argument with V about what happened in a novel. Since none of us had yet graduated to discussing whether books were any good, or how or why they were any good, V was our very own professor of Politics and English.'

Miss R scrambles for her notes.

'V knew books that Mr V and his wife had already absorbed for the corroboration, or otherwise, of their political hopes, hers well to the left of his. Copies of Dickens and Woolf were not merely Campbelled and digested but gutted, chewed and spat back between their plastic covers. Sometimes there was evidence of fatherly pleasure, the *Annals* of Tacitus on paper so thin that his ticks for Seneca dented a dozen pages behind each one.'

'Or there were crosses of dissatisfaction, pages brown-inked "progressive cant" or ripped away completely. Words from the past were as serious as any screams of the present.'

'And your own family?'

'Between the Stothards and the Vs was not the tiny gap in employment status that exercised my mother and father, my mother most of all, but the massive gulf between silence and the clashing of ideas. V's was a family where books and politics were one, a conservative vs two socialists at a time when under the Conservative Party we were told we had surely never had it so good. In my own house there were only five books and never any talk of politics at all.'

'But you kept in touch with Mr V?'

'For thirty years after that long-ago time he sent postcards and letters written in pale brown ink, mainly in the 80s when he noticed some egregious failure of mine to support Mrs Thatcher's position in an argument, afterwards when his target was some incompetent whom he thought I might influence, the Secretary of State for Work and Pensions (the Work always deleted) or the Governor of the Bank of

England (on a bad day he deleted England).'
'Ours was a one-sided correspondence.'
'Are these all of them?'
'Everything that is left is here, but not for long.'
She shuffles some frail pages.
'I replied to Mr V only a few times. He did not want replies in 1987 any more than he had in 1962. My one attempt to answer a question he posed about the world's oldest parrot fossil (found a few hundred yards from his front door) produced a fusillade of abuse. He wrote like a man with a gun, "fire and forget" as the missile men of Marconi used to say.'

21.5.14

Miss R is calmer this morning, her hands almost still and retracted neatly from sight. She has time. Perhaps she knows she is in the right place. Her new patience is like my own in these days of limbo.

Next on her list is Ronnie Millar, my man 'who put the words in Mrs Thatcher's mouth'.

'Was he a friend to David Hart?'

'Ronnie said so, especially at the start.'

Miss R says nothing more until she asks with her most mechanical voice, crossing her legs, tapping her feet, like a moving mannequin in a shop window: 'When did you first see Sir Ronald?'

That is the question on her list, the one she should have asked before.

'It was at the end of 1980 in my second year as a journalist', I reply.

'This was two years after I first met David but well before I had any power, indeed before there was any likelihood of that.

I was still not yet thirty. It would be six years before the newspapers moved to this watery patch of London and I moved to the "executive Mezzanine". Yes, I was on the other side of town then and, as it seems today, on the other side of time.'

'Ronnie Millar was my earliest guide into the court of Margaret Thatcher. When I first spoke to him it was on his sixty-fourth birthday, only a year older than I am now, and he said that he had her on the piano. He later somewhat changed that story. He did sometimes change his stories. But the time of my telephone call to him is clear in my diary, the afternoon of his birthday, November 12th, 1980, and he had absolutely no idea then who I was.'

'I was sure of that. Unlike David he had not sought me out. At breakfast I had seen his name on the Court and Social pages of *The Times*. As the Prime Minister's speechwriter he had won an official eminence that plays and films had never brought him. Later, at lunchtime, I shared a bottle of white wine with a fellow reporter, both of us anxious about where our next story (though, in those opulent days, not our next bottle) might come from. That afternoon I looked up the name Millar, R in the telephone directory, a source then of contact details inconceivable today, and called to wish him Many Happy Returns.'

'A lilting voice immediately mentioned Mrs Thatcher and the piano. I said that I was pleased that she was sitting on the instrument and not under it. There was a pause, then a light sound that I optimistically took for laughter: "My dear, we've been rolling around on the carpet for an hour". I asked if I might come round and talk for a birthday hour about life, work and Prime Ministers. Absolutely, came the reply. Why not right now?'

'Two hours later he had given me some jokes and stories that I could use in the *Sunday Times* and many more that I could not. For my reporter's notebook he rejected any sug-

Sir Ronald Millar   :

gestion that he and "dear Margaret" were like characters from *Private Lives*: "I mean to say, we don't roll on the floor while a record player blares out 'Some day I'll find you'".'

'I pointed out, politely I hoped, that he was the one who had made the comparison. He spoke about her the whole time as though she were the star of his *Robert and Elizabeth* or *Abelard and Heloise*, one of his once famous musicals, a singing poet or nun. He treated me as though I were still some sort of theatre critic: what did I think, how could she improve, why was the rest of the cast so jealous and useless? I don't think that he had then met many journalists. We drank the champagne that she had sent round, snipping the dark blue bow around the bottle's neck with nail scissors.'

Miss R frowns. She is becoming anxious again. She begins to look as though she has been in the same position too long, her legs in tight trousers today and splayed over old Oxford lectures.

'You've told interviewers this before', she says.

There is a mild menace in her tone.

'I am saying only what I remember', I reply.

'You mean, what you have said before to other people?'

'Partly, but also what I wrote in my notes.'

'Has anyone else ever seen those notes?'

'No.'

'Did Sir Ronald talk much about himself?', she asks.

'I have told you all I can remember. I'm sure that I was drunk', I say, 'and so was he. It was his birthday.'

The mention of drink makes me want a drink now. I would like to offer Miss R a glass of wine but Wapping has always been hostile to wine. Office alcohol was one of the vices that in 1986 the new world of newspapers was meant to leave behind.

We sit against the darkening sky, each of us with a plastic cup of water.

'Ronnie never gave much of his privacy away', I say, 'not even when we were alone. He had a preference for personal discretion that contrasted sharply with his indiscretion about others, the MP whose philandering would always keep him from the Thatcher court, the minister who collected miniature spirit bottles and had tried to interest Margaret in this enthusiasm.'

'With some difficulty I learned about his schooldays at Charterhouse. This was Charterhouse in Surrey, successor to the London site occupied by numbered pensioners where we said goodbye to Richard Brain. With even more difficulty I learnt how in 1940 Ronnie had been a classicist at King's College, Cambridge (his fees paid by a secret benefactor) before first, Her Majesty's navy and secondly, Her Majesty's Theatre had claimed him as their own.'

'He approved of secret gifts?'

'Yes, so did Seneca. They were the purest kind'.

'His first political speechwriting was for "Mr Heath", two words always spoken softly at this time, but his commitment to the art came with "Margaret". His voice was low that very first afternoon. The piano was silent. His mother was asleep in the second bedroom.'

'On his bookshelves were three copies of Sophocles' *Antigone* in Greek (one of them marked up phonetically for the actor playing the part of Creon, the wicked uncle), some blue-and-white scripts of his own musicals, a paperback of the *Satyricon* in English, the copy now here in my office, and two OCTs, both bound in blue leather, some of the Cicero speeches that have long been deemed "improving" in certain sorts of schools and some of Seneca's letters and plays that mostly have not.'

I look down into a large brown box and pull out an Oxford Classical Text to show her what I mean by an OCT, a severe volume of Latin without a word of English encouragement. I add that on the lid of Sir Ronald's piano, reflected in the black polished wood, was a photograph of Britain's first female Prime Minister in a silver frame.'

'For the next seventeen years, as he grew ever closer to his "Margaret", we spoke every week, sometimes several times a week. And yes, he and David seemed to be friends as well as allies at the start.'

'When did you first notice them together?'

I am beginning to anticipate Miss R's questions before she poses them? I reply quickly.

'It was in the Falklands War. This was the event, more than thirty years ago now, that saved Margaret Thatcher's career. It was also the first event that alerted me to your four courtiers, the ones who became my Senecans, how they worked together, how they did not and how sometimes they failed to know the difference.'

22.5.14

Miss R has found the Seneca pile. She opens a battered red book, a Loeb edition of essays, and reads the titles of the chapters aloud.

'*On the Value of Advice, On the Usefulness of Basic Principles, On the Vanity of Mental Gymnastics, On Instinct in Animals, On Obedience to the Universal Will.*'

She speaks mockingly with pauses as though waiting for me to stop her.

'Which of these is your favourite? Did the Senecans have a favourite?'

'The Senecans did not yet exist, not as a group', I tell her. 'You are losing your chronology.'

She looks anxious as though that is what she has been particularly instructed not to lose.

'At the beginning of April, 1982, Millar and Hart were still merely separate names in the contacts book of a political reporter. I knew as little about their contact with each other as I did about the Falklands. They knew nothing of the Falklands either. No one did.'

'But the Argentine invasion of our South Atlantic islands was unexpected, embarrassingly so for the beleaguered Thatcher Government. The Prime Minister might either be blamed for allowing an enemy in or praised for throwing an enemy out. Who could know which? There were suddenly big prizes on offer to those who learned to care about South Georgia, those who could appreciate what a transforming story this might be. Millar and Hart lacked nothing in "animal instinct".'

'Yes, I see. Which animal were you?'

'You decide. Generally I prefer birds.'

'I had moved on a bit since that day in 1980 when I first wished Ronnie his many happy returns. I had risen from the reporter's room of the *Sunday Times* on the Gray's Inn Road into the job of leader-writer and factotum editor at *The Times* next door. This brought with it a junior observer's position at Margaret Thatcher's court. I was lucky. I argued about M1 and M3 and other 'money supply targets' with motorway names. I knew about the throw-weight of missiles that might threaten Moscow.'

'On the afternoon that war began I was also one of many journalists still trying to find the Falklands in an atlas. Our designer had a book of penguins from which he was hoping to produce illustration for the empty sea. The islands themselves, numerous and spread throughout the unexamined pages, were hard to discern. Some of the names were in Spanish, some in an obscure numerology. No one cared. There was a much more important football World Cup in the offing and the Princess of Wales was for the first time pregnant.'

Miss R presses her elbows to her knees, leaning forward as though this is my first fact of real interest.

'One ordinary morning Charles Douglas-Home set off grumpily for the Ministry of Defence. My Editor at this time had a limited patience with officialdom, a limp and a lump on his head, the latter two signalling the cancer that would kill him just before we left for Wapping. Before he left the office there were other anxieties on his mind too, the imminent visits of the Pope and President Reagan, Margaret Thatcher's maladministration of her own policies, her equally imminent electoral defeat, and the health of his cousin, the Princess.'

'By the time that he returned, his limp renewed as an uneven stride, there was only one issue. We were "all Falklanders now".'

'Obedience to the Universal Will?', says Miss R coldly.

'On Fleet Street even those who despised principles on principle discovered righteousness and self-righteousness with precise simultaneity. In the newsroom we just had to find out precisely where all "we Falklanders" were supposed to be living. It was all quite comic before sailors began to die'.

'Yes', she says.

23.5.14

The stage below is shifting as though for some new scene, maybe a new act. The protected trees around the pit are now part of a fence. The wooden boxes were moulds for concrete cubes and have fallen away. I was wrong last week. There are no new trees. There never were any new trees, only posts. The site of the pit now holds a cage for what is perhaps a particularly valuable JCB. A picket could still hit it with a carefully lobbed bottle.

This time, for the first time, I am looking from my window at the right time and can see Miss R walking towards me, watch her pick her way past the relics, watch her taking photographs, talking into a phone. She has the shoulders and colours today of a toy figure, a poster-paint postman on my old Essex train set, bright blue between the square red plant of Lego and our Rum Store, a plastic model farm.

'Two years ago I was in Argentina myself', I begin, taking the initiative after ten minutes of her desultory sifting through books and papers. She puts down her notes. She does that when I abandon her chronology.

'Three decades on', I report as though to a newspaper news desk, 'there are still Falklands protests, "Fuerza CFK" protesters supporting Cristina Fernandez de Kirchner, a President who likes to compare herself for glamour with Margaret Thatcher and John F. Kennedy, while decrying their views. They wave their placards at everyone whom they deem to be British, a group that, on the morning I was there, included a Danish couple, their small dog and a thin Canadian with a Father Christmas outfit in a carrier bag.'

'There are also balsa trees', I add.

She grimaces.

'Inside the army museum there is a map on the wall of the Salas Islas Malvinas which would have been very useful to us at *The Times* in 1982. It is not a very big Sala, more of a corridor between massive celebrations of victories against nineteenth-century Brazilians. On one side there is a boy's bedroom of plastic aircraft, Mirages and Lightnings, on puppet strings. On the other a glass case contains three blue-ribboned medals, a model Mercedes truck and a green bottle of Tierra de Malvinas dry mud.'

She closes her eyes.

'A sign to the toilets leads the careless eye away from a sailor's hat with the name General Belgrano, a bright colour photograph of a warship and the names of 323 "heroes" who were drowned when Margaret Thatcher ordered torpedoes against a "fleeing enemy". A plastic Sea Harrier completes the scene. The sinking of the *Belgrano* was Millar-Hart-and-Wyatt's first joint move in my direction, May 2-5, 1982.'

Miss R opens her eyes, picks up her book again and begins to write. She has a curious knack of asking for explanation without saying a word. I give the answer that I think she wants.

'The British Task Force (a curious name that for reasons unknown had attached itself to the available ships of the Royal

Navy) had by early May, after many a nervous moment, reached its distant destination. The diplomats were in disarray. The war had begun. A torpedo in the side of the battle cruiser, *Belgrano*, a ship in the wrong place at the wrong time, seemed a reasonable response to reasonable fears.'

She makes an electronic note. I am back on the right lines.

'News of the sinking arrived slowly. Slowly too there emerged awkward questions about our target's position. This was not a total war. Diplomacy still decreed its wrong and rights. Those who knew about 'rules of engagement', including the newspapers' Defence Correspondents and their friends at the Ministry, said that the *Belgrano* was outside the combat zone and moving away from the Task Force at the time, that the attack was a disgrace, should never have happened, that admirals' hats should roll, ministers too.'

'There were politicians in all parties who hoped that a sunken ship might even sink the Prime Minister. My first call was from a Labour friend, ringing to explain how helpful this former cruiser could be to her cause. She was not a senior figure. Her name was Jenny Jeger, the J in 'G, J, W' a newly fashionable company formed by a young Socialist, Liberal and Tory to lobby on behalf of companies.

'Individually these three were not important: G, a languid Liberal of the then dominant Scottish aristocratic kind; J, a bouncy niece of a battle-hard Labour aunt and MP; W, a witty art collector who had worked for Ted Heath. But together they represented what was still the orthodoxy of all party elders, a yearning for the days before Margaret Thatcher was invented, a return to normality that could surely not be far away and that a war crime in a botched war might bring closer.'

'In Margaret Thatcher's inner court this was a problem.

Millar and Hart were just two of those who had the task of tele-
phoning the press, pioneer Falklandistas, part of a campaign of
military precision to ensure us that the experts were wrong,
that the Belgrano was an acute danger to our sailors, that it
was 'zig-zagging' to evade pursuit. How could anyone tell in
what north, south, east or west was its due destination?'

'When Ronnie called his voice was more than usually like
Noel Coward's, strained in the intensity of the role he
thought might impress me most, the patrician head of an
Oxford college, disappointed in the cleverness of his charge.
He said loftily that I should see our ships as scholarships and
that, if I did so, I might better prize their survival.'

'Beware the vanity of mental gymnastics', says Miss R softly.

'Yes, that was more or less what he was trying to say.'

'David Hart, decades younger, fit and full of purpose, was
on a slightly different track. He arrived at the front door of
The Times in an armoured car. SAS colonel? Cruise-ship
crooner? He attracted suspicious newsroom attention.'

'Once behind brown wooden doors he was calm and con-
fidential. He had already advised the Prime Minister that a
major Argentine ship needed to be sunk. It was what the
people wanted on "the street", those beyond the political
class, the football fans who, when Britain played Argentina,
wanted a result. He wanted one or two aircraft too, definitely
more than one, a black eye for "Johnny Dago", a carefully
calibrated black eye.'

'"The sinking should be cause for celebration", he confided
in a whisper. "GOTCHA" ran the first-edition headline of the
Sun when the news arrived. There was also, of course, the
very serious threat to the Task Force from the *Belgrano*,
the ease with which a ship might launch weapons while
appearing to be in flight and the fact that, as a man of
scholarship (was that the only kind of ship I cared for?), I

should know better than anyone about the Parthian shot, the arrow shot from horseback by enemies of Rome in a seeming retreat.'

'David did not deliver his message as succinctly as Ronnie had. But the taunt and purpose were the same. Later on the same day our columnist, Woodrow Wyatt, followed their lead. Between them they ensured that *The Times* saw the issue as it was meant to be seen, while avoiding any tasteless triumphalism that might trouble our readers.'

'That was not the last time that they worked together but for a while it remained the clearest.'

Miss R turns to a new page and draws two horizontal lines in blue.

26.5.14

'After that it was Ronnie who became my closest political "source", the word that journalists use for the most useful of their friends. David knew less and was less reliable. Ronnie seemed to know everything and events usually confirmed what he said. In the following year, 1983, we were together in Blackpool for the fall of Cecil Parkinson, the party chairman who led her we-won-the-Falklands election campaign, a pale and flat-faced man, the kind she appreciated most and hated to lose.'

Miss R stares into the outer office. A pencilled picture of a past *TLS* editor stares back at her. She blinks first and bids me to go on.

'It is odd how so many of Margaret's allies looked the same, the polished brows, cheeks that made mirrors, noses that in profile almost disappeared. Cecil was the model but I am remembering too Lord Hanson, the "asset-stripper" who helped to finance some of David Hart's campaigns, Lord Quinton, the President of Trinity College, Oxford, who offered Roman philosophy and jokes – blurring faces now, men, always men, in whom she could see her own reflection. I am not being unkind to those men. It was Ronnie himself, who carefully shared this look, who first observed the pattern, treating himself like a casting agent, as though he were outside his own appearance, judging, deciding, noting what made Margaret feel good and what did not.'

'The Times, to his great regret, was the tripwire for his "dear friend" Cecil, whose mistress, Sara Keays, gave us an "exclusive interview" about their love affair, her pregnancy and his failure to leave his wife. This was a story that most of us on The Times too would prefer to have analysed than reported. Even the journalists who were given "the scoop" were embarrassed. But there was nothing that they could to stop or even control it.'

'The front page on the last Conference day was sensational. The Times was inexperienced at sensation and some of its Tory readers, an angry crowd of them harassing me on Blackpool Station, said that they would never read the paper again. What upset Ronnie most was that the revelation ruined the impact of the Conference speech. No one cared about his carefully crafted prose when there was a scandal.'

She smiles.

'In 1984 we were together again at the other seaside end of the country, in Brighton. He was the first to give me an insider's account of the bathroom bomb in room 629 of The Grand Hotel, the blood in the rubble, the calm of "the Lady" who came so close to being killed by gelignite in clingfilm. He watched her leave in the back of a black Jaguar, "waving not driving" he said: Ronnie could not resist a literary joke in even the darkest times.'

'He survived the blast himself, he said, because at the beginning of the week he had demanded a room that was closer to Margaret. It was on the back side of the corridor but he had seen the sea view quite often enough. His first thought as the ceiling crashed and he hit the staircase wall was "My God, the speech" and he collected its scattered pages on his hands and knees before joining the survivors in their deckchairs on the promenade.'

'Ronnie saw politics overwhelmingly as the product of speeches. Writing for his mistress became the most important part of his life. He was jealous of her attention. He deplored rivals and knew how to make her deplore them too.'

'He kept in his pocket a cutting of a sketch by Frank that described "the left-right conflict which dominates our time" as the one "between her left-wing speechwriters and her right-wing speechwriters". It was almost a talisman. He lilt-ingly mocked the chauffeur-delivered jokes from the novel-ist, Jeffrey Archer. He crumpled David's cream-vellum couriered phrases too. It was at speech-time that I realised what Ronnie had and David most wanted, proximity to her person, and how Ronnie would never let David have it.'

'When the two of us were alone together he liked to speak about politics and classics as one and the same. I told him about the sycophants' lunch and he talked to me about Petronius. He told me about Denis Thatcher's seventieth birthday party, a "gin and golf" affair where he sat between an unhappy Mrs Parkinson and an unhappier girlfriend of the Son, "Mark the menace" but still less of a menace in Ronnie's view than the Daughter, whom her father called Carol Jane. Ronnie quoted lines about Trimalchio's gold-grasping wife, Fortunata, and paused so that I could praise his powers of memory.'

THE SENECANS

'A speechwriter needed to be close to his client's family, Ronnie explained, just as Lucius Annaeus Seneca had been, the first speechwriter in the tradition in which Ronnie saw himself, a manager of Nero's mistresses as well as one of the very first men to understand the principles of writing a speech for someone else to deliver, the science of it, the setting out of arguments that the writer would not necessarily use himself, the ranking of them in order, the grace notes for sliding from one to another, the way to memorise and deliver the words. What, why, when and how? Both he and Seneca knew why a speech had to answer those questions and how, by weighing the answers, a good speech could be distinguished from a bad one.'

'Mrs Thatcher's original voice oscillated in the range between parrot and owl. Ronnie and "one of her PR friends", dealt with that together despite Ronnie's belief that he could quite easily have done it alone. It was, in any case, a superficial problem. The permanent danger was that so many people hated her, particularly and most dangerously the people who said that they did not. "She used to spit out her words like my Latin teacher in Reading", he recalled. "But when you think of the snakes that surrounded her, she should have turned them to stone. "Nero forced both Petronius and Seneca to commit suicide", Ronnie added tartly, "although that would be quite inappropriate today".'

27.5.14

Before Miss R leaves she asks if I was ever tempted from the outside into the inside of politics.

'What about you?', I counter.

'My mother and grandfather were political enough for all of us', she snaps.

'Only once did temptation come', I tell her. 'It did not stay long.'

'That moment was in 1985, the year before Wapping, when there was a move from somewhere to put me into a "Policy Unit". The idea sounds even more absurd now than it was at the time. It would have been a bad mistake for everyone. Fortunately, the Mandarins, as Ronnie discovered, deemed me insufficient of a "team player" and "too liable to confide in others".'

She is almost out of the door, with her short blue jacket over her shoulders, when she asks a different question.

'Did you ever meet a man called Sir John Hoskyns, Ronnie's fellow plotter in the earliest days?'

'Yes, I did.'

'Was he really the clearest and cleverest man she had?' She asks as though reading from instructions.

'Well, he was the straightest-backed of the flat-faced men, a strategist trained in soldiery and computing. Clear? Yes. Clever? Yes. He produced a paper on how to crush the Left called *Stepping Stones* which even the boldest thought too bold. He was a good source to me. He trusted *The Times* in what was almost a family way. His wife was an artist friend of Charles Douglas-Home's mother, the woman whom both John and CD-H called "the Queen of Norfolk".'

'Ronnie and I watched John Hoskyns as Margaret Thatcher drove him mad, as he tried to escape, as she would not let him go, as he tried to escape again and did. She accused him of wanting to hurt her cause by publicly leaving it. He thought that to be a suggestion from a tyrant. Ronnie asked if I remembered that scene where Seneca is trying to resign his offices and the mad, bad Nero refuses to let him go? I nodded. I knew it better than any scene in ancient history though Ronnie did not know that.'

'I never spoke to anyone of Mr V in Walton. This was also the first time I heard a friend refer even obliquely to Margaret Thatcher's madness. Her enemies spoke of it all the time.'

'John wrote her "that cruel letter", Ronnie whispered. He sneaked to her room like "a ghostly apparition" and left it where she could find it by herself, alone, with no one to help her absorb the shock. A military man in a hurry, he thought she was missing so many chances, letting herself and the country down, preferring her own "intuition" to his own inexorable logic. She had never received anything like that letter before in her life'.

Miss R moves back from the door, lays down her jacket and stops me there, just as I am about to reprise the importance of resignations, attempted resignations, failed resignations.

'I already know what you are going to say', she says.

'What is that?'

'You're going to tell me the story of the "slipper wheel", the warning that the most important position is the one from which you are about to fall.'

She says the words slowly, challenging me to contradict her.

'Maybe we'll come to the "slipper wheel"', I reply.

'So why', she asks, shifting direction as she so often so disconcertingly does, 'do you recall your time with Ronnie so well?'

She moves her shoes closer together, white again today and almost side by side, edging away a pile of Seneca's essays and letters, *On Anger, On Mercy, On the Shortness of Life, On Style as a Mirror of Character*.

'Because, as a young reporter, I took good notes and because today I am older and leaving this office, leaving

Wapping and in a mood to remember. Is that not what you want?'

She looks out at the dirty sky.

'And because Ronnie is worth remembering, worth reassessing. He took his responsibilities seriously, a seriousness that was hidden because he came to be known best of all for his jokes, his style, his *elocutio* as he put it. He was not a scholar. He affected a genial disdain for the professors whom he had left after his one Cambridge year. But it was dangerous ever to assume his ignorance. He once surprised a speechwriters' party with his knowledge of a teacher at the court of Henry VIII, who translated works that he thought were by Seneca but that are not. In the 1970s he had wanted such a character for a Tudor play.'

'Politics and writing were all part of the same business, he used to say. It was the business of being human. Some of his theatrical friends used to snipe at his working for "that ghastly woman". Some of his political friends looked down on him as a showman. Their shared error was one of Ronnie's favourite themes.'

'Sometimes he took her on theatre trips, for pleasure, not instruction, the pleasure for her, most of all, of being applauded as she took her seat, a response that took him risk and trouble to arrange. Margaret the performer must never become too theatrical: actors, as Seneca knew, were not trusted to tell the truth. But neither must she neglect the artifice of the stage: if she was not noticed she was nothing. Politics was an art irreducible to logic – and Ronnie was a modest master of it, telling me many things and teaching me more.'

Miss R turns a page in her book of roman numerals.

June

Stand, who so list, upon the slipper wheel,
Of high estate; and let me here rejoice
And use my life in quietness each dele,
Unknown in court that hath the wanton toys

—THOMAS WYATT after Seneca, *Thyestes*

1.6.14

It is much easier to write about Margaret Thatcher now that she is dead. This is not because last year I might have libelled her. I would never knowingly have done that. The dead cannot be libelled (that is one of the first laws that a journalist learns) but my ease in talking and writing does not come from freedom under the law. It comes because her ghost has gone too. She was a ghost even while she was still alive, someone whom journalists and politicians began to understand less and novelists rather more. It is better not to look directly at a ghost. This office is full of novels that Miss R should read, English not Latin, modern stories by Beryl Bainbridge, Philip Hensher, Alan Hollinghurst and Ian McEwan, as well as those by Seneca and Petronius who were on the shelves first.

2.6.14

Miss R has not enjoyed her journey here today. I know this from the way she sighs and seizes the chair. She has come here not by car but on foot, avoiding the simplest route, varying her journey away from the clogged Highway to the path along the concrete banks of the canal. Searching for her notebook, chuntering to herself as much as to me, she complains of sweating roads, a jungle churchyard full of tropical birds, parakeets and budgerigars.

'Are they escapers from a zoo, she asks, 'or immigrants with nowhere else to go?' This is not a good day for her white shoes.

I know exactly where she has been and why she might feel sick. She has visited the site of the Latin lessons. She has put off till today the task of seeing the pub where Frank and I declined nouns and conjugated verbs. She has pushed open a door into the most ponderous of Hawksmoor's churches. She has found a Bangladeshi playgroup in the gloom. She has walked the side roads where Ronnie illegally parked his car. And finally she has looked through broken windows at the place where we learnt *The Usefulness of Basic Principles,* where David showed off his homework and Woodrow checked on our progress and the problems of *I Claudius.*

Sensibly, she did not stay there long. The roadside by The Old Rose is grassed and fetid now on even the best of days. The path down to the river will become even more disgusting until someone pulls a lever to put the canal water back. Maybe there is a leak, maybe the harbourmaster has lost his job. Whatever the cause of the drought each separate section of the Thames dock channel has suffered a separately shallow fate, the first part holding just enough cloudy river for a diamond drift of oil and leaves, the second dried and steaming, the third clear but toxic, the fourth full of floating blossom in a Petri dish of golden brown bubbles.

I walked this way myself last week. It ought to be a way to avoid the polluted Highway. Instead, the air smelt worse – of vomit and of dead birds, visitors and natives, afloat on green slime as flat as a snooker table. As soon as the canal was behind me, even the fumes of limousines heading to Canary Wharf came as relief, even the lorries the length of small trains heading to the east coast ports.

In 1987 The Old Rose was a haunt for drinkers, drunks and five Latin students. It is closed, planked and boarded now. it was the last survivor in what was once a string of pubs serving beer and petrol fumes, entertainments for Jack the

Ripper's victims, his tourist pursuers and the mistresses of J.
M. W Turner, the "little fat painter", as the locals knew him.
Still standing, more or less, it is now the last survivor of the
club that gives this book its name.

No one should take this canal route till the water returns.
Perhaps that will happen when the newspapers are gone.
Sometime I have seen school parties here, groups led by
anxious teachers seeking a brick-and-water classroom aid, a
reminder of Britain's sometime supremacy at sea, the decades
when this channel connected dock to dock in a chain of
trade that stretched almost to the coast.

Sometimes the children are learning how to canoe.

4.6.14

'How about Lord Wyatt', says Miss R, her mouth suddenly
a thin red line of exasperation. 'Newspaper columnist, bookmaker, diarist, wine-snob, friend of rich and Royalty.' She is
speaking as though reading. She is leaning forward. 'There
is much to say.'

'You could have asked me before. The most important
fact to understand is that Woodrow was a master of flattery.
Visit Churchill College, Cambridge, the last resting place she
chose for her papers. Look at the obsequious letters from
those offering help. At the height of her power Mrs Thatcher
attracted devotion of the kind that is good for no one,
hymns to her virtue that eventually deafened her to all good
sense. But the prime flatterer's role – in this highly compet-
itive field – was the one that Woodrow Wyatt held.'

She scribbles in her book.

'He didn't hide it. He flaunted it. He used to boast how
he telephoned to "cheer her up", to tell her facts of her suc-

Woodrow Wyatt

cess that were "hidden from her by ministers", to pronounce upon her natural virtues, to accept her gratitude for his laudatory columns, to say how good her own newspaper articles had been, articles that she had sometimes never even seen before Woodrow praised them.'

'Didn't David and Ronnie do the same?'

'David never came close enough to compete. Ronnie was a ruthless critic of Margaret by comparison with Woodrow's Voice of Reason. Look in her archives for yourself. The longer that she remained in Downing Street the more dependent on nonsense she became.'

Miss R signals for me to stop. 'Go back a bit', she says. 'Start at the beginning, always at the beginning.'

I'm going to make us both more comfortable. I point to a small padded sofa by the door, too old for the new offices, about to be abandoned in the move. I should help her but she does not wait to be helped. It is light enough for her to grasp it with one hand, a surprisingly strong right hand, to drag it across the paper stepping stones. She draws her arm across the view as though she were pulling aside a curtain. For the first time we sit down together, looking together down the cobbled road.

'Woodrow and I were never close', I begin – in pre-emptive defence of my failing to help her with whatever history faculty question she is working to answer.

'You say you are interested in David Hart, Ronnie Millar, Frank Johnson and Woodrow Wyatt? Well, Woodrow and I spent the least time together of all the four men on your list. He was the most difficult. When he was alive we shouted at each other as much as we spoke.'

From the new comfort of the sofa I point out some of the places where we used to shout, the collapsing upper floors, the barricaded doorways, the mangy plots of lawn behind the gates.

'That was then and this is now', she says, moving away from me along the seat where there is little room to move. 'My job is just to find part of the picture. There are people working on this all over the place.'

I don't fully understand her. 'What picture?'

She does not want to answer and looks as though she would prefer to take back what she has said.

I still feel mildly confused. I should be sharper to talk about Woodrow, the man who will be at the heart of one of the strangest Senecan stories. Miss R almost relaxes as I begin with what was once well known but is not known so widely now.

'Lord Wyatt of Weeford, as Mrs Thatcher later entitled him to be known, was a man of frail appearance, strong opinion, moderate skill in many things and magnificence at flattering the powerful. In 1984, when I met him first, he was already a veteran moth at the flame of British power, a famous host who poured out fine wines and fierce words, most of them in the cause of his friends. I saw him then as a populist snob, a proud man who prided himself on knowing the People's opinion. He considered me to be a non-populist snob, much the worse kind.'

'But you worked together for years', says Miss R, for the first time seemingly surprised by my answer.

'Yes, we needed to work together', I tell her. 'That did not mean that either of us wanted to.'

'Yes, he worked for *The Times* and he had his weekly column in the *News of the World*. But he exercised his zealotry in the cause of characters who ranged rather narrowly, I thought, from Margaret Thatcher to the Queen Mother.'

'Although he brought fun into a room, he brought trouble too. He was loyal, which was a virtue of a kind, except when he sat at night with a dictating machine in his hand. Many were the friends who thought him loyal until they read his diaries after his death. He was generous with his gifts, particularly to anyone who could help him in return or with whom he had shared his childhood. His "Voice of Reason" was a title held with a wide smile without irony.'

Miss R circles her hand towards her body, her way of saying that I should start further back.

'So, yes, when he first invited me to lunch it was to abuse me as "a naive intellectual" and to use me in some way if he could. That is what he told me later. He wanted to talk about short stories and plays, his own in particular, the virtues of Robert Graves's *I Claudius* and the possibility of his writing a novel himself, maybe on a Roman theme.

'Did he mention any other Senecans?'

'He told me that David Hart was a maniac, a security risk, more libertine than libertarian but somehow influential on Margaret. When he spoke about Ronnie, he used the term "hired hand" – even though Ronnie was never hired, never paid anything for his speeches, and Woodrow himself was always desperate to be paid. We drank wine of which he was volubly proud. His diary recorded the name.'

'And about Frank Johnson?'

'Woodrow thought that all wit was dangerous around Margaret Thatcher, but that Frank's wit, being the subtlest, was some of the safest. She did not always understand it.'

Miss R looks unimpressed. Is that all?

'I could tell you much more about Woodrow Wyatt', I say, 'but not from the first time we met. The first time we talked (I was alert now to all her distinctions of seeing, talking, sharing food) was on the *Belgrano* day when he delivered the identical 'scholarship' message to me that David and Ronnie did.'

'You should have mentioned that before', she complains, more like an interrogator than a historian.

'I don't think so. Woodrow was less directly concerned with me that day than were the other three. He aimed always at the highest point in any social or editorial pyramid – and that was not me on that day, nor on many others either.'

'There were many later lunches, like the one at which he used Kingsley Amis to stop me trying to reduce his contributions to *The Times*; or the many times when he abused me for reporting the "madness" of John Major on Black Wednesday; and when he invaded my office with Frank Johnson on the way to a *News of the World* party and put his finger through an oil painting.'

I expect Miss R to ask for more about that Black Wednesday, September 16th, 1992. It was a well-known date once, when suddenly an economic policy collapsed, when speculators spread the political reputation of a Prime Minister across their trading room floors. It is one of her subjects, possibly her main subject. Instead she stares through the glass walls of the *TLS*, imagining some impossible past in which oil paint might have surrounded us instead.

'Was Woodrow Wyatt, the *News of the World*'s Voice of Reason and dinner host to a Queen and Prime Ministers, a regular wrecker of art?'

'No', I say. From a sharp angle I can see her own face in the glass, querulous and broken into parts by the remains of transparent tape which, till yesterday, supported a calendar.

'Woodrow was a connoisseur. He knew about paintings, particularly those by his ancestors. That was the day when he tried to show off his knowledge of the dull brown portrait of an artist at his easel that hung behind my office door. It was a 'novelty item', he said, that had entered the *Times* art collection only because its subject, a pseudonymous Jacob Omnium, who also used the name Belgravian Mother, was a once renowned writer of Letters to the Editor.'

'"The small black dog playing around its master's shoes", he added proudly, "was from the brush of the lion-maker of Trafalgar Square, Sir Edwin Landseer". Woodrow was still explaining this to Frank, as though to a moderately damaged child, when he touched the creature's tail and a large patch of brown paint and varnish fell into his hand.'

Miss R smiles into the smeared mirror.

'Frank Johnson was a wary friend to Woodrow as was I. On that picture-punching afternoon Frank stood beside us like a don about to enter a brothel, sardonic, contained, certain that he should not be on his way to the *News of the World* party but looking forward to "the copy" for his diary he might get from the night.'

'As the tail pieces fell to the carpet he bounced up as though he were about to dance and smiled at me as though he had planned the embarrassment himself. Frank was impressed neither by Woodrow's art conservation nor his art history, not at all when he noticed the little plaque at the bottom of the six foot picture that clearly identified Landseer's sausage dog.'

'As the tour continued, Frank smiled kindly only on the faces of Henri Blowitz and William Howard Russell, reporter heroes of the second half of the nineteenth century, the first fortunate enough to have been painted by the fashionable Frenchman, famous portrayer of Hamlet and Queen Victoria, Benjamin Constant, the second by a hack who made a decent job only of the Crimean tent.'

'Both men pointed to the only female figure on the walls – and in the whole *Times* collection – a woman who had married a former proprietor, lived with him for a year and then died. Beside her was a peculiarly beautiful lily, with, in this case, no indication that the flower had come from a superior artistic hand. Frank smiled again. Woodrow scowled.'

Miss R is making me nostalgic, normally what she wants to avoid. Or maybe it is the looming sense here of departure and destruction.

'These paintings were what everyone expected at *The Times* when I was there – antique, imposing. My walls themselves, however, were not at all what visitors to the newspaper imagined. They were low and windowless, their proportions liable to oppress even a captain of submarines and to delight only an interrogator of evil intent.'

'When the journalists of *The Times* arrived at Wapping in 1986 our place of work was that long tube of brick that you can still see, corrugated-iron roofed, beside the main plant. At the far end, where the cartoonists sat to catch the light, there is the wide door for Charles Douglas-Home's wheelchair, the door that he did not live long enough to need.'

'In the then new red brick offices there was room only for machines, managers and the journalists of the *News of the World* and the *Sun*. So our home became this so-called Wapping Rum Store, built, it was said, by prisoners of Napoleon's wars in grey and yellow brick and apparently set to survive now again, as expensive shops for the expensive flats when the latest Wapping revolution is complete.'

Beneath the mezzanine

'No new window in this brick was then allowed. Before we moved to the London docks in 1986, few had even known of the Rum Store – and none had cared. But architectural conservationists became rapidly romantic. Some of those who sympathised with the print union protesters found it easier perhaps (and more soothing for their guilt) to put up small obstacles to our business than large ones.'

'Perhaps the "rare French brickmanship" around us was indeed a masterpiece. Whatever the reason, all queries about whether a hole might be punched in our office walls for natural light, or for any reason other than a wheelchair, were met with shrugs. It was as though I had walked the two hundred yards up river to the Tower of London and asked for a white plastic conservatory on William the Conqueror's White Tower.'

Miss R has had enough. This mention of King William is too much. She is getting anxious about her 'chronology'. I have come to recognise when this happens. She fears a return to Thomas More. She wipes her face, complains about the dust in the air and studies her notebooks, the electronic pad first, then her SENECA.

6.6.14

Immediately below me I can see what will happen next. The last parts to be built are the first parts set to go, the glass tower of lifts and gardens and atria that grew from the western side only when it was safe for there to be glass on the plant at all. In 1986 there was only brick. Any panes then would have tempted bars and ball-bearings from those opposing Margaret Thatcher, market capitalism, Marxist groups deemed traitors to the Marxist cause, scab journalists, scab electricians, scabs of every kind who were doing 'print-workers' jobs'. In minutes it will be glassless again.

Yellow cranes carry crashing balls of steel. There are grey concrete ramps where escalators once gleamed. Blocks of ceiling-lights, anonymous parcels of weight and black tape, hang down from cables like bodies brought down from a mountain. Fountains of water play on the pillars, no longer to create the illusion of calm but to prevent fire.

Miss R has a map and photographs. She prods and asks, asks and prods.

'High under the roof is the dining room where we once entertained visitors and did not dare to invite Margaret Thatcher in February 1986.'

'Go on.'

'There would have been a riot outside if we had tried. She might have been tempted to come through the gates. She would surely have been advised against doing so. Some of us liked our lunching box in the sky. We wanted it to be seen. We thought about its redecoration. We thought what we might serve for lunch. And then we played host to her in the Mikado room of the Savoy Hotel. 'Three little girls from school are we, ending our career with a touch of glee', sang Frank, who loved opera, even *The Mikado,* and, as a schoolboy extra, had shared a stage with Maria Callas.'

'I was the one sent ahead to check the place cards. Thus Margaret and her civil servant, who liked to be punctual, and I, who had my job to do, were beaten to the room only by a man with a Hoover who worked on till he had cleaned every corner. She seemed younger than at the sycophants' lunch, more crisp, less motherly, less and better perfumed. We mused on whether patients should pay for bed and board in NHS hospitals and if not why not. We remembered Anthony Berry and his dogs.'

'She had seen an excellent idea for advancing wider share ownership in *Good Housekeeping* magazine, "such a good guide to our culture" she told us when the lunch finally began. David had wanted me to mention his name at some point so that I could report to him her response, a warm and favourable reaction, he hoped.

Somehow the opportunity never came. I blamed the man with the Hoover.'

Miss R points at the black hole that, till five minutes ago, was our office dining room.

'Beside what is left of where we ate is the last girder of the corridor where Woodrow once pushed me against a wall. I was sure he was going to hit me. This was soon after the *Good Housekeeping* and Hoover lunch. He was enraged that a *Times* political writer, in a formally arranged interview for Good Friday, had asked the Prime Minister about her personal shares, her dealings in those shares and whether share-dealing was something that prime ministers should do. "This was a disgrace", he screamed. "None of her responses should be printed. It was a breach of an agreement made at the lunch".'

'Not the lunch I attended', I said.

'"Then it had to be another lunch", he snarled back.'

The setting for the whole scene has been struck by steel now. For the first time Miss R is watching with clear attention. 'What was that share business all about?'

I too am rapt by the wrecking balls. 'At the beginning of 1986 even her most loyal courtiers were beginning to be concerned at what was then called "sleaze", not yet a cliché. David saw "spivs" everywhere. Business supplicants saw David Hart and no less firmly held their noses. Ronnie feared that a little PR man, the same little man who wanted to share his elocution classes, was entwining Westland, Mark Thatcher, a knighthood for a tobacco boss and a request to sponsor a motor racing team.'

'But Woodrow was furious at the calumnies. Surely we had not asked Margaret about such nonsense? She was quite right to ask that, if she did not like the interview, we should not publish it.'

'I told him that I didn't understand. An interview was a theatre show for her. She had to be calm and she, if not he, surely would be.'

'Woodrow retorted that she had "quite enough real enemies" without my becoming one, "friends of yours", he sneered, John Mortimer and Antonia Fraser who were modelling their plots against her on the plots against Hitler. She needed protection. Our interview was intended to be about "popular capitalism", the "way ahead", "trade union intimidation at Wapping", "the 'next big challenges", more specifically, if that was strictly necessary, about the future of British car production, the question of whether patriotic customers might buy more Land Rovers if the Land Rover company remained in British ownership.'

'This last unlikely theme, I guessed, was one proposed to her by Woodrow himself. He did not hit me but he did hold my jacket and push my shoulders hard against the plaster. The government has not "lost its strength", he said. It is not "accident-prone". Margaret will "without equivocation lead the Conservative Party into the next election".'

'That wall cannot have felt the like until the iron ball that has just now crashed it into sky. I told David what had happened, hoping for some sympathy. He said that Woodrow was absolutely right; that *The Times* was "out of control"; that the Editor and I were not sufficiently loyal to Margaret; that Frank was furious with me; that, if we were not more careful, it would be time for the "Colonel and the Wild Beast" to take over. When David was angry he often spoke in code. He never seemed to mind when this stopped him being understood.'

Miss R has been listening with an ever more puzzled look. 'I thought that you did support Margaret Thatcher in those days?'

'Yes and no. *The Times* was in a difficult position. Whatever the Editor, Charles Wilson, and I, his deputy, thought of her and her policies, at least half of our readers hated both. Unhappy readers were always liable to defect to other newspapers that made them happier. Defecting readers meant lost money. Too much lost money might mean lost editors.'

'Where did we stand? We drew a triangle with a long horizontal base to mean support, a shorter upright to show attack and an acute line between them. We stood on that "acute".'

Miss R gives a sly look of understanding. She taps her SENECA notebook. She wants me back with Lord Wyatt.

'Any attack on Thatcher at all', I tell her, 'made Woodrow angry. Fortunately for both of us, he could never remain angry for long.'

'When he invited me for lunch at his house the second time, a few months later, he had more important anxieties than the Prime Minister's Australian mining portfolio, and why it had taken six years of power to put it out of her personal control, or about promises to ennoble sponsors of racing teams. He again feared that I would try to remove him from *The Times*.'

'Woodrow was right about that. I still did not like his unswerving support for his dinner party guests. I still did not appreciate his weekly claim to Reason. He thought that if I ever had a chance I would probably "kill" his contributions (killing being the verb of choice for removing unwanted articles from newspapers). He was right about that too. Those were impeccable reasons for a lunch.'

'That was the day he invited Kingsley Amis too, one of Woodrow's many friends who had made the meandering journey from left to right over their years. When I arrived Amis was already there, seething quietly in a tweed jacket beside a table on which his Booker Prize-winner, *The Old Devils*, sat. Woodrow told him that this study of sexual rivalry among Welsh pensioners was a masterpiece. Woodrow was ever adept at praising those who did not need more praise. He thought I needed extra lessons in that art.'

'Our main topic was to be money. Amis was to be his support. Woodrow was never as wealthy as he liked to seem. Difficult marital unions as well as the industrial sort had seen to that. His difficulties were real and freely confessed, albeit of the kind, he said, that could not possibly last. Unlike David, Woodrow was without codes. He was direct. Few ever misunderstood him.'

'Woodrow was confident, enthrallingly so as it seemed to me in our good times. He had been briefly rich in the past. He had owned his own small newspaper which he would have liked to be a large one. He once wrote a short story about a get-rich-quick scheme and published it himself as if to make the fiction true.'

'He always liked to live as though he were inevitably (and soon) about to be wealthy again, about gently to rejoin his school friends, racing friends and royal friends in worry-free consumption – in his own case in the cause of the public good. As for the present, the money from his column in *The Times* mattered to him a good deal. He was keen that I properly understood this tiresome but temporary problem.'

'As other guests arrived there was a brief diversion. The subject was the appropriateness at dinner parties of serving good wine at one end of the table and bad wine at the other. Woodrow said he did this all the time. It was fortunate, he said, that young people normally preferred to sit together even if it meant that their champagne was from Sainsbury's.'

'Amis said that the practice was fine as long as one's own position at table was guaranteed at the good end. I said something haltingly about the dinner of Trimalchio and how the satirist, Juvenal, had howled when the rich of Rome tried this trick on their guests. Amis mentioned an awkward incident with an Arab ambassador. I said nothing. Instead I watched our host pour pale wine from old bottles, and listened as he asked if Juvenal and Petronius had parts in *I Claudius*. He did not recall them there "creeping and poisoning about" but those were the Romans that he liked best.'

Woodrow was a latecomer when we began our Latin lessons at The Old Rose. But he successfully annoyed Frank with the amount he could remember from his schooldays. And he loved Robert Graves. A Roman bestseller, packed with parallels between then and now, was one of the kinds of novels he most wanted to write.'

'Which Roman "enemy within" was most like Margaret's

"enemy within" and would-be successor, Michael Heseltine? Which bore was most like her early supporter and estranged foe, Sir Geoffrey Howe?'

'Before I could stumble to an answer, Amis quoted the appropriate wine lines from Juvenal – which made me wish that I had never raised the subject in the first place. Woodrow assured us that we were not to be drinking Sainsbury's champagne any time soon. Amis grasped nervously at his glass of Scotch and we went in to lunch. This menu too would be committed to his diary.'

'Afterwards Amis signed the copy of his book on the library table. Woodrow smiled and praised the sagacity of the Booker judges. He was as keen a collector of books as I was, one of our earliest bonds. Most of the recent winners, he said, were rubbish. In the year before *The Old Devils* the substantial cash prize, satisfyingly free of tax, had gone to a book about a deaf-and-dumb Aboriginal: the money had been collected by a women's collective, a conga of Maoris creeping around the dinner tables. It had been a fiasco. He thought the prize would never survive it.'

'And then, why had his friend, the black-haired beauty, Beryl Bainbridge, never won? Maybe "beauty" was not quite the right word for Beryl. She had a simian appeal at best, he said, but sexy, certainly sexy. She also wrote very good books, though not as very good as Kingsley's, of course. She was a fine painter in oils and charcoal. She was from Liverpool, via Camden, and a "general good thing".'

'As I left to return to the office, Woodrow put the signed copy into my hand. I looked surprised. I was surprised – and pleased. The black-ink inscription read "Jolly good lunch and cheers to old Peter, Kingsley Chez WW, 1986". This was the first, but not the last, time that I was 'Woodrowed'.'

'Woodrow mentions in his diary of this lunch Amis's admission of having given up sex. I did not hear that myself. He also notes the 1964 Cos Labory and the Graves Royal 1947, wines that I drank without discrimination. After that we became almost friends. I did not try to reduce his contributions again, or at least not for another eleven years.'

My 'first edition' of *The Old Devils* is now by Miss R's feet. She stacks it carefully on one of her piles before getting up to leave.

She is going to miss the main show of destruction today. At Wapping this afternoon, Woodrow's corridor has already gone. The floor half-carpeted in blue for the most senior managers has gone. The zone with the sign welcoming visitors to Sun Country has gone.

The grandest offices of all are to be crushed by the claws of the highest crane. A man in a blue overall points up to a place in the sky. I am trying to remember the pleasures I took there, the storytelling, the hunts for stories, the successes, the wit and wisdom of friends. Instead I am seeing all the aggrieved subjects of newspapers in the past thirty years who would love to be driving that smash-and-grab machine, would probably pay to be driving it.

'Just think, Miss R, of all the people who hate the newspapers that were in those offices, sometimes with a reason, often with none.'

She stops. Perhaps for once she is following me rather than leading. She seems keen to leave as fast as she can.

'Think of the pickets of 1986, the Tories too fond of schoolgirls, the celebrities with mobile phones, the "scroungers", the Prince of Wales (for reasons, architectural, political and personal), that Karmic football manager, that other football manager whose face was turned into a turnip, the doctors in bed with their patients, the Cabinet ministers who did not have sex in football kit or keep a Miss Whiplash in their basement.'

I cannot remember all their names. All I can see of Miss R now is the back of her tight belted coat as she leaves the room, just like one my mother once had. I am even remembering the rock star who did not surgically silence his guard dogs, who sued, and won a grand apology. I am thinking on and on, of worse and worse, because bringing back bad memories is what the dying of a building, like the dying of a person, seems to do.

12.6.14

'Margaret Thatcher was not one of those who hated newspapers, not in her high days in power anyway. The *Daily Telegraph* was her paper of habit and the *Daily Mail* was a reliable supporter. She also once mentioned to me her reading of *Today*, a "plucky newcomer in the middle of the market". This paper, now dead, was edited briefly at Wapping at the time by the fierce Labour Party supporter, Richard Stott, a master of editorial disguise, author of *Dogs and Lampposts*, soon to be available again in a nearby Oxfam shop.

From the rest of the press her courtiers aimed to manage her moods, ensuring that she should read only the parts that she would like. Columns by Frank Johnson were often in her cuttings file. She best enjoyed sketches that compared her to something conquering and stately, a galleon perhaps or a giant gun.'

Miss R looks surprised. 'Did she have a sense of humour?'

'No, she often failed to see Frank's jokes, but laughter was not what she was looking for. She was not even unusual in that. Most Members of Parliament liked to be sketched by

Frank. Unlike a cartoonist he did not exaggerate their thick necks and noses. Any minister who had made a speech might find himself the butt of an extended parody but this was at least some proof that the speech had been made. Even *The Times* had stopped recording speeches in any other way.'

'When did you and Frank Johnson first meet?'

This time I snap back at her. A greater variety of approach would be good.

'Rather than keep asking the same questions, you might do better reading what Frank wrote about Margaret Thatcher herself. He is still a good guide to how she wanted to be seen – as confident, motherly, harder working and farther seeing than the rest of her kind.'

She asks her question again. She has her list and she will not be deviated. She is comfortable and has adopted the two-seater sofa for her own.

So when was it? She has made a strange game for us but I am in it now. I must not be caught out. Frank and I must have 'brushed by' one another often after 1978 but when did we first 'meet'?

I take a longer pause. 'The date that Frank and I sparred our opening rounds, shadow boxing, the role we came to occupy for the rest of his life, was probably in 1985. I remember the scene if not the precise date. It was another mark in that crowded year before we moved to Wapping, when newspaper revolution was in the air for those keen to sniff it, even if the exact form that it might take was known to very few.'

She makes a note on her SENECA pad.

'We were both looking out over a different London skyscape at the time, one just as little known to me in detail as the one we are looking out at now.'

'Are you proud of that?'

'No, I am not proud. Everyone should know the names of the landmarks outside their windows. It is only polite to be able to do so, to make visitors feel at home or at least to feel that they are with a host who is at home.'

She looks around the piles of personal and professional relics, the two types indistinguishable among the removal piles.

'We were at a party on the roof of what "in 1929 had been the tallest office block in London, 55 Broadway, headquarters of London Transport, a masterpiece of Art Deco, all grey limestone and Murano glass with a statue of the West Wind by Henry Moore". But it required Frank's companion to tell me that.'

'Who?'

'Well, at least he seemed to be Frank's companion. I knew Frank then only as the wittiest journalist to have ever worked in parliament (thus almost never in the offices of *The Times*) and as our present Bonn correspondent (posted temporarily abroad at his own request on an assignment for self-improvement). The authority on Murano and Henry Moore turned out instead to be the companion of our party host.'

'It was a summer night and this very learned visitor from Canada was here looking to "buy properties". He leant against the roof-garden wall and looked like a pile of gift boxes, battered but expensive cubes loosely tied with string, his square face scouring the skyline ten degrees at a time, naming, turning, naming, turning, naming, turning until he saw the Houses of Parliament where he stopped.'

Miss R turns her own eyes too. So do I. We each embarrass the other.

'The visitor was challenging Frank or me or anyone to say Big Ben, to embarrass ourselves by naming something so obvious. No one was so foolish as to speak so, in the next ten minutes, Mr Black, who had dressed for the night in the darkest shades of brown, had identified every office, church and tower block that we could see.'

'It was as though he were responding to questions that he alone had heard. Over there was the glass tower of New Scotland Yard.'

With no sign of thinking Miss R signals student dissatisfaction at a mention of the police.

'And then there was Falkland House, home base for our watery colony, the Equal Opportunities Commission, from whose clutches all had to be saved, or so said Frank. Mr Black ('Conrad' as we were to call him) agreed.'

'It was thought that this distinguished visitor might soon own the *Daily Telegraph*, where Frank was once a star. So there was a small crowd around him, individuals trying hard not to be a crowd, who listened as he spoke, laughed at what they hoped was a joke, and worried that the visitor might ask one of them a question about their home city that he could not, or chose not to, answer himself.'

'The head of London Transport, Keith Bright, an equally polymath businessman, had to parry the most dangerous thrusts. He was the only man I knew in London life who had also known my father as a laboratory colleague in Essex. I very much wished Max Stothard had been with us on the rooftop that night. The two men shared Marconi sports days. We talked about those, the cream cricket flannels, the distinction between engineers and technicians, between the cakes (good) and the sandwiches (poor) which we took at tea.'

'After fifteen further minutes on top of the capital's most artful underground station, Frank was firmly in charge of the senior conversation, saying that Henry Moore's "West

Wind" was the finest work on the building but that Jacob Epstein's "Day" might have come close had it not lost an inch-and-a-half of penis to the censors.'

'"And what do you think happened to the rest of the penis?" Frank smiled his question. Conrad Black laughed. There was even louder laughter from his circle of listeners. After that Frank and I noticed each other more and more, warily at first, testing each other like boxers, trading insider gossip to impress where we could. He said that he was keeping a diary where one day all would be revealed.'

Miss R is taking lengthy notes now. Occasionally she looks out east where we first looked when she first arrived. There will be no good for her today in playing the Conrad Black game and asking what buildings we can see. Yes, I have worked in this sliver of riverside land for almost thirty years. I ought to know. But most of the time I was in that thin brick warehouse down on the ground. And, even in the best of circumstances, I can understand geography only if I do it as though for an exam. In today, out tomorrow.

As for this particular spot, I am a newcomer. I have been in here, up here, overlooking the Wapping plant site, on the sixth floor of Thomas More Square, for barely more than a year. There has been no time to change the spatial incuriosity of a whole life.

Next month everyone in the *TLS, The Times,* the *Sunday Times* and the *Sun* newspapers is moving west a little, to a new home beside London Bridge Underground Station. One of the titles that came here is missing. Woodrow's old home at the *News of the World* has disappeared in recent scandals which, as she quietly makes clear, stand outside Miss R's period of study.

'Nothing after 1997 please', she says, clinging to her calendar.

Outside this window the rubble is piling. The gatehouse has gone. Yellow-jacketed men pick over the flat remains like scavengers on a toxic copper mine, gingerly turning over the relics of security gone by. A small crane eats the few pieces of metal and plastic worth placing in its mouth. The next occupant of this office will not care what was there before. There used to be a grey-box bridge across the cobbles, like a sea-container washed up after a storm. I wonder what happened to that. No one will need to explain this place to visitors, not ever again.

'And no, Miss R, don't test me. No, we cannot see the execution grounds where More and so many others met their ends, not unless we go to the other side and look out west towards the underground at Tower Hill. We can see some Hawksmoor churches and their graveyards for exotic trees and birds.'

She makes a querying note.

'Any grotesque church around here is quite likely to be by Hawksmoor and, unless you are unlucky enough to meet a polymath like Lord Black (O yes, he occupied his newspaper property, and his peerage, before spending a little time in an American gaol), you can reasonably safely pretend.'

'Look instead at the Highway as it stretches out to the east, the Ratcliff Highway of the old marching songs. Watch for the dry-docked sailing ships that were once supposed to entertain shoppers at Tobacco Dock. There is no point in going back too far (thirty years are enough for me) nor going too far away. Most of what you seem to need happened in the hundred yards I can see without straining or thinking. The Senecans can properly be bade goodbye from here. It is too late to learn the names of the tower blocks now.'

July

To shower bounties on the mob should you delight
Full many you must lose for one you place aright
—ANONYMOUS
Cited by Seneca in *On Giving and Getting*

9.7.14

This morning Miss R is dressed like a builder or protester, heavily jacketed for a warm day. She has her silver SENECA notebook in her hand, her pen poised to write, when, outside the window, down beside what was briefly in April the pit, a crowd begins to form, a swirl of men, workers in search of the right entrance, a cloud of yellow jackets like bees blown by a wind. Mixed among them stand starkly outlined figures whom we know by name.

The first swings like a drunk between the new trees set in their metal boxes. Then comes another, clasping the black brick wall beneath Thomas Telford's stencilled alphabet. Further ahead are two men enfolded in polythene wrapping, protection for that part of the plant wall that is not yet ready for felling. Smoke belches sideways into the narrow road. Among the flow of demolition men our class is once again leaving the plant for its Latin lesson, dodging, diving, hiding as it used to do.

The view is not exactly as it would have been in 1987. We rarely all walked together then or even as far apart as the figures are now. Only Frank, Woodrow and I ever walked in Wapping much. Ronnie drove his bronze Rolls Royce and parked it with impunity. David walked only on his own property.

Today the four seem as one with all the other walkers. As the smoke swirls and the plastic billows a ragged line forms, fast at the front, a slower gradual exit for those behind. It is like closing time at a bar, or the few minutes before the end of a football game when the knowing leave for the car park, or the flight of animals from a forest fire.

David Hart is the first, the most hurried at the head of the line at the farthest end of the narrow cobbled path. Close beside me Miss R is unpacking her case, a blue satchel designed in expensive imitation of schooldays. I have told her much about David already, not all of it good. What to add, if I am asked, now that he is closer?

One thing is for certain, one of rather few certain things about him: of my three metaphors for his exit from the stricken plant he would have accepted only the forest fire. David did not go to football matches or, except for Latin lessons, drink in bars that closed at legally designated times. Yes, he was a "man of the people", trading forever on his reputation as the representative of popular will; but, no, he did not do many of the things that "men of the people" do.

It was Ronnie, the figure swaying third in the line, who first told me some of things about David that later everyone said: that he was a bankrupt and not to be trusted; that he kept women in different parts of London and was not to be trusted; that he claimed to be a confidante of Margaret Thatcher but was not trusted by her at all, especially not in the election campaign of 1987 when no one was to be trusted; that he hunted crypto-communists in the media, a sport that, while virtuous in intent, was, like communism itself, more effective in theory than practice.

I must remind Miss R that Ronnie was David's friend. His enemies made charges that were much worse. David did know a lot about a few things, including about animals and forest fires. Piero di Cosimo's panel landscape of fleeing birds and deer, based on Lucretius's philosophical Latin poem, *De Rerum Natura*, was one of his favourite things. He said that if he could steal a single object in the world, that would be the one. In Oxford's sleepy Ashmolean Museum it would not even be hard.

David was also knowledgeable about sixteenth century Italian sex manuals, the woodcuts and prints known as *I Modi* that were destroyed in their original form by the Vatican but survive in variously disputed copies. He could recite some of their accompanying sonnets. He admired their writer, the courtier and pioneer propagandist, Pietro Aretino. He used the words *cazzo* and *culo* for cunt and arse. He was always going on about the right positions, on tax reform and strategic defence but *I Modi* were The Positions that he liked the most, he said. He turned to sex whenever the talk in our Latin lessons of 1987 turned to an election topic on which he did not have a position. Wapping to him meant *The Times* and Jack the Ripper. Sex was his "default".

Miss R sees a Position on the floor and frowns. It is a grey image of fornication, not one of a too outrageous kind. But I forget that in a woman of her age a liberal tolerance and an acute sensitivity to the appropriate sit unpredictably side by side.

Some of *I Modi* show vigorous sex from the front, some from behind, positions with one, two, three or four feet on the floor, 'sixteen pleasures' in all. They are sometimes known as 'Shakespeare's pornography', notable more for the muscled equality between the sexes than for erotic charge, nothing that would shock or arouse in the internet age. Miss R seems unhappy at these 'buttocks of the night' nonetheless.

'Were these David Hart's own copies?, she asks.

'Copies of his copies', I say.

'David liked to tell the story of their original creator, Giulio Romano, who avoided Papal persecution when his engravers did not and is the only contemporary artist named in a play by Shakespeare, Act V, Scene 2 of *The Winter's Tale*. He said he liked the later versions of *The Positions* best, the ones in which the 'cocks and cunts' belong to Greeks and Romans, gods and goddesses, heroes and heroines, Mars and Venus, Antony and Cleopatra, false names designed to deceive the censors. While Woodrow's introduction to the court of Nero came from Robert Graves, Ronnie's from King's College, Cambridge and Frank's from a Wapping skip, David's came from the image of Claudius's third wife, Messalina, taking up a not especially adventurous position in a Roman brothel.'

Miss R ensures that the Position is hidden before cupping her ear that I should continue.

'David loved to claim expertise. He "offered" obscure types of nuclear technology, Middle East security, polling statistics, property tax reform, Moscow bank accounts, most of which, said Ronnie, were hardly known to him at all.'

'Ronnie did concede sometimes when David made a sound literary point, about D. H. Lawrence's admiration for Petronius on one unlikely occasion. David had a fierce dislike of Lord Byron, which Ronnie shared, and for any other "subversive of the Left" wearing the label of the Romantics. An early appeal of the classics for David was that in many books it is deemed the Romantics' foe.'

'Ronnie accepted, too, David's knowledge of *I Modi*, the imminent publication of a first English edition, the secret ownership of a single surviving sixteenth century copy, while adding in his haughtiest manner that the "insatiable prostitute" calumny against Messalina was false propaganda from Nero's mother, her successor in the imperial bed. He asked questions about *The Winter's Tale* designed to show that David, while knowing one abstruse fact about the play, had probably not seen or read it.'

'Woodrow Wyatt, walking second in line today, saw David

hardly more favourably. Woodrow was quietly jealous of libertines and liked only the rich who, in his view, deserved to be rich, a group that did not include the sometime bankrupt son (yes, that was true enough) of a Jewish banker, a phrase he was not afraid to use in 1986.'

'Seneca was harsh on bankrupts, those who deliberately did not return what they had taken. That was a Roman position to which Woodrow would from time to time return. He thought that David's mysterious influence with Margaret was absolutely to be resisted in an election when she was beset by far too many pedlars of novelty.'

David's face is wholly shrouded in cloud. Miss R looks blankly into the same cloud.

'Woodrow used to joke that David looked like Lord Lucan, one of Woodrow's aristocratic acquaintances, who disappeared from Belgravia in 1974 leaving behind a dead nanny. He joked about this resemblance so often that he seemed to be trying to make it more than a joke. Ronnie, whom David called Rondino, used to reply that David was no more like Lord Lucan than he was like the poet, Lucan, Seneca's nephew.'

Miss R calls a halt. 'Two Lucans?'

'The ancient Lucan was the greatest writer of Latin epic after Virgil. Like his uncle he was implicated in a plot against Nero and forced to commit suicide, declaiming his own works as he died. But Woodrow wanted nothing of Lucius Annaeus Lucanus. One Roman writer at a time, he thought, was quite enough.'

Frank, the backmarker but walking now the fastest, was the Senecan who was the most suspicious of David. He had good reasons, he said. He did not elaborate what these suspicions were, preferring to be strictly factual except when he was writing his sketches.

'To Frank, David was mostly as David saw himself, an

avant-garde film producer, property speculator, seigneur of country estates and writer of various fictions; but also Mrs Thatcher's unacknowledged ruffian, insecure conspirator, alert conspiracist, agent, spy, man of enormous wealth that he justified for the public good, wordsmith and a monger of mashed ideas. All of this was true.'

Woodrow stumbles and raises his hand like an umbrella to steady his fall. He is squashed flat against the black walls by wind but, despite the swirling smoke, he seems today the man most comfortable in his ghost walk to The Old Rose.

'Woodrow was always the Senecan most comfortable in Wapping, the man without whom the plant might never have produced a newspaper, the Labour MP turned Thatcher-loving lord, whose links to the anti-communist Electricians Union were vital in allowing the plant to produce newspapers without printers.'

'Woodrow was the most practical about the threats from "the Left". In the late 1980s, once the coal miners were conquered, that meant most of all the dismantling of trade union controls over the press. He was suspicious of us all as dilettantes just as we were suspicious of him.'

After ten minutes all four figures have turned the corner towards the Highway and our unlikely place of learning. Miss R watches me watch the scene.

She bites her lip. I feel anxious. It is not easy separating the then from the now when the then is obscured by time and the now by dust and thistledown.

The men on her list are sketched in barely more detail than an alphabet, expressionless today in the dusty distance except in soft charcoal outlines, Hart as a bulky letter H, feet splayed and grounded as though for a fight, Millar as willowy letter T, a tall man taking inspiration from the upper air, Wyatt as a lop-sided L-shape, sniffing the slightest breeze,

Johnson, a slim and compact J. But there is no doubt to me who they are.

10. 7.14

'H was for Hart, not because it was his initial but because he looked like an H. T was for Millar, L for Wyatt, J for Johnson. This alphabet trick was one I learnt early from Ronnie. It was a variety of abstraction, an everyday discipline of his art. Look at that one, he used to say as we sat in my office. His target could be anyone, a sub-editor, a sportsman, a lawyer, a man filling the drinks machine, almost always a man. What letter is he, an O, a P, a Q, an X?'

'We had a vantage point in the Rum Store roof, a gallery mocked as "the Mezzanine" by those who worked on the news desk below. From there Ronnie could see almost as far as the distant Sports department ("surprisingly full of O and B, don't you think?") and over the partition walls to Fashion and Arts ("lovely I and T"). One day we visited the cellars where every copy of *The Times* since 1785 was bound and caged, where pale librarians ("barely semi-colons") kept our cuttings in buff envelopes and readied us for the digital age by issuing books with no insistence on return. There was everywhere less alphabetical order than he expected.'

'Yes, Miss R, Ronnie was in every possible way a man of letters. In his youth he was grateful to a family whom he called the Ks who had helped him to Cambridge from his birthplace in Reading ("a town in southern England that, if conceivably possible, one should try not be born in"). I told him about my Vs.'

'We had a mutual friend called Mr G who lived on the Isle of Dogs.

It's out there under the farthest cloud to the right, the one shaped like a submarine'.

'G had also migrated from Heath to Thatcher in search of continuing influence. My first visits east with Ronnie then were to G's house, flat-fronted yellow brick beside swirling water, where around a circular table of Chinese food the ambitious men of the Tory Left, Messrs M and B and F, traded tactics for their journeys to the Right.'

'There was much tasting of wines to lend legitimacy to these evenings of plot. Ronnie's favourite party piece was about letters, letters as people, letters excluded from names as courtiers fear exclusion from court, a recitation of some feeble scraps by Alexander Pope, lines from a comic poem about the characters of the alphabet excluded from the name of the fashionable playwright, Thomas D'Urfey. It was absurd but, once it had been explained to her, he told the munchers of sweet-and-sour, it made Mrs Thatcher laugh.'

Miss R does not laugh.

Pope's excluded courtiers were the P and the C. They were characters both alphabetic and human. They fear to be ignored. They want to be close to their master, to be part of him. They profane and protest. I can still remember the lines even though I can't roll them out like Ronnie did, making his points to his Margaret with all his theatrical authority.

P protested, puff'd and swore,
He'd not be served so like a Beast;
He was a piece of EmPeror,
And made up half a PoPe at least.
C vow'd, he'd frankly have releas'd
His double share in Caesar Caius,
For only one in Tom Durfeius.

And so on. I have to keep the lines silent in my head this morning. Miss R is in no mood to be amused. Are they funny? I thought so at the time. Pope was a bit of a Senecan himself and when he saw discord around him wrote that it was merely a failure to see the secret harmony. Was that a survival strategy at court or the sound of a man burying his head in the sand?

14.7.14

Today it is Miss R who is dressed for a funeral, long skirt, too long, almost trailing on the ground, black shoes, stockings, no nail varnish, black sweater and jet stone around her neck. I ask her.

'I hope it's not someone you were close to.'

'Now for the Latin lessons', she says, ignoring me as though I had made what was once known as 'a personal remark'.

'Surely all that Senecan study was just another cover for your plots?' In church she would be like a mourner disbelieving the encomium to a departed crook.

'No. I can see how our Latin lessons might seem. In the summer of 1987 there were many Tory plots, and many journalists on the trail of them, all more or less cleverly concealed. But the main point of our meetings at The Old Rose was to study Latin. This was not a cover story.'

'Who suggested the lessons first?'

'The class was Frank's idea. He and I had good times and bad times but he has to get the credit for that.'

'We were never close in the way that Ronnie and I, or even David and I, were close. We shared a space on the Mezzanine. We had sometimes shared assignments too. We

Frank Johnson

were together on the morning after the Brighton Bomb, I with a hangover, he writing with high style of that "great and terrible thing", of silk pyjamas on the sea front and the bright moon in the dark blue sky.'

'More often we were in different places. We were very different kinds of journalists, more different than in some respects either of us wanted to be.'

'As others occasionally pointed out, we shared a similar background in the lower reaches of the English class structure, I from my Essex housing estate, he from the London East End, Shoreditch, not far from here. But this did not make cooperation any easier. The biggest difference was that I had taken the then available "direct grant school" route from Essex to Oxford, a free education among fee-payers for the academic poor, and he had failed his Eleven Plus exam and missed university altogether.'

'He was not proud of his Minus Eleven, as he called it, but he had proudly missed what he learnt to see as the ubiquitous Whiggism of academe. He had worked his way through newspapers from the messengers' floor, speculating about which senior women journalists he would most like to fuck, teaching himself, and being taught later by the then Tory intellectuals of the *Daily Telegraph*. He wanted the Latin that he thought they all had.'

'Frank liked to argue, as much as possible from first principles or from classic texts, ideally those that were somewhat obscure. He first mentioned his lack of Latin to me when talking about one of his favourite history books, *The Rise of the Dutch Republic,* written in the 1850s by the American anglophile, John Motley, full of aphorisms, drama and a deep suspicion of Catholics. Frank wanted to read for himself the language of Cicero and Tacitus that had kept the brave tribes of north Europe, the Batavi and the Nervii, "after almost twenty centuries still fresh and familiar in our minds".'

'I knew nothing of Motley then and little now, an ignorance that in his mind helped to counter my Latin advantage. His head was full of the failings of Charles the Simple and Philip the Good, names with clear meanings, generalisations of the sort not now allowed, "the German who was as loyal as the Celt was dissolute", the funerals of the Gauls that were "pompous" while the Germans stood "unambitious at the grave".'

'Free Hollanders were good, Tyrannical Spaniards were bad. This was the style and certainty that Frank, as describer and commentator, appreciated most. The Dutch Republic was unfashionable, studied by few of his friends, a field on which he was safe from surprise attacks. He saw in Motley a dramatist of the kind that in miniature he had become.'

'But he still wanted Latin. When he decided to begin the lessons he had missed by missing university, he thought, reluctantly and only for convenience, that I might be the one to teach him. He wanted classics for wisdom – but also for adornment, for its help in creating the illusion of what was wise, one of the commonest of all uses of classics in those corridors where the powerful prowl, primp and preen. He wanted the Latin of the more learned characters in his parliamentary cast.'

'It was Frank who first found our textbooks. It was he and I, in fact, who saved the entire *Times* classical library from fire and shredder. We rescued every book from a skip just like the one that is now there again, taking away dust and iron and plaster. It was our first joint enterprise. We sweated side by side in that loading-bay. Neither of us could resist the lure of the Loebs, reds and greens, those useful student texts with English on one side and the ancient language on the other, valuable both to those who read Latin and those who would like to and do not.'

'That was a triumphant day, probably the best time we ever spent together. Against the yellow of the skip the red Latin books looked like tomato ketchup on the yolk of eggs, the green Greeks like salad on mayonnaise. Geer's Diodorus, Watts's *Pro Archia*, Sir James Frazer's *Fasti*, Warmington's *Laws of the XII Tables* and, the one that came to matter most, Seneca's *De Beneficiis, On Giving and Getting*, as he elegantly called it, translated by John W Basore, all of them once considered essential to the *Times* library, but in the new era deemed not even a luxury.'.

'Frank and I saved those texts that day like antiquarians at the dissolution of a monastery. As soon as he could read a Latin sentence, and I encouraged him that this need not take long, he wanted to begin with Cicero. He knew already of the *Pro Archia*, now available to us in the 1923 *Times* ex-library copy, Cicero's struggle to win citizenship for his poetry teacher Archias. This was a founding document for the history of the Renaissance, he insisted, daring me to challenge him. For the history of Cordoba and of flatterers too, I might have said but didn't. Cordoba was not then so important in my mind and I tried not to enter unnecessary contests with Frank.'

'So yes, Miss R, Frank genuinely wanted to begin his assault on accusatives and the pluperfect. He genuinely wanted to move his Cicero in English to a Cicero in Latin, from the right-hand page of N. H. Watts's edition to the left. And I was the one to help him.'

'But in the meantime we had troubles. His other reason for urging me to a petrol-polluted pub in the spring and summer of 1987 was]political, to stress my responsibility (not yet being met) to help Mrs Thatcher's re-election. He did not like the necessity of this either.'

'Nothing with Frank was ever easy except his appearance, plain, handsome, saturnine, self-consciously without show. It was only by unfortunate accident that we were on the same Mezzanine at the same newspaper. Life would have been much quieter at *The Times* in Mrs Thatcher's third and most fraught election campaign if Frank had remained a writer, outside the office and responsible to someone else. But his position had turned into that of an editor and suddenly he was responsible to me.'

'How exactly?' She is twisting her jet beads as though in genuine mourning.

'All newspapers liked to mount "talent raids". Frank was a *Telegraph* man at heart. Mr Black from Canada had by this time completed his skyline ambition to buy the *Daily Telegraph*, our main commercial rival and the traditional voice of Tory England. Frank's old home and school wanted him back.'

'My Latin pupil was made easily insecure by stories elsewhere in the press, often and transparently in the *Daily Telegraph* itself, that his *Times* bosses were about to be fired. On this latest occasion he had been offered a 'safe haven', as he described it, as editor of the *Telegraph*'s comment and leader pages. He would have accepted had not, against my advice, *The Times* made him the offer of exactly the same job with us – and for more money.'

'Frank could be a careful editor but for the most part he wanted the status more than the work. Like many great writing journalists he had a variable enthusiasm for improving the words of others. My own view of the *Telegraph* tactic, which I ill-advisedly set out in an office memo, was that it would be better for us if Frank "fucked up" the heart of the opposition paper than ours. But this wisdom was ignored and by May he was working directly for me in *The Times*'s most sensitive parts, plotting for pleasure every day.'

'On a good day on the Mezzanine Frank saw me as merely "misguided", one of his favourite words. He considered that I had made my name by doing exactly that of which he disapproved, reporting hidden facts that Mrs Thatcher and her friends preferred not to be reported. Frank's fame came, as he liked to see it, from seeing more of what could already be seen, much the more desirable talent.'

'He prized analysis over investigation – and made it clear that his was the only right way. He liked words in a leader that benefited a good cause. If he deemed an action likely to help a Conservative cause, he would want to do it. If a hundred businessmen wanted to sign a letter to *The Times* declaring obsequious allegiance to Mrs Thatcher, where was the problem? If a hundred schoolteachers wished to do the same for Labour, we could simply say no. Consistency was an overrated virtue, hardly a virtue at all.'

'After the *Telegraph* raid I was Frank's boss on the letters, leaders and opinion pages. This suited neither of us. Most routine political leaders in *The Times* in those days were tactical advice for ministers and the Prime Minister about how best to achieve their ends, where they should trim or tack to reach their destination. Frank deemed these to be vulgar, preferring that every point be backed by stated principle and quoted text, from Hobbes or Machiavelli or even John Motley. Turning a draft leader that Frank wrote into what *The Times* could say was a trial. Frank disliked our arrangements in every respect except that I had Latin and Greek. Maybe he could profit from that.'

'And Seneca?' Miss R looks up from a slew of notes within her funereal garb.

'The choice of our teacher from the past was mine.'

'Why?'

'I knew that Frank would like him.'

'Seneca was good, a realist, a hypocrite when he had to be, a force of moral restraint. Seneca believed in a deity that was everywhere and not too troublesome. So did Frank, who called himself a deist when he talked of his religion at all. Seneca both understood power and used it. He was not a favourite of liberal academe. Many educated people knew nothing about him. He was ideal.'

This morning there is a wrecking-ball hole in that place where there once squatted that skip, where *On Giving and Getting* began its journey to The Old Rose. Miss R spends the last part of the day among my files and boxes. She is both distracting and helpful. She leaves much later than she promised. She has no funeral to go to. I am beginning to prefer it when she does not promise times at all.

15.7.14

'At the first lesson with Frank in The Old Rose Ronnie Millar arrived by mistake.'

Miss R looks away. Chance is no use for her 'Thatcher project'. She wants links and intentions.

'No, that first group lesson was wholly unplanned. Someone sent Ronnie on to us from the Mezzanine, keen to get rid of him, I suspect. Newspapers hate visitors, just as actors don't want their audience backstage.'

'He had "an important message". He had abandoned his bronze Rolls Royce in the car park where the pond and fake trees are now. It was only a short walk but Ronnie had a very Senecan policy of walking as absolutely little as was necessary. My theatrical friend was somewhat frayed when he finally stepped from the traffic fumes into the bar.'

'The scene inside was one that Ronnie must often have

imagined. East End pubs were a comic cliché and 'there was nothing wrong with a good cliché, my dear'. No book was so bad that a good line should not be stolen from it. This was the piece of advice from Seneca that he used the most.'

'The Old Rose was not, however, the kind of common-place that this West End man had experienced directly. On his right as he stepped through the door was a solitary woman, straight-backed, her hair set like pink cement. On his left was a young man, no less alone, with shiny black hair, gelled as though with tarmac. As Ronnie stumbled, he only barely avoided the need to grip these human supports.'

'He did better once he was inside. He dipped his head beneath a low-hanging fluorescent tube. He conjured a drink with speed and style – as though he had known the barman in his Beverly Hills days – and sat down gratefully on a beer-stained wooden chair. Frank and I were "in the back" already doing our verbs.'

'Which verbs?', asks Miss R, more like a journalist seeking "colour" than a researcher in search of understanding.

'Dabo, dabis, dabit, dabimus, dabitis, dabunt. I will give, you will give, he she or it will give, we will give, you (plural) will give, they will give too. We had decided always to begin each session with some grammar and we stuck to that decision. We maintained the idea that we were language teacher and student even when Frank's greater concerns became great Roman principles, plus the latest political failing by myself and *The Times*. The angrier that Frank became the more useful the Latin was.'

'Once Ronnie had settled, his welcome message to us that day was of the "utter shambles, my dears" within the campaign to win Margaret Thatcher her third general election victory. "To be David Young was not very heaven", he said, citing Wordsworth in support of Margaret's current Cabinet favourite and twisting the words as he always liked to do, imagining some speech ahead.'

'Our contrasting message to him (which he did not see as a welcome at all) was fo, fas, fat, famus, fatis, fant. Ronnie reinforced his no-time-to-waste look. He was determined and urgent. Our words were not even Latin although, as Ronnie knew well, do, das, dat, damus, datis, dant would have been an accurate conjugation of the present tense. Frank invented famus, fatis, fant. His usual drink at The Old Rose was Fanta, some sort of ironic reminder of his childhood.'

Miss R smiles.

'Frank and Ronnie both thought this funny too. Woodrow and David would not have done. Frank and Ronnie respected one another's wit. Woodrow and David shared a mutual wariness which only resembled respect. The resemblance sometimes deceived even the two men themselves.'

'Late-learners of a language take a different approach from the young. Frank liked to contrast words that might have existed in Latin (like "fant" if there had been a verb, "fare"), with those (like Fanta) that could never have existed and that, indeed for all three other Senecans, would better not have existed. Fare, he proclaimed, "two syllables like X-Ray", meant "to fuck up a newspaper or an election".'

'"Fa, magister", intoned Frank. "Fuck it, master. The magister is in the focative case. We had better all believe it".'

'The news that Ronnie brought about the Conservative campaign launch of 1987 was that every senior participant thought that every other senior participant was "fucking it up". Some top Tories brought mere sartorial problems, hair too long, waistcoat too yellow. The Prime Minister herself brought the TBW, That Bloody Woman problem, a verdict from the opinion polls which required more delicate handling and was not getting it.'

'Ronnie must have thought that you were mad.' Miss R screws up her nose as she screws down her pen into her pad.

'Yes, Ronnie did not like the cod Latin. He was the only Senecan to be trained as a classicist himself, a King's College student of Greek, influenced, though not economically, and certainly not in Margaret Thatcher's hearing, by John Maynard Keynes.'

'But Ronnie was also a veteran playwright. He had thought hard about the relationship between politics and language. He saw Seneca as a model. He saw emulation as a potent reason for reading the classics. But he did not want to talk about Latin while there was an election to be won. He was sure that Seneca would have agreed with him if he had agreed with democratic elections which he most certainly would not have.'

'And Frank himself?'

'Frank was torn between learning and life, scholarship and the Ship of State. He wanted victory for the Tories and civilisation for himself. He was still a bit stunned by attending a pre-election dinner which featured the adoration of Mrs Thatcher by a drunken cricketer and the abuse of her government failures by one of the men most responsible for them. We were at a party for a think tank. Frank sneered out the words, "to, tas, tat, tamus, tatis, tank".'

'In the first of these party-pieces, as Frank recalled, Sir Keith Joseph, anguished minister, scholar and wise tutor of her first phase in power, had torn apart the education policy that he had himself imposed as Secretary of State for Education. In the second, a purple-faced Sir Denis Compton plainly thought that his role was to respond to Denis Thatcher and not to Margaret herself. The once famous batsman and Arsenal footballer, still a hero for certain Tories of a certain age, made several jokes about being the night's "second Dennis" before collapsing into abuse of Opposition "bouncers". The Prime Minister maintained a face like glass throughout.'

'Frank was in self-mocking despair for days. Ronnie reminded him that Denis Compton was renowned for forgetfulness. He had once had to borrow a bat from the Old Trafford museum to make a test match century; he so regularly ran out his partners that a call for a run from Compton was deemed "no more than a basis for negotiation". Frank snarled. He hated sport. He hated anything that a humorist could not make more absurd than it was.'

'Yes, Margaret was wasting her time on nonsense. Yes, too, he was keen to start our lessons. He liked The Old Rose, 'our purple place' as he called it. He liked how it teetered beside the lorry-lines of the Highway, suitably coloured, we thought, for the study of empire, and how, early in the day, we wouldn't be expected or disturbed. He would have preferred Ronnie to have stayed away.'

18.7.14

Miss R made an appointment to come yesterday and cancelled it. This morning she says again that she is on her way and will be with me soon. She has to speak first to her mother who is visiting her grandfather and needs her help.

I will see her approach only if she comes in on the Wapping side, past the pile of logs where the fir trees used to be, past the nest of concrete cubes that last month I thought were tubs for trees. More likely she will come by the execution block from Tower Hill.

Whichever way she comes she won't see inside the new kidney shaped pool and L-shaped trough behind the new grey steel wall, not until she arrives up here on the sixth floor. Three quarters of the upper offices have gone. The hose-pipes play on.

I am packing and staring out the window. It does not matter if she comes or not. She has begun something. I have the note-books and the letters. Now that 'something' goes on without her.

It was May, 1987, the Thursday that the Senecans took a new turn. Woodrow arrived at The Old Rose before Frank did. The Voice of Reason was not sure what was happening on the Highway but he did not like the sound of it. At first, he seemed determined only to show me that, out of all of us, he was the most at home in a Wapping pub. He succeeded in that.

Woodrow could act many parts. A sometime soldier in wartime and socialist causes, he had sought votes in harder places than the Highway. Short in stature he could be combative or cringing as required, bow-tied in a boulevardier's or bookmaker's way, depending on how he wanted to look. Somewhat bandy in his legs, he might have been a master of fox hounds or have begun life in the docks.

It was important to Woodrow that he alone was the true man of Wapping. He considered Ronnie and David, who had never veered from the Right, to be untried by life. I was even worse, he thought, although he knew nothing of my life before he met me. He bought two pale ales ('nothing that isn't from a bottle in a place like this'), somewhat breaking his 'man of the East End' spell, and started giving me advice.

He had heard that there had been a difficult leader conference at *The Times* the previous day. He sketched the scene in the long windowless room on the Mezzanine as though he had been there himself, with Frank arguing Margaret's case, me playing the part of her would-be replacement, Michael Heseltine, with various colleagues taking the roles of other ministers and shadows.

We often did this, I told him, overtly or almost without thinking. The best way to work out a policy for *The Times* was to play out how the politicians were planning. We all took our roles and we could usually agree a result. It was the part of the newspaper day that I always enjoyed the most, not taking ministers to lunch but understanding what they might mean.

Miss R is not concerned with Cabinet ministers. Others on her team, senior figures, are attending to those. But if she wanted to find out anything from me about Michael Heseltine I could tell her more from arguing his case than from seeing him, meeting him, or sharing drinks at a party.

But Frank had explained my advocacy quite differently. And Woodrow was supporting him. Even to countenance the view of Margaret's most dangerous enemy was a heresy. *The Times* should be aiming to advance her case better, not to test it as though we were in some useless politics department of a university or playing parts on a stage.

For almost an hour there were only the two of us at the table. We discussed what it meant for a newspaper to have an opinion, how at the *Guardian* the leader conference was open to all, how on the *Telegraph* that Frank had joined the writers were personal acolytes of the Editor, virtually the only staff that the Editor had who were free of the dictates of news. The leaders of *The Times* were, in Woodrow's view, the only ones that mattered as leaders had mattered in the past. I was their steward and I should step up to my role, my role as defined by him.

He spoke much more freely than he had ever done in the office or at his house. He said I had too little idea of the dangers of the world. Life was a "slipper wheel". As well as slipping, there was always the risk of falling over or being pushed. Everyone needed a protector – and mine should be the man who had improved my Kingsley Amis collection.

What was this "slipper wheel", I asked after he had used the phrase several times. He intoned the lines to The Old Rose. It was hard to keep such sonority to a single table. He looked a little embarrassed. It was the only time that I ever saw him embarrassed.

> *Stand, who so list, upon the slipper wheel,*
> *Of high estate; and let me here rejoice*
> *And use my life in quietness each dele,*
> *Unknown in court that hath the wanton toys*

He stopped. This 'slipper wheel', he whispered, was a quote from the sixteenth-century poet Thomas Wyatt, not, he insisted too loudly again, his relative. He and his children were related to the other Wyatts, the architectural 'Wexford Wyatts'. He had a mad aunt who was always trying to link the family to the Tudor courtier and inventor of the English sonnet, the lover (or not) of Anne Boleyn, the queen who did for Thomas More. It was nonsense but she would not stop. But it was a good quote, even if it was from outside his family. *Dele* means *part*, he said, as though that were my last remaining query.

The longer that we sat together, the other two seats of red and green leather still empty, the darker the domain of danger that he painted, a place of paths that he knew and others that he did not. All power was at the centre, in politics and in newspapers. I was privileged and powerful and did not recognise what I was. All life now was a court, a network of help and hindrance and 'frightened little people'.

The slippery wheel was originally a phrase from Seneca,

he added. I looked surprised to hear him mention the name. Don't think I don't know what you're doing, he laughed. Frank must have kept him informed of everything. He said he wanted to join in. The quote was from *Thyestes*, he went on, not wishing me to miss his knowledge of the most brutal tragedy from all antiquity. Woodrow left on that occasion even before Frank arrived.

Miss R arrives as though on cue to pick up the next part of the story. She sees me writing. She has her cold gaze. She is looking far away or as though I am the one far away, far from the subject she is seeking.

'What was Frank attempting to do – improve his job prospects, improve Margaret Thatcher's prospects or improve his Latin?' Answering her is suddenly like answering a statue in a cemetery or in the last act of *Don Giovanni*. But this time I do have an answer.

'I've told you already. Frank wanted to learn Latin because he thought that a civilised man should know Latin – even at the cost

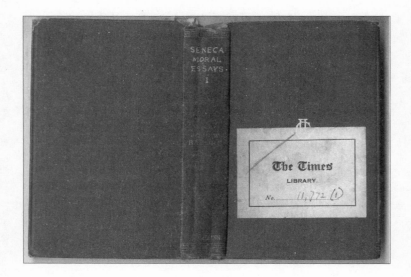

of learning it from a colleague whom he did not see as civilised in the best sense. He wanted to know about one of the great ancient speakers of Latin. He might have chosen Julius Caesar, where his hero John Motley and many students once began, or Cicero, where many of them too early ended. Instead he had our copy of the Loeb Seneca, *Moral Essays Vol 3*, newly rescued from the skip, not read since 1935 according to the *Times* library ticket.'

'On that May day in Wapping, with Woodrow on his way down the Highway, he opened it and read aloud from the English page:

Among the many and diverse errors of those who live reckless and thoughtless lives, almost nothing that I can mention is more disgraceful than that we do not know how either to give or to receive benefits.

'Ahah, my boy, he said. Whatever else was on his mind there was no warm-up to Frank's enthusiasm for this text, a product from the first century AD that set out a survival guide for rich and poor, strong and weak, controversial, practical. The Latin was a catalyst, a comfortable base for an awkward thought, the first of many.'

'For Frank the tension between learning and life was low. He wanted the one to illuminate the other. Seneca was the servant of a new kind of government at Rome. Seneca took Frank directly to the impact of newly centralised authority upon people still adjusting to that change. It took him to the Tory party whose tired leaders, at what should have been the height of their power, were quarrelling their way through the election, feeling unappreciated, failing to appreciate each other, fighting each other much of the time.'

'Frank loved novelty as long as it was old. The giving of benefits explained so much. Thatcher is hopeless at giving – honours, houses, anything', he said. "She never wants anything for herself and thinks that that makes meanness alright. No wonder even her friends are beginning to hate her".'

'"I sensed that problem right at the start", he said in a rare act of boasting. "At first I thought it good that MPs cheered her because they agreed with her, rather than in the hope of distant knighthoods or peerages. Now I am not so sure".'

'This was our first political conversation that did not concern such now neglected topics as Michael Heseltine, numbered money supply targets, nuclear MIRVs and the reform of the Rates. It was about how giving and receiving were arts in Seneca's time, lending too, and that it was a dangerous mistake, in Seneca's view, to look for loyalty or gratitude from a gift or loan, certainly not immediately, directly or from every act, and that the powerful, especially the very powerful, should give as though the act of giving were the virtue itself.'

'A long pause followed this first extract from the age of Nero, a silence broken only by the sound of a single glass settling on beer-sodden crisps. Frank nodded in agreement. He even made a note in his little pocket book. He then asked me sharply why, if this were so, I behaved as though it were not so.'

'Because his second point was about journalism, a directly related problem, in his view. There were two kinds of journalists, he went on. And lest I was in any doubt, I was the wrong sort and he was the right sort.'

'I might be a deputy editor and leader writer now: but fundamentally I was the kind of journalist who, when I saw politicians saw backhanders and backscratchers, and when I spotted the smallest exchange of benefits smelt a corrupt deal, a cover-up, a crime – or a story of a crime. In spirit I had never left the *Sunday Times* where I began. He, on the other hand, studied why people acted not what they did, ideals as virtues in themselves, intentions more than outcomes, the good above the true, the links that bound the world of politics together, without which there would be nowhere for me to dig for dirt, nothing political at all.'

'We talked about Latin for two hours. It did not take many Latin sessions for Frank to be sure that he and Seneca and Margaret (never mind about me) were made for one another.'

21.7.14

Miss R turns a new page in her SENECA notepad. She also has a red-and-black-squared calendar for 1987 on her knee and a slim edition of 'On Gifts' in English from an American university.

'How much gratitude should parents expect for gifts to their children?'

It is like a test. She stops before I can give Seneca's best reply. She points to her list of dates and names, all of them still from the 1987 election. 'What was all that about heaven, or not heaven? Who was young? Go back to The Old Rose. Go slowly.'

'Fine. I will. Concentrate. We will be talking about forgotten politicians.'

'When Ronnie arrived and sang out to the bar that "it was not very heaven to be David Young", he was referring to a court favourite of the time, a tall telecommunications tycoon, one of the flat-faced men, then famous for his reputation as "the man who brought Mrs Thatcher solutions" when other ministers "brought her only problems".'

Miss R makes two vertical lines to form what could be a chart.

'Young's unheavenly battle at this time was with the party chairman, Norman Tebbit, nominally in charge of the election campaign, still blasted by pain from the IRA attack on the Tory conference hotel in 1984, bitter in personality and appearance, and considered by Young to be Margaret's current biggest problem.'

'There were writers fighting on all Tory sides. Tebbit had a novelist assistant called Michael Dobbs who later became Baron Dobbs of Wylye. "Why lie?' by name; Why not lie?" That was David Hart's response when he heard the news of the honour he would have loved for himself. Dobbs had the doctorate in nuclear deterrence strategy that David did not, and his enviable bestsellers starred a machinating minister, Francis Urquhart, ("you might very well think that: I couldn't possibly comment") whose plots owed much to the Tory politics of his time. Dobbs was another survivor of the Brighton bomb and Ronnie deemed him a dangerous opponent for anyone.'

'The party's most successful writer was Jeffrey Archer, later Baron Archer of Weston-super-Mare but at this time no longer even Conservative Deputy Chairman because of an imminent libel case about a prostitute at a railway station. He was still available to the Tebbit side and on offer to the Young side or to any other that would have him. I remember how Frank always defended Archer to me, suspecting that I had some kind of jealousy towards him, while invariably abusing him to anyone else.'

'Young, said Ronnie, complained of every day walking on eggshells, watching his ankles for wild animals. The draft Election Manifesto had three different covers from which Margaret Thatcher had to choose, each with supporters for whom variations in cream and blue card were versions of holy writ.'

'A core reason for the election date, which few agreed was the right election date, was the fear that, with further delay, the would-be-winning team would have turned its razors on itself. Already there were stories of one man's cocaine habit and another's sexual appetite for boys, each charge delivered, and duly tagged, to any journalist who might believe it.'

'Young had his own team of writer-plotters, Ronnie himself, who was a help, and David Hart, who mostly was not. David's newest interest at this time (and his newest was always his greatest) was in a new party, its symbol a splayed capital M like a gull in flight, which could take over the Conservatives from within. Its shock troops were to be Conservative students with a penchant for rough stuff at meetings; and some mothers from the outer London borough of Haringey (not a place that David had ever been to) who disapproved of gay rights.'

'As we sat at the back of The Old Rose, Ronnie was just about to give his latest report, about to count the Tory Party casualty figures, when Frank motioned that he should stop and began reading loudly in Latin.

'Nec facile dixerim, utrum turpius sit
His style was to stretch all the vowels like a headmaster acting the role of priest,
infitiari an repetere beneficium; id enim huius crediti est, ex quo
making it clear that he could go on forever if necessary,
tantum recipiendum sit, quantum ultro refertur. Decoquere vero
and that we had no choice but to listen.
And then he began the same lines again.'

'These were words that he had not studied before and did not understand. This was Frank's test. He was challenging Ronnie to keep up with Seneca's syntax, anything, it seemed, to stop the stories of electoral strife. Ronnie stopped and stared at Frank as though at a mad man.'

'There were secrets, Frank said in explanation, that should not be revealed in front of journalists, even friendly journalists, indeed especially friendly ones like me because they were often the most dangerous of all. I sometimes wore a red tie, as David Young had been heard to remark, suggesting that red allegiances were not far away. I was sometimes heard to praise Michael Heseltine. I was severely prone to the "error Heseltinensis".'

'This tactic achieved its end. A Latin lesson might stimulate political discussion. It could also close one down. Frank was beginning to sound like Seneca himself, spraying dark aphorisms of anxiety behind columns of purple.'

22.7.14

Miss R and I begin easily now where we stopped last time. She is back in her power jacket. She is writing detailed notes as well as checking her recorder. She is in the middle of a story that she wants to hear.

'A week later, after a week of rage within the Tory camp, David came too to our retreat. I hadn't invited him. I thought that he would prefer his splayed letter M party to our own. Frank would certainly never have invited him to our lesson. Surprise appearance was David's usual way. The man who looked like Lord Lucan often disappeared like him.'

'David was an especially disappointed courtier at this time, a man behind the political curtains who feared that he would be stuck there. He yearned for the recognition to which a trusted adviser was due. He saw a world of important meetings happening elsewhere and in his absence. He would have loved to spend time in those offices of Wapping that are now empty air and black holes. He would have loved an open welcome in Downing Street. He was never encouraged to come to either place.'

'So he came to The Old Rose – in shorts, sweatshirt, cross-garters and with a bodyguard who shared both his helicopter and his armoured car. He noted the same woman and man who had first greeted Ronnie, the regular guardians of the

Highway doors. He commented loudly, as Ronnie had not, that their tarmac and concrete hairstyles well suited the road outside. This pub, he complained, was virtually a part of the road. Except when he was reporting on "real Britain" for "the Lady", anything as real as The Old Rose offered David few charms.'

'His first topic was the allegation that the wealthy shire Tory, Peter Morrison, Margaret's confidant, senior party aide and critic of homosexual law reform, had a police-recorded penchant for the buggery of boys. Woodrow said that the man was "useless" to Margaret anyway. Frank, freshly imbued with the example of Seneca, wanted to discuss whether hypocrisy (though not the sex with boys) was quite as bad as we liked to think.'

'David's main message to us was that he had been doing some "tags" and that he knew where some of this "muck" was coming from. Frank told him that in The Old Rose we had Stoicism and the fourth declension on our minds. This in no way dimmed David's desire to tell us what he had exposed. As soon as he had acquired a drink (which took him rather longer than it took Ronnie), there was no option but to listen.'

'I already knew about these tagging tricks. David had boasted of them before. No good ever came from them. During the Miners' strike he had arranged for an untrue "exclusive" about the Chairman of the Coal Board to be passed to a suspect reporter; and he had delightedly read the story the next day in reports by that man and his fellow-traveling friends.'

'During the Falklands War he had invented a weakness in the Task Force defence and "fed it", in the jargon of journalism, to a hostile critic. The recipient of the fabrication had been too smart to use it himself but had passed it on to several left-thinking colleagues who were not so squeamish and one whom David was most surprised and pleased to identify.'

'This sort of behaviour gave David the keenest pleasure. It was better than sex, he said. He pretended to use it primarily for his *British Briefing*, a photocopied monthly list of secret subversives in responsible places, particularly in newspapers and the BBC. He knew how unreliable the method was and how, for journalists of every political persuasion and none, there were stories that were simply too good not to use if others were using them. He just couldn't help himself.'

'Tagging gave him thrills, the closest thing, he used to say to screwing a tight *culo*. David used to speak often of fornication, one of his favourite words, but this was a strong simile even for him. That was how important 'tagging' was.'

It is also strong language for Miss R who, when I repeat it, grimaces as though to a swearing child. 'Normally he restricted himself to talking about his pleasures through his collection of *I Modi*, those tastefully classicised positions in which the *culo* and *potta* belonged to an Ariadne or Venus or Messalina.'

Miss R again gives her 'where are we going now?' look.

I apologise. 'There will no more references to sex in this story if it continues on its current course.'

She now looks disappointed.

'So, just for the purposes of completion, Ronnie was not a very sexual man. He was widely believed to be a 'closet queen' (to use the language of that time) and only the occasional 'Downing Street garden girl' (80s language again) contested that this was the truth.'

'And Lord Wyatt?'

'Woodrow was a veteran connoisseur of the female form, as his published diaries show, but the only yearning he ever suggested to the editor of his columns was for the novelist Beryl Bainbridge. Perhaps he thought it the only one that would interest me.'

'Frank Johnson?'

My level of intimacy with Frank was lower still. He was handsome and admired by numerous beautiful women, justly proud of his hair and later married to an elegant Scottish aristocrat. Sexually for the Senecans, that is the sum of things.'

'No new lines of inquiry will be necessary in this area', says Miss R in a rare attempt at humour. She sounds like a probation officer.'

'Back in 1987 in our Latin corner of The Old Rose David was still attempting to engage us with his latest tag-data. He had incriminated a distinguished journalist for passing scandal about one of David Young's alternative election team. Frank covered his ears. He refused to listen. He was being purist and Frank "did purist" very well. Unless David was going to talk about Seneca, he did not want to hear from him.'

'David was not to be so easily discouraged. If Seneca was the price of entry to our party he was well prepared to pay it, much better prepared for a Latin lesson than any of us expected him to be.'

'From his country house in Suffolk he employed many savants in disciplines that he might sometimes need. There was an anti-Darwinian ornithologist, a theorist of watercolours, some varyingly disciplined relics of the CIA, an Egyptologist who believed in pyramids built by visitors from space. He fed them all fine wines and chocolate squares and they fed him cues for his erudition or his jokes. He knew of the new Latin enthusiasm at Wapping and from one or other of these men he had already begun his studies.'

'So David sat back smugly in the best Old Rose chair, the only one with arms. He began talking as though from a script, an actor confident in his lines. He was always ready, he said, to sniff the ancient air, to hope to absorb learning as perfume was absorbed in a shop, as Seneca himself once said.'

'Frank began to snigger but, when we looked longer at each other, we could not stop showing that we were impressed. David had assimilated some Senecan axioms that suited him well. If we wanted to talk Latin when we ought to be talking elections, he was happy to join us, to check that he had understand each ancient point properly so far.'

'First: was it really true that vast wealth was no bar to virtue, that Seneca saw money as of only secondary importance? He very much hoped it was. He had had no idea that Thatcherism was born so early.'

'Second: was it true that poverty did not matter either, that some people were always going to be poor, that virtue and poverty sat easily together. In his view, (and might Seneca have agreed?), no British voters in 1987 were truly, materially poor. Some were grateful for their benefits but many were not.'

'Third: Seneca did not have to deal with the bloated modern welfare system. What Margaret Thatcher's voters lacked was not money but soul, nothing physical but something spiritual, ideals to aim for, to miss, as ideals were always missed, but to aim for again and again.

David had already written a pamphlet on this theme, *The Soul Politic*, one for which, he believed, he had himself benefited much less than he deserved.'

'Hypocrisy, he went on, challenging us to stop him as we usually did, was a charge too readily hurled at Seneca. And anyway was hypocrisy much of a crime? David Hart was rich and others were not. Britons were good Stoics, not obsessed by economic advance. Nor did they care about what journalists called "double-standards" but most saw merely as ordinary life. Frank nodded his agreement at this, silently suggesting that, if a true Senecan myself, I should abandon my investigation of Tory election troubles and get back on the path of helping the election to be won.'

'Just as Ronnie had begun to agree with Frank, more loudly than usual, "readying myself in the wings" as he used to say, David's driver burst through to the back of the bar and said that "the best friend" wanted him immediately on the car-phone. With expanding smugness David smiled and, without having discussed in any detail what his tagging might do for his "best friend", or any other friend, returned to his Mercedes.'

'Frank and I looked at each other again, even more ruefully than ten minutes before. We had not learnt what we had planned to learn; we were behind in our grammar book; and we had heard a set of Senecan questions that hardly disgraced the unruly questioner whom intellectually we liked to look down on.'

'It was always easy to underestimate David. He studied as though in an anthology or dictionary. But in tiny shards he studied with care. He cited Seneca against giving universal benefits, against giving indiscriminately to the undeserving. I listened to him despite myself. Margaret Thatcher too, his "best friend" also listened to David Hart despite herself – and also despite dozens of others saying that she should not.'

'She was said to like his flamboyant militarism. Maybe she did. If she chose her funeral service herself like the characters on that Greenwich stage on the night I first saw her, she shared a self-image with the most bellicose men of Rome.'

'David was always keen to be seen as an army man. Like

Seneca, David saw life as a war even though he had never fought in a war. He used to apologise to her for his artistic and philosophical temperament but say that art and philosophy was what her warrior's character needed most.'

'He affected to despise the merely material. He wrote plays about ancient religions and played the thinker himself. He believed in the power of an idea to change a voter's mind, a belief that surprisingly few politicians hold. He talked much of democracy even though he was not much of a democrat.'

'In David's absence, as though to avoid commenting on what he had said, Frank and Ronnie began a discussion about how rich Seneca had really been. The richest great writer who had ever lived, said Ronnie. Richer than Tolstoy?, Frank countered sceptically.'

'The Gerald Grosvenor of his day, said Ronnie, a Roman Duke of Westminster owning huge areas of the city centre, Italian estates and a retreat in Egypt; and the Rothschild of his day too, lending across the known world, furnishing mansions with his famed collection of ivory-and-lemon-wood tables. "So yes, richer than Tolstoy".'

'No, as Frank saw it, Seneca was not really rich. In the most vicious autocracies, with no power beyond the palace, no one ever owned anything. The Emperor could always take away what he allowed a man to win. That was surely why wealth was secondary in Seneca's philosophy. It was always about to be lost. If a man was lucky he might be allowed to retire and keep a part of what he had but many were not lucky. I pushed my chair back against the wall.'

'So, no happiness under a Labour government, Frank added, anxious that we had made our lunch unnecessarily dark. Unless Margaret gets a grip that is exactly what we will have, said Ronnie. *Nil desperandum*, said Frank, applying his new knowledge of the Latin gerund as David returned from his carphone and spat his Old Rose wine back into its glass.'

'There was briefly a sense of anticipation, the hope for fresh "news from the front", the latest instalment in the Tory plotting that so consumed us all. But David had no news. He was even more morose and wanted to talk only about himself. Because we were expecting better, we listened longer than otherwise we would have done.'

'He was frustrated, he said. He wanted his benefit. He had earned his due. When Margaret Thatcher was at her most depressed, he had given her hope. She had become cut off from what he always called "the street", those who had first put her in power, the people who she needed to keep her in power, the young who lived beyond the influence of the media, the men and women who sought moral leadership.'

'He imagined a source of power – and, like a sorcerer, had told her that he was the link to it. To help prepare her for a trip to India he had cited a Tantric Swami who was guiding the Thatcher spirit from the Ganges. She had thanked him; he had made her laugh, or so he said.'

'But in 1987 it was two years since David Hart had been at the height of his influence in Tory politics. He genuinely did dominate the defeat of the Miners' strike, by being the first to define it. He took his literary alias and, as David Lawrence, tramped the streets of mining towns. He claimed direct connection to hidden realities. He enraged the conventional. He used his own money, his own lawyers, even his own helicopter.'

'By the summer of her last election, in his shorts in the back of a Wapping pub, he was merely wanting to write a book about his role, at least to write a book that would place himself in what he saw as his own story. Margaret said that this would "break our understanding". Ideally he wanted to be powerful again but he should surely get the honours that he felt he had waited for long enough. Surely Seneca, who urged against expecting rewards directly for good service, did not see reward as never coming at all?'

23.7.14

Miss R is becoming accustomed to my office furniture. She no longer sees books and boxes as obstacles, more as stepping stones. She stumbles, catches her low, blue heel in a red ribbon and splashes letters in pale brown ink across the floor. Her next question is brisk.

'Did the Senecans meet again before election day?'

She straightens her skirt and leans against a bookcase, one that is emptier than when she first arrived but still solid by the shifting standards of this room.

'Yes, we did, about three weeks later. This time there was only one topic of conversation. This was the first day for the words "Wobbly Thursday", June 4th, the day that the opinion polls showed the wrong opinions, when the Tory leadership thought that they might lose the election and began their most serious bout of tearing each other apart.'

'Not even Frank wanted Latin lessons while this was the show on the other side of town. The Senecans were loosely distributed among all the warring factions whose very slightly different remedies were under vicious debate. Ronnie and the "no heaven to be Young" team were demanding a more central role for the Prime Minister and a more positive defence of her achievements. David argued that by seeming to reject retirement, telling a questioner that she wanted to "go on and on", she deserved still greater obscurity. The party establishment view, with Norman Tebbit in the lead and the Senecan support of Frank, argued for a more aggressive approach to the Labour alternative.'

'It all sounds ridiculous now, a set of "so what" details. But, like so many stories, like most of what goes into newspapers, it was the most serious of matters at the time. David Young himself telephoned to complain that our reporters were too kind to Labour. Ronnie complained that the TV cameras were too kind to Labour. Geoffrey "G" Tucker rang to say that Norman Tebbit was finished and Michael 'House of Cards' Dobbs too. He rang back ten minutes later with details of exactly which rooms in Downing Street were secretly occupied by his anti-Tebbit advertising agency clients and how the Prince of Wales now wanted their services for himself.'

'Woodrow tried to remain above the fray, boasting of his direct line to Margaret who always "takes my calls". He promised her that he was writing weekly in *The Times* instead of every fortnight so that he could "keep the muddled egg-heads in order", me prominent among them, as well as "the masses" in the *News of the World*.'

'Every time that something appeared in *The Times* to upset her he said that I would lose my place on the "slipper wheel". If the Tories did lose the election, I would definitely lose my job and deserve to. He described Young and Tebbit as "partners in panic", the first as "distant and weak", the second as "confused and hopeless". He wanted more emphasis on tax cuts to feed the voters' greed. Wealth and the fear of losing it was what moved votes, whatever the nonsense about virtue that Frank Johnson had picked up in The Old Rose.'

'Woodrow also wanted much more Margaret on show even if she was That Bloody Woman to the pollsters. Woodrow, like David, enjoyed citing his close hold on public opinion, based in his case on the word from far-flung race courses which he ruled as Chairman of Britain's state-owned

bookmaker. The further he travelled from the Thatcher
court the more that he found the people fearing and respect-
ing her. And let them bloody fear her, as long as they voted
for her, he snarled, quoting the Emperor Caligula and, as if
to fit in with the Latin lessons, attributing the line to Nero.'

'Beneath this battling at the top was an underworld of
businessmen seeking their own benefit from victory if it
came. To Frank's especial dismay (he despised commercial-
ism in all its non-theoretical forms) there were two advertising agencies in this war, the incumbent holder of the party
accounts, who had for eight years profited mightily from
that position, and a rival, represented by Genial "G" Tucker,
who wanted the same benefits for itself. So now, Mr G, left-
ist Tory and sometime champion of the Chinese food table,
was a secret solicitor for an insurgent challenger backed by
the farthest of the Tory Right.'

Norman Tebbit (right) with David Young (centre)

'Woodrow deplored "the Whitehall farce" in which one set of advisers hid in prime ministerial bedrooms to avoid being seen by another. He mocked the pathetic competition among ministers to appear in Party Political Broadcasts and to stop their enemies appearing. He attacked Ronnie, Frank and me for confusing the issues – and David most of all, for being "a fucking nuisance".'

'David was not part of any team. Snubbed by the Young faction (or so he thought), seeing Tebbit as barely more than a butler and Margaret as betrayed by everyone bar himself, he was planning a £200,000 campaign of his own, financed by himself and a few friends. He sat out the campaign in Belgravian and Suffolk exile, producing barely legal advertisements of sycophancy and abuse, lobbying for reduced rates in the newspapers to unleash them on the electorate.'

'On Wobbly Thursday itself Tebbit and Young came to blows, or close to blows, the closeness of their fists depending on whose account was later believed. With seven days to go to the poll itself, their supporters gathered eagerly behind them. There was grasping of lapels and the rattle of abuse. Share prices fell – and maybe were pushed. Profit made the strongest alliances.'

'In Ronnie's account there was rage like he had never seen in his political life, a destructive demonstration of the claim that 'no plague has been more costly than anger to the human race'. He spoke these words in his sing-song quoting voice. Frank sneered and David sniggered before they realised that Ronnie was in theatrical-philosophical mode. This was still formally a Latin lesson. Seneca, he reminded us, had been very sound on anger, arguing that all rage was an affront to reason and that political ideas were as nothing to rage in brutal force.'

'Even Frank, normally the purist in protecting the original purpose of our meetings, said that this was Seneca to excess. Our ancient mentor always put practice first and theory in its service. Could we please return to the anger among the Tories. Exactly who did what to whom? Why did anyone believe any of them?'

'All sides, said Ronnie undeterred, had identified groups of voters that their opponents could not reach. 'Our side has the "belongers", he proclaimed as though this were some extraordinary discovery. For the duration of the campaign, he lost his dramatist's irony altogether. Frank replaced his abandoned sneer with another fresher version of the same.'

'The "belongers"?', says Miss R.

'Yes, the "belongers". These were not little people from a story for children, not "the Borrowers", indeed often not borrowers of money at all but "quiet Conservatives" who prized their positions in life and their privacy, kept themselves to themselves and hated Norman Tebbit as "the coldest man of the age". There were temperature charts of names and chilliness-ratings to prove this point, said Ronnie in his own purposefully matching chill voice: "We need to win them back or Labour will win and where will any of us be then?".'

'"Still here", said Frank, consulting his Swatch watch, the only kind he ever wore, smoothing his Marks & Spencer suit, ditto, sipping at his Fanta as though it were Puligny-Montrachet and studying his book of verbs.'

'Immediately before Ronnie arrived with his news, Frank and I had been planning to move on from our verbs to some real Latin, a sentence or two at a time of Seneca on some appropriate topic. Possibly *De Ira*, Seneca's youthful denunciation of anger designed to shame the Emperor Claudius. We had the full text, if we wanted it, in its fresh, unread-for-forty years *Times* Library edition.'

'We also had Seneca on the ethics of buying white shoes', I add, worried that I might be losing Miss R's attention. 'Should a virtuous man pay for white shoes if the shoemaker has died?'

'Obviously not', she says.

'Or we could read more from other parts of *De Beneficiis*, some further discussion of gratitude for gifts.'

'But, instead of reading any of these, we had to listen to Ronnie's description of the Tebbit dining room at Tory Central Office where the serving women, trusted secretaries from the Chairman's outer office, wore pinafores inscribed in italic red with the words "Norman's Nosherie".'

'If only those *Guardian* writers who call us "cut off from ordinary people" had the slightest idea', said the Prime Minister's speechwriter, ordering some nacho chips from the barman whom he had adopted on his first visit. 'You must promise me that none of this will be in *The Times* until the election is over'. I promised that I would not write a word till then and, after a few feeble attempts on deep-yellow salted corn, he left.'

'Once Ronnie had gone, Frank decided to postpone our Senecan studies a little longer. As a reporter, I was pleased by what Ronnie had revealed. Wobbly Thursday, the day the Thatcher dream nearly died: this was a *Times* story, even if I had to wait till the last vote was counted before writing it.'

'Frank was concerned that I should be even thinking of publishing any of Ronnie's story, even when the election had been won, as it was surely going to be, despite the madness of the campaigners, indeed because of the madness, since, if there were really a chance of the Tories losing, everyone would surely be behaving better.'

'That was the way in which Frank liked to think, with a studied realism which, with good intent, could be made real. Publication of "dirty Tory washing" would not be right at any time unapproved by him. It was not what he thought we should be doing. He agreed with Woodrow that our leaders in *The Times*, almost always my own leaders in *The Times*, were insufficiently supportive of "the greatest British leader since Churchill".'

25.7.14
'The 'Wobbly Thursday' Tory scare, like so many election scares in every campaign, was more a safety-valve than a signal. On the Saturday after polling day Ronnie was sitting at the Trooping of the Colour beside the safely re-elected Prime Minister, she herself sitting on a House of Commons majority of more than a hundred and a gilt wooden seat that was not quite so comfortable.'

'He would have felt more comfortable himself, he told me, if *The Times* that morning had not published a lengthy account of Downing Street rages, nerves and wobbles. It had all been "a lot of nothing", he complained. I had quite spoilt his conversation with the ambassador of an African country whose name he forgot.'

'Thankfully, Margaret had not seemed to mind, taking a certain satisfaction from the sight of the Queen for the first time processing beside the Scots Guards in a carriage rather than on horseback. Age was catching up on some. Others could go "on and on".'

26.7.14
'Margaret Thatcher won the election but, in truth, she lost it. Her body might "go on and on", or until someone pushed

it out of the door, but the spirit was past. That was David's ever clearer view, delivered some eighty miles northeast of Wapping, as he stretched out on an August afternoon in the garden of a house that, as he much liked to boast, was once home to a Gunpowder Plotter.'

'Coldham Hall was a large red house at the centre of David's deep green Suffolk estate. He and his friends were often franker there than they felt safe to be in London. At Coldham they could plot without codes. What better place to plan a coup, he laughed as I sat on the sloping grass, looking about at his guests and challenging me not to laugh back.'

'I hope that I laughed both at him and with him. I don't properly remember. I do remember the cast of regular other visitors, bird-painters, unemployable biologists, soldiers from small countries, businessmen in businesses from aircraft to high fashion, a pack that was constantly reshuffled but never changing very much.'

'A coup?', queries Miss R. 'Really?'

'Well, in their jokes and maybe in their dreams.'

'Coldham's best known previous plotting owner was Ambrose Rookwood, a leading Catholic enemy of James I, disappointed in his country's choice of despot and hopeful of faring better under a replacement. "Uncle Ambrose" was a man of principle in David's minority view, a man more generally deemed deserving to be hanged-drawn-and-quartered, as indeed he was, no mercy shown, just as none had been shown to Guy Fawkes.'

'David saw himself as a worthy successor to this "uncle" and his own reputation as similarly divided and traduced. He raised a toast to "owners past" every Fifth of November.'

Miss R gives a tight smile.

'David loved his house. His personal improvement to the

Plotter's legacy was a "Garden of Eastern Peace", a circle of seats and Buddhist statues, all set at a sympathetic distance from where he landed his helicopter. This suited the prophetic and philosophical part of his nature which, he said, was too often misunderstood.'

'His main prediction that day was that Margaret, for all her magnificence, would be gone within a year. Ronnie, sitting uncomfortably among minor masters of tranquillity, disagreed, angrily by his own peaceful standards. Grass, he said, always made him angrier than he would ever be in the Haymarket or The Old Rose. The two men would soon have sorely tested the local gods had there not been two others present who disagreed with each other more.'

'Why were you there yourself?' Miss R regularly interrupts any line of answering that she fears might fail to interest her. She is as constant in this as in asking 'when was the first time?' Sometimes I think her rude, sometimes as failing to recognise her own story, sometimes as pursuing a different story, one that I do not know.

'There was good company. Ronnie was my best source of information on the Thatcher court', I reply.

'I know that already and this was not Ronnie's house.'

'Ronnie said that he would only go to Coldham Hall if I did. By being close to Ronnie there were so many duller people to whom I did not need to be close. David was useful in the same way, less useful but again never dull.'

'I knew other Tory politicians too, Geoffrey Howe and Michael Heseltine who never became Tory leader, Michael Howard, who did, Norman Lamont, Woodrow's great friend: that is just to remember a few who haven't disappeared from history entirely. Don't think I spent all my time with the Senecans and their kind. '

'Were there really others of the same kind as the Senecans?' She does not seem to believe me. 'Why was everyone else there that day?'

'We were supposed to be talking about foreign policy', I tell her. 'Only when an election is safely over does anyone want to talk about places other than here. David always liked to have his own foreign policy.'

'That afternoon, two of his friends were in the Peace circle, Edward Teller, an elderly American known as "Father of the H-bomb" was arguing with Vladimir Bukovsky, a former guest of the Soviet Gulag, about the best way to deal with Mikhail Gorbachev.'

'Saying what?' She puts her notebook down.

'Do you really want to know? Teller talked about the "nationalist Russian adversary whose nature was manageable by tough, traditional diplomacy". Bukovsky preferred "helpless leader of an alien inhuman state". Teller wanted "Reagan to be Reagan". Bukovsky wanted desertion from Soviet armies and the arming of their Islamic enemies. That was the basis of it.'

'David too was enthusiastic for teaching Islamic Russians to use American missiles. That was the consensus of the Peace Garden. Only Teller seemed opposed. We could say he showed the greatest prophetic wisdom of the afternoon.'

'Yes, you could', she says.

'The talk turned to one of David's favourite causes of the time, SDI, the Strategic Defence Initiative, a sky full of American satellites that would destroy nuclear warheads. David loved to draw diagrams to show how it would work, with lines and triangles linking continents from space. If you look long enough around you there will be dozens of these, probably on the back of Messalina's Positions.'

Miss R stays still.

'His problem was Margaret, who wanted to please Reagan, wanted US arms spending, particularly that part spent in Britain, but did not want any shield that stopped British nuclear missiles being our "independent deterrent".'

'Teller did not care about Britain's deterrent which he knew was not independent anyway. He agreed with Reagan, that this "Star Wars" shield should be developed, built, deployed and its protection shared with the Soviets; neither rival need then fear obliteration by the other.'

'Bukovsky said that this was idealism at its most dangerous, an absurd risk. Teller thought that Gorbachev was a man with whom business could usually be done, that Margaret Thatcher was right in her assessment of him in 1984. Bukovsky did not.'

'Neither man thought that Margaret Thatcher was more than a booster of business. She never wanted to see defence in space. All she wanted was the diagrams and the dreams, British profits to back a President's fantasy. The Prime Minister was a woman who dreamt – as she slept – as little as she possibly could. Teller laughed at his own joke. '

'David wanted to agree with them all – with his distinguished guests and with their masters whose dissonant spirits hung behind the Buddahs. This became harder as the afternoon in the garden wore on. Sweating around his neck and wiping his forehead with a giant red handkerchief, he suggested that 'Thatcherite ideology' might form common cause between them.'

'Teller sniffed and said the West had no surviving ideology, that this absence was, in fact, it strength, since it could not fight an ideological war, always the worst kind. Bukovsky sniffed too, saying that Margaret Thatcher had no ideology and that to pretend otherwise was a self-deception.'

'David's one thought for the afternoon was dismissed. Ronnie was then rash enough to say that, from everything that he had heard in Downing Street, SDI would not work anyway, that, however many of our missiles we fired at theirs, one thermonuclear intruder would always get through. It was a "Maginot Line in space".'

'This brought down upon himself a direct assault from the two scientists. Ronnie was even more rash to defend himself by citing Mrs Thatcher as the scientist from whom he had heard that then heretical view. This provoked yet more abuse, this time on the Prime Minister herself whose contribution to science (if not her fellowship of the Royal Society), said Teller, was in 'the chemistry of whipped ice cream'.'

Miss R laughs loudly as though in a group of friends.

'There was a hush at this offence to local proprieties. We could suddenly hear wood pigeons and the hum of distant farm machinery. The Buddhas of Coldham Hall were not used to hearing David's "lady" described in this way.'

'Nor was another of the silent guests, the young MP, Michael Portillo, David's protégé of the time who took Anthony Berry's seat in parliament after the Brighton Bomb. For David he was long the Thatcherite most likely to succeed, the most worthy of his money and support. This was not, however, a subject to dislodge the higher arguments of the foreign guests.'

'Discussion of Margaret's future, high in all our minds, was postponed for later. When the British side gathered again that evening in the gallery of the Gunpowder Plotters, the choice of a new Tory chairman, the virtues of the new Poll Tax, and the means by which our host might have a bigger public presence at the forthcoming Tory conference, were discussed before the main course.'

Miss R stiffens as though she has heard something she has not wanted to hear. 'Who won the great "Peace Garden debate?" she asks mockingly.

'Our ice-cream chemist was absolutely right about SDI. But Teller was the winner in the verbal battle that afternoon. The Father of the H-Bomb was a veteran of Washington lobbying and an astonishingly successful advocate for the billion dollar shield. He began the afternoon as an old man, with trousers twisted round his belt and a long stick, and ended it with the vigour he deployed upon US presidents. Bukovsky began with icy passion but ended by agreeing to be a warm-up act for David at a Party Conference rally.'

'What?'

'Yes, while matters of higher principle swirled around his statues, this "Freedom Rally" was the most present problem in David's mind. Ronnie was trying every possible means to stop it happening at all, fearing that the Tories could look, 'quite unfairly, of course', like Fascists. His stated reason was that it could be hijacked by the French National Front leader, Jean-Marie Le Pen, who was also on his way to the Tories' post-election triumph by the sea. David said that he would stop Le Pen coming. He had friends in Paris who would do that for him.'

'Ronnie lay back with me in the grass, observing that the whole event was like Bernard Shaw's play, *Heartbreak House*, recalling a production from his theatrical youth, "all those dynamite-destroying psychic rays, bombs in a country house garden, the ship of England heading to the rocks, 1919, a fantasia in the Russian manner on English themes". Michael Portillo smiled but this was another subject that David did not want. He suspected Ronnie now and he suspected me and he especially suspected any comparison to a play he did not know.'

'It was upsetting enough to him that Margaret Thatcher, in the greater scheme of the world, was minor and irrelevant. He was content to write her off himself but he did not want two of his American heroes saying that she had never mattered very much. It took a long and elaborate dinner before his own mood lightened and he began to talk about a private play that he could produce next time upon his own Tudor stage, some work in which he might himself have an appropriate role.'

'Seneca's plays were for small, discriminating audiences. Was there one suitable for Coldham? Or would he have to write a play? He was full of plans for who and what should follow the Thatcher era, the "who" being ideally Michael and the "what" including a much larger role for himself, on stage and off. His benefits were still to come.'

27.7.14

When Miss R arrives today, I am checking some TLS proofs. While she waits, she picks up a copy of a novel by Beryl Bainbridge, *Winter Garden* (1980), a black comedy about a trip by British Council intellectuals to the USSR.

'Woodrow loved that one', I look up and tell her. 'It is about very complicated adultery.'

She continues reading.

'He surrounded himself with the latest books. He always liked to keep up with novelists and publishers, even with the "useless literati" whose members he blamed for his own early rejection as a short-story writer and for the cold reception of his plays.'

'How did the literati think of him?'

'Badly. Mrs T was a talisman. Woodrow wore her initials on his sleeve. That was enough.'

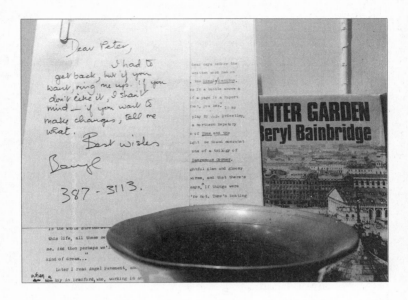

'Woodrow held a special personal grudge against *Winter Garden*'s publisher, a one-time friend of Frank and full member of the literati called Colin Haycraft. This was not because Colin was a man of the Thatcher-hating Left (he was not) but because he entertained many men and women who were, and more precisely because he was Beryl Bainbridge's publisher and was not, in Woodrow's view, behaving well.'

Miss R rubs a plastic-ringed finger over the *Winter Garden*'s grey onion-domed cover.

'Why would anyone ever have bought something so dull?'

This was a view that Woodrow often uttered himself. I can see what he meant (and what Miss R means today) although the grey-and-black of this and many of Beryl's books never bothered me when I began to collect them.

This one stars a man who takes a fishing rod when he accompanies his mistress to Moscow, an accessory that he has added in the hope that his wife will believe he is in

Scotland. There are predictable consequences in Soviet-era baggage halls and bars. Miss R reads several pages, laughing from time to time. She seems just about to read a passage aloud (what worse fate than to be read aloud to when one cannot escape, thought Seneca) when she asks a question instead.

'How about you? Were you with the literati then too?'

'No, not exactly, although in that summer of 1987 I was on the list for Colin Haycraft's most famous literary party, the one in which we celebrated the 200th anniversary of Edward Gibbon's *Decline and Fall*.'

'Appropriate?'

'I didn't think so at the time but, yes, the Thatcher foes were out in force that night. They sniffed generous alcohol and like-minded company. Declining and falling made the perfect accompaniment.'

Miss R makes a note in her Seneca book.

'This was not the main intention', I say. 'It was not a political party. Colin almost always put classics first. Beryl put fiction first, particularly when she was with Woodrow, who rarely allowed anyone to criticise his beloved Margaret. But it was a literary party and in those days that meant politics too.'

'After 1987 Margaret divided more than she had ever done, demanding loyalty, dispersing hatred, discouraging any mixture of the two, encouraging her enemies despite herself. This was nothing so unusual for the end of an imperial reign, said Colin coolly, who was himself dressed as Gibbon for the evening.'

'Curiously, I can now see Woodrow there with him, bow-tied and with a toga on his shoulder, even though I am sure he was not. He could not have borne the knowing sneers that his "lady" was "on her last legs". Nor would he have liked hearing Beryl, his other lady in the room, relate a "rough trade" one-night-stand with the musician, George Melly.'

Miss R looks curiously across the room and into the sky.

'Woodrow would most definitely not have felt at home on Gibbon night', I repeat. 'But if he had been there, he would not have been alone in hostility to Colin, an "acquired taste" not acquired by a good many people, including many of his guests.'

'Beryl's publisher, possibly her lover too, was a much too showy classicist for ease, even more likely to quote Latin than Kingsley Amis was, and also, as Woodrow argued from his own experience as a publisher, an exploiter of Beryl, whose best-selling novels for the Duckworth Company supported many a low-selling work on Cicero and Seneca, a tradition that went back to Virginia Woolf.'

'Woodrow even warned me that Colin was not a man whom I should meet. He only knew one thing about him, he said untruthfully, and that was that his father had been an army officer murdered by his own men, a story for tragedy, its own truth uncertain. He asked if maybe I could find out more.'

'I said that I would, but without sincerity. At that time I was in some awe of Colin, who was a bit of a boaster but the greatest independent publisher of books about Greece and Rome, a bit of a showman but for more than twenty years the face, body, brain (and Woodrow-like bow-tie) of Duckworth, promoter of his novelist wife Alice Thomas Ellis as well as of Beryl, Alice's friend (and often non-friend). On good days, I held the hope that one day Duckworth might publish a book of mine.'

'Colin impressed Frank because he was a model for any-one who likes to see the world through ancient eyes, one of those rare men who inhabited antiquity as though it were his house. It sometimes seemed as though he inhabited antiquity all the time.'

'No modern publishers, even publishers of the classics, sprinkle the promotion of their books with sparks of Seneca, judging such displays pretentious, elitist – or, more likely, impossible. Colin was not afraid of anything like that, not even of being deemed superficial. There was virtue, something neither to be hidden nor denied, in a light covering of Latin and Greek. It was central to his sense of himself – a flamboyant, fancy bow-tied example of the keys to his ancient home.'

'Colin was too like Woodrow for either's comfort. As a seller of books he was happy enough to be called pretentious, if that was the price he had to pay. He could ape the "ape in purple", he used to say, challenging visitors to note what he meant, that he did not mind being likened to one of antiquity's fake philosophers identified only by their coloured cloak. He enjoyed the simian wordplay of aping the ape, quoting the words in Greek and reminding everyone that A. E. Housman had used them too.'

'And he liked to tell his life story in classical quotation – from Aristotle, tutor to Alexander the Great, to Ausonius, tutor to the Emperor Gratian, the not very great. He strode through Latin and Greek from Mediterranean schooldays to Wellington to Oxford to a start in publishing when his task was to condense Gibbon's *Decline and Fall* for modern readers, missing out, as he said, most of the Decline.'

'This was maybe the version that my friend V had in her box room. She was sometimes very authoritative about Gibbon.'

Miss R has put down her *Winter Garden* and picked up her SENECA notebook. She waves for me to continue, like a football referee playing the 'advantage rule'. It is getting late. The office outside is empty.

'In that summer of 1987 Colin was at the height of his powers as a gentleman bohemian in a publishing age that was beginning to reject both. He hosted his party to celebrate Gibbon's centenary by dressing as his hero and reading aloud, to a hundred or so of his friends and neighbours.'

'Memory of this is as fresh as anything in these memories. There we all were on a cold summer night, almost three decades ago, in a tiny, liberal enclave of Camden, the part belonging to playwrights and grand pianos, not ecstasy and bondage trousers. Colin stood high against the London sky, slimmer than Gibbon, disguised in frayed eighteenth-century frock coat and buckled shoes, less fastidious in attire than his hero but consumed by his part. Inside we had the words of Gibbon and outside the police sirens sounded.'

'In Colin's garden the mood was political, literary, elegiac. Outside it the noise was of sullen opposition to what the electorate had just decided, stone-throwing, the defiance of keys against the sides of costly cars.'

'Down beneath the speaker's podium, there were political commentators talking about Thatcher and Gibbon, variously speculating on which evil Emperor she resembled the most. A fashionable playwright was playing the textual critic of Gibbon, talking about whether "date" or "fate" was correct in Colin's speech and when both alternative readings would apply in Downing Street. Grand lady book reviewers were talking about Gibbon and the sexual preferences of the Princess of Wales, the subject that was just beginning to be a party subject at this time – and about how much Latin was required to be a gentleman – in the 1780s, 1880s and the 1980s, in Gibbon's day, in Trollope's and in their own.'

'Ferdinand Mount, a future editor of the *TLS*, a rare friend to Margaret Thatcher on this Gibbon night, was fending away discussion of a piece about her in the latest issue. The *TLS* classicist and controversialist, Mary Beard, was there too although I did not know her then. The mother of a Tory MP was complaining that anti-Thatcherites had trashed her son's car.'

'Away from politics, Beryl and the Booker Prize were the subject of bibulous debate. The chairman of judges in 1986 had been the poet Anthony Thwaite, the most likely candidate in London, it was said, to choose Kingsley's book about drunken old men who took an hour at least to dress themselves in the morning. In 1987, the chair was another of Woodrow's female favourites, P. D. James – and there would doubtless soon be a well-spoken lady winner, perhaps even a writer of detective tales. That was how prizes worked. Poor Beryl, dry, thin and laughing with her Liverpudlian vowels, would win when someone like her was in charge. No one was quite sure who or when that might be.'

'Woodrow deemed Beryl a teller of old-fashioned stories, the kind that he had promoted (and written) in the 1940s. He liked most her early books whose themes were a better past, darkness, childhood hauntings and cautious adultery. He was fascinated by the story of her father, plunged into rage and poverty by the depression of the 1930s. He liked *Winter Garden*. He never saw her more Booker-suited later novels, *Master Georgie* (a Crimean war story shortlisted and beaten by Ian McEwan's *Amsterdam* in 1998) and *According to Queeney* (her account of the last years of Dr Johnson).'

'When he was with Beryl, or talking about her, Woodrow could play the Senecan role of the literary man for whom politics was a secondary pursuit. This was a conceit but a pleasant and sometimes useful one. He often praised her ribald remarks about trade unions in *The Bottle Factory Outing* (1974). He joked about her odorous cats and lavatories. He was generally contemptuous of Colin, who taught Beryl's children Latin, whose father's fate remained a mystery and whose business acumen was not so very different from his own, similar too, he noted, to that of the classical hack in Beryl's *Watson's Apology* (1984) whose translations earn between £5 and nothing but still keep him from holidaying with his about-to-be-murdered wife.'

This was the time when I seriously began wondering whether I should try myself to sell Colin a book. I had a long neglected project on Cleopatra. Beryl was muttering something about Bernard Shaw and Cleopatra – and resting her ashtray on the back of a stuffed buffalo. Maybe this was my chance. Maybe Colin could help. Maybe he would have done but I never asked him.

29.7.14
Down below us, just inside the gate, there is a single small triangle of grass.

'So that was where you used to have your lunch.'

'Some of us, I suppose. Sometimes. Not me. Not very often.'

Miss R is asking about 'daily life' in old Wapping. While she adjusts the line between her skirt and blouse, she sounds like a teacher preparing a history lesson for a class of low academic ability, less politics and power, more sandwiches and soft drinks.

'What did you use to do on sunny days? Did you stay behind your windowless brick? Did you walk within the walls like zoo animals? Did you eat at your desks from trays or outside on camping tables?'

She has heard that, even when the siege of Wapping was over, we still behaved as though the barbarians were at our gate, like prisoners whose guards have fled but who have become accustomed to their cells. There is some truth in that.

'Yes, I almost always ate in my office from a tray, often from the canteen's peculiarly thin trays. Who else have you been talking to?'

'We never reveal our sources. You should know why.'

'Yes, that triangle of grass was one of the few places in the sun where we could eat or sit or walk with anything but concrete beneath our feet. In 1987 it was a little larger than it is today. It was also much, much brighter, a chemically fuelled green place, the only kind of lawn that could survive. On a Wapping lunchtime dozens of newspaper people used to sit there.'

She scribbles a note.

'It was hardly a pleasure park', I insist. 'Once the eating time was over, hardly anyone ever sat there for long. It was not just the garden-centre smell of fertiliser. This was a lawn much too exposed for most pleasure, or even leisure, the closest thing that we had to a stage, useless for hiding, useful only for wanting to be seen when few of us did want to be seen.'

'When do you last remember sitting on that lawn?'

I tell her. 'It was a few weeks later, in the middle of a hot afternoon. Colin Haycraft had said that he might drop by. He had books to promote to me, payback for his Gibbon invitation, and I had one that I hoped to promote to him. Ronnie wanted to talk more about David's Heartbreak House weekend.'

'It was Ronnie I was waiting for most anxiously. I did not mind being conspicuous. I wanted to be seen. I did not want to miss him. I wanted to intercept him before he met anyone else. I was being careful, respectful I hoped, keen to ensure that he bore no grudges – and not just about our afternoon in the Garden of Peace. My story of election rage was still a bit of an issue between us. There had been other stories too in other papers, "follow-ups", the same events seen through different eyes with aims of different advantage. I knew that he was displeased.'

'I also felt slightly sick. It was a day like today, fumes steaming from the water that we could not see. I needed whatever fresh air I could find. I was working while I waited. I held the draft of a difficult leader for *The Times* on property tax reform, the product of an angry morning on the Mezzanine.'

'Property, rates, the Poll Tax', she spins out each word one by one.

'Yes, the Poll Tax. It may seem ridiculous but taxing houses is often awkward, often worse than awkward, and at this time in 1987 especially so. The colour of the grass, even the chemicals that made it green, were welcome distractions from the PT, the initial letters of the words that no one wanted to say, the policy that within three years would bring Margaret Thatcher down.'

Miss R stands up and splays her feet in a position for attack. She has the expression she wears when she suspects I am going to tell her what she already knows, the same one as when she thinks I am going to talk about sex. But she does not stop me. She still has her notebook open.

And then she sits and begins to talk, first in halting half phrases, then in a stream of words. I listen and I keep listening. This is the point where everything here changes.

Suddenly she has her own 'first time'. There is no rise in her voice, no questioning, no sharpness, no certainty. She is dressed today as she was when she arrived in April: blue skirt ruffled shorter over her left thigh than the right, flat black shoes, a black clasp in her bobbed black hair. Only her shoulders seem narrower, not so padded for power, a different jacket.

Her tone is flat like a mobile phone voice overheard, personal but with no listener in view. I try hard to hear but in wondering why she has changed I miss some of what she is actually saying.

When I recover, her subject is 'the horses'. She repeats the words and shifts her position on her chair as though posing for a portrait photograph, stiff and still before moving her right hand above her knee and turning her head ten degrees towards the window, each change distinct from the other. She lifts her eyes away from the muddied grass and out past the brick walls of Mr Breezer, the painted A, B and C on his warehouse, as far as the clanking traffic of the Highway.

'There were metal bars', she says. Her voice rises very slightly. I assume she is asking a question because questioning is all that she has ever done here.

I begin to answer. 'Yes, there were still metal barriers beside the road in 1987, no longer strung out in an iron wall but stacked in piles, in case the pickets were to return.'

She is not listening. 'When a metal bar meets the thigh of a horse', she continues softly, 'there is the softest thud before the squeal.' This time there is no rise in her voice. She is neither listening nor asking now. She is remembering.

Miss R says that she remembers directly the Poll Tax. That is not, of course, the payment of it (she was too young) but the riots against the tax which took her to London 'for the first time'. She moves her head a further ten degrees away from our line of sight. This is the first time she has used her favourite phrase about herself.

'There were galloping grey horses. A "gallop" is only what horses do in stories until its direction is towards you. There were straps around their riders' necks and fists.'

I must be looking sceptical. 'Are you sure you're remembering?'

'I remember what my mother told me but also what I saw, the hooves, the iron bars, the traffic cones like hats for Noddy

(or was it Big Ears?), the burning cars and broken glass.'

'The battles of the Highway here were nothing beside the battles of Trafalgar Square', she adds, returning to her academic stance.

'David Hart used to say the same', I reply, encouraging before pausing. 'Were you really there? You could have been no more than six years old.'

'Yes and when I first heard the words Poll and Tax I thought the subject was a pole for prodding police horses.'

'So that's my PT story. How was it for you then?' She breaks out from her distant stare, asking the question as though seeking reassurance about a film or a fillet steak or a partner's position beyond the range of the Renaissance erotica that lie around her feet.

'Embarrassing', I reply. 'Treacherous. Worse than any other dispute we had.' She nods in an attempt at agreement. For the first time it seems that we might be speaking on equal terms of giving and receiving.

'Snap', she says. 'Snap! Snap!' She means that she knows exactly what I mean. Another first, I say in silence. It is years since I have heard anyone cry 'snap' to signify similarity, the matching of clothes and cards, a red tie, an Ace of Clubs, not maybe since I heard my mother use it last at home.

'The troubles of *The Times*', she says, 'can hardly have been worse than those of the places where I spent my own last Thatcher years. Sometimes I was by the sea with my grandfather, a fervent Margaret man, mostly with my mother, an even fiercer Poll Tax opponent. That was why I was on the march.' She is almost whispering now.

'The only concession by my mother was that we should choose the route from Kent, re-enacting the first Poll Tax march in 1381, rather than the more convenient road from Essex. This was for my greater education. But all that I have ever remembered was the sound of metal on horseflesh. My mother and my grandfather did not speak for a decade after the battle and the tax were over.'

Miss R checks herself. She brushes her skirt down as though it has been temporarily occupied by an intruder. She gives a long sigh.

'Chronology, chronology, chronology', she whispers. That march was 1990, the year she fell. You must stay for me in 1987 when Thatcher still felt that she could do anything she liked and that people like you and your Senecans would happily follow wherever she led.'

'Not very happily, not at all', I counter.

'All of you on the triangle, what did you think of the Poll Tax?'

She pauses, as though challenging me to object to her change of tone.

'Grandad was a bit of a Senecan himself', she adds as though an afterthought. O yes, he knew a bit of Latin. He was a very self-styled man of virtue, a hypocrite to everyone else, not, unfortunately, very rich, indeed not rich at all. Not stupid either though.' Her words are now staccato, strained, almost strangled from her throat.

I am readjusting my place in this interview now. If I had a different chair I would sit in it. But there are still only two chairs, still stuck on the same small pieces of bare carpet, still with the same view down to the chemical lawn, surrounded, if that were possible, by yet more piles of letters, books, erotica, politics and personal tat. Miss R juts out her jaw, posing as though to match a photograph.

I am hopelessly thinking back, stuck with the question she has asked in words. What did we all think of the Poll Tax? Not the same thing. That is certain. Disagreement among the Senecans was by 1987 almost guaranteed.

I start with the easiest answer. 'David Hart did not care about the taxation of "domestic property", as he called it, distinguishing this from taxes on office blocks and stately homes. So yes, he said: in an unimportant way it was unfair that, before the Poll Tax, four salaried teachers in one side of a semi-detached house would pay the same rates bill as a single pensioner on the other side. A new tax on every head seemed fairer. But this was not the kind of fairness he cared much about.'

'Seneca, he reminded us, was particularly sound on orders of importance. Rates reform, the switch from payment by house to payment by individual, was down in the fifth order, well behind Gorbachev and Star Wars, Marxist trade unionists and meddlers in Brussels, maybe even lower. David had long admired Margaret's "thinking of the unthinkable" but, if this had been reduced to "reform of the rates" it was further proof that she was finished.'

'And Ronnie Millar?'

'Ronnie did not agree with David. What mattered to Margaret must necessarily matter to him, and to all of us if we were as loyal as we ought to be. As Seneca would have seen it, there were issues on which the Emperor has to have his will. This was one of them. The Poll Tax was a promise from her heart. It was also opposed by all those ministers who, in their deepest and dirtiest hearts, had opposed her on almost everything else.'

'Lord Wyatt?'

'Woodrow agreed with Ronnie although he understood the problem rather better. His best case for the Poll Tax was that most of the money for local councils, for schools and police and refuse collection, came from local businesses which, unless their owners lived where they worked, could not vote on how their money was spent. Councillors, for example, had no incentive to control their trade unions (or be economical in any way) since they were elected by voters who paid almost none of the bills. The Poll Tax restored a fundamental principle of taxation and representation. Margaret was right to insist upon it.'

Miss R is listening patiently to the answers she has asked for.

'Yes', she says, 'but under the Poll Tax the Duke would have paid the same as the dustman, the David Hart the same as the man on the Essex council estate where Peter Stothard used to live.'

She has a photograph of herself with a 'Duke and Dustman' placard. She pushes her right foot through a pile of my own old photographs which merely show examples of ill-fitting suits.

She waits for me to say more. I have no wish to do so. The last few minutes have been like a leader writers' morning on the Mezzanine. The words are hard even to type any more.

In front of me, however, is now a very different Miss R from the one who appeared here four months ago. Her chronology has reached the time of her own life. Seneca and the Senecans have left history.

'It was Frank', I tell her, 'who first called it the PT. As usual, he liked to think he had a more sophisticated understanding than the rest of us. This PT, dear boy, was a proper case of applying classical principles.'

'I can still hear him saying those words, down there where we found the books in the skip. As well as "dear" and "boy" he spoke of great men of reason. The Poll Tax came from All Souls, Oxford, and a Rothschild Bank. It made a logical sense.'

Miss R nods.

'Every user of public services, Frank said, should pay the same single tax because the available services were the same for everyone. He called this the "benefits received principle" of taxation and derived it as far as he could from ancient models.'

'Was he right?', she asks.

'No. But the relationship of the Poll Tax to the Romans, however attractive to Frank's mind (remember: he was a comic fantasist by trade), was the least of its difficulties.'

'Even at the age of six, you were right and he was wrong. The PT defied the common kind of sense, the kind of the losers, the many, the young, the surprised, the angry mothers of girls with placards. To almost every politician apart from the philosophers who had conceived it, the 'fairness principle' that the rich should pay more than the poor, while in some sense less classical, took a priority that was self-evident.'

Miss R frowns.

'So, the Poll Tax was difficult for all the Senecans but particularly for the two of us at *The Times*. It was a test not of tax policy but of loyalty. Frank's notes for a leader, the one I held in my hand that day on the chemical lawn, pretended to argue that the rating system was undemocratic as well as inefficient; that there were principles at stake and surely I should approve of principle. It praised the wise men of Oxford who had invented the Community Charge, as the Poll Tax was known to its friends, a radical way of restoring lost simplicity. It was surely very Roman, easy to collect, equally burdensome on all. Seneca would have approved.'

Miss R crosses her legs and smiles.

'But Frank, of course, did not care at all about logic and the rates. Any principle was only a pretence. He could hardly say the words "rateable value" without polishing his wit. He cared solely about tests for supporting Margaret Thatcher. Would I pass or would I fail? Anyone, he said, could support her when she was popular, when she was doing what she had done

at winning elections for almost 200 years, did espouse belief as a virtue – and not just her own beliefs. She expected others, her friends, advisers, courtiers, even her opponents, to be comfortable in the territory of the believers too.'

'Seneca was a good man to think with. Ronnie recognised his territory as his own. Frank observed. Woodrow exploited. David depended absolutely on the place where, more than any other courtier, he needed the queen or king to be. Dogged adherence to the Poll Tax was the last error of her political life but it was important that she be replaced by another believer.'

'David was certain that she herself could not be saved. Ronnie still disagreed. More importantly, David feared that he would never be even half accepted once she was gone. Ronnie, Frank and Woodrow knew that this was true.'

Miss R picks out a white card with wishes for a Happy New Year. She smiles a silent question.

'As 1987 came to an end, David sent that out with a quote from *Ecce Homo*, the last book that Nietzsche wrote before he became insane. He described its recipients as Argonauts, the name that some of Margaret Thatcher's earliest supporters had given themselves, the characters central to Seneca's impossible "Medea, M'dear" play, pioneers in uncharted waters, journeying to a land beyond all known lands.'

'He offered "Best wishes for 1988" from his latest libertarian base of protest, the Committee for a Free Britain. Frank showed me his copy at the bar of The Old Rose, tore it into four pieces and filled an ashtray.'

'David needed a new court where conviction was again the currency, the more contrarian the better, a court where power was pulled to the centre and could be swayed and moved there. David wanted new days on which he would resign in the morning and be welcomed back as irreplaceable in the afternoon. He wanted the tools for swaying and moving to be those not used routinely before. He wanted novelty and the advantages that novelty brought.'

'To play the Thatcher game had long required the player to be alert, to recognise rules and arguments not learnt at every school. Virtues were good and good intentions from good characters were virtues. A virtuous intent was a Stoic idea very attractive to David. He noted how Stoics liked to set the moral bar high, sometimes ridiculously high, in the confidence that a high aim missed through human frailty was better than a low aim successfully achieved.'

'He did not want this spirit to die.'

Miss R has scribbled a large blue line and turns a page. 'Next!', she says, as though she is casting a role in a film.

She writes "RM" and a question mark. She has ceased to be helpful. She is as impatient as on her first day here. She kicks a pile of texts that tumble around her feet, challenging an answer to come directly from the books themselves so that she no longer has to listen to me.

I answer her as best I can.

'Ronnie saw Seneca as a subtle source of philosophy, a studied transformer of obstacles into advantage, of enemies into allies, a man skilled in survival, from an ancient time which was, like the Thatcher time, still adjusting to concentration of power. Seneca was a pioneer writer of speeches for the source of that power, a political adviser who had to curb power's recurring mania, an artist who saw politics as theatre, and image, his own image, as his greatest legacy.'

She rolls her eyes and turns her head, circling her chin across her neck as though she has been shot. She checks her recording machine.

'Ronnie's Seneca was not a thinker who brought solutions. He saw problems. He understood problems. He helped others see and think and understand. He saw the need for the artist in politics, the difficulty of the artist in politics, the absurdity of the politician who prefers to be an artist. He implemented compromises while calling for steadfastness to principle. His success was always underlined by doubts about what success really was. He stuck by a mad leader in hopeless attempts to make the madness less.'

'Ronnie knew enough about Seneca to talk about him as an historian would. Woodrow yearned for *I Claudius*. Frank pronounced the virtue of making the bad in a state less bad, but he was practising Latin translation at the time, a code that allowed him to disavow anything he said. David began asking technical questions about Senecan drama for the small stage. He had plans for a "Tragedy of Margaret Thatcher" at Coldham Hall.'

'Virtue was the word they all liked the best. Their time was a time of high moral tone, the tone that Margaret Thatcher bequeathed to Tony Blair, the heir under whose thoughtless stewardship it died.'

Miss R is startled. 'Tony Blair?' I have opened a new door into a time where she may not want to go. She continues the exercises for her neck. She reaches down to the floor. She starts filling a box of her own with books and papers I have said I no longer need. I am wondering if this might be the last time we talk.

She keeps a tight hold on her SENECA notebook, the SCHOOLS OF THOUGHT from Foyles. She pushes it towards me and puts on her 'question face', a lip and eyebrow different from her 'quotation face', different from her many expressions of impatience.

'Yes, Seneca did try to do good. He was most of all a servant. He served the Emperor Nero before he took power. He helped Nero to present himself as a man of power. He helped him to outwit his enemies. He did not help him to kill his mother but he did help to clean up the mess afterwards. He was a big help.'

'Yes, there was his self-serving justification of extreme wealth and serving revenge cold. He could be cruel. But he had to live his life under three autocrats, three unlikely heirs to the throne, the last leaving no one in his family alive to succeed legitimately at all. The appearance of stability was essential, its reality hardly being required, its images requiring to be constantly made and remade.'

'Would Seneca have liked the Senecans?'

Miss R sometimes still surprises me with a different kind of question, the sort that seeks merely an opinion, unanswerable in any truthful way.

'He would be pleased to be remembered by successors in his trade. He would not have minded charges of inconsistency, still less hypocrisy. Life at the top was difficult, difficult for a thinker most of all. He was a realist about politics. He tried to resign. He failed. He tried to make Nero a well remembered monarch and he failed. He would have been well satisfied to be any example at all. To leave an "exemplum vitae", a lesson of his life, any lesson at all, was his last wish when, as a result of a plot that probably did not involve him, his pupil's soldiers came to tell him it was his turn to die.'

Miss R continues her packing of plays and prose, noting titles and dates of publication. Each one of my Senecans had something in common with Seneca. Each was something of an artist in politics, a much better role than being a politician in the arts. They wrote stories. They passed on truth and lies.

August

Tell me. What are you doing, Seneca?
Are you abandoning the party?

— SENECA *On Leisure*

If you know what another should not tell,
then tell it not yourself.

— SENECA *Phaedra*

5.8.14

We are not long now for this place. A hot, grey day is keen to bid us all the more swiftly goodbye. Sweating clouds squat above the men in yellow who are doubling the thickness of the grey steel fence down below. It is as though they too, like Miss R and I, are back in the Thatcher years.

On the side of the plant the red steel gallery that once looked down on Advertising Sales is ever more sharply exposed. The cream atrium roof above it is spattered blacker. Soon, like a pleasure balloon or hang-glider, it must all soar away with the birds.

Yes, all the birds. When Miss R first mentioned that she'd seen budgerigars and parakeets in the churchyard I thought she was exaggerating from ill temper with the heat. She was not. From what I saw there this morning she was understating the invasion, underestimating the escape. Singly, and in groups, there are dozens of parrots in the trees above the graves, not all small, some of them of proper value to a zoo or pet-shop, I would guess, vivid examples of creatures who live wild even in captivity, and when free shout 'pay attention, pay attention' while not wanting any attention to be paid.

Only an expert (or more likely a fraud) would say precisely what types of parrots they are. Psitticids, as Mr V used to say with learned realism, have ordered their parrot family very little over the millennia, sometimes troubling to differentiate their males from their females, their young from their old, their individuality over that of another, but mostly not. Birds of every sex and size wear the same black-and-yellow or white-and-blue, like families in their favourite football club strip. For once I wish that he was here, just to see them.

Or to hear them. From every group comes a uniform cracking of che-chek, che-chek, che-che or ruh-ruh-rah, killing the efforts of any bird with pretensions to sing its own song. A scarlet-rumped parakeet, one of Mr V's favourites and one of those very few parrots that can hold a tune, would have no chance in competition against these black-fronted, green-bellied, ring-necked screamers.

There is no space for the birds that once flattered Roman lovers in Indian dialects and Greek. This is an urban mob in urban skies over urban trees. The higher shit on the lower. That is just the way it is in this air today full of noises.

Meanwhile on the ground below, the crows are wise and stately, ruffed and gowned, deep-thinking that with effort and patience they might become ravens of the Tower. They stare at the workmen and the workmen stare back – for hours on end if they wish.

Where is Lord Wyatt when I need him? Woodrow would have appreciated these hot and hopeless black wings. He would have had pink silk around his neck and pink champagne in his hand. He liked to see himself as something of an ornithologist. He always liked both to look at birds here and to bait protesters, baiting protesters perhaps the more so.

Even up here on the sixth floor there are green wings beating beyond the glass. The heat drives the parrots either to high windows or the shade of churchyard shrubs. The temperature is not what even a tropical bird is used to in England. It has, however, improved the mood for me and Miss R.

A call comes from Reception. She has returned. I was wondering if she would not. Four months after her first arrival, there is still space for misunderstandings. I know little about her work. I don't ask her enough. I am too content to be asked. Sometimes I feel I am being interviewed by a pedant historian, at other times facing an analyst, a doctor, a casting agent, or a patient.

When she walks through the door I am assembling boxes for the books I used to care about the most, not those on the Seneca shelves but novels most of them. Miss R again offers to help. She is not dressed for removals. She is wearing a pink silk suit with short skirt and jacket. She looks as though she is on her way to the last garden party of the season. Instead she makes and stacks boxes.

'You must have been mad to keep all these', she says.

'It was a long time ago.'

Together we skim across the paper surfaces, scraping dust onto our thumbs, finding evidence of me and against me, the price-tagged reminders, embarrassments now, of the three decades in which I suffered from a book-collecting disease.

She opens each title page and checks for dates.

She is looking for books from 1992, she says, 'the next year on my list', the year that John Major had his much alleged 'breakdown', Ian McEwan, *Black Dogs*, Proof, Mint (£275); Michael Ondaatje, *The English Patient*, First Edition, Fine (£110); Barry Unsworth, *Sacred Hunger*, Edited Typescript, Slightly Foxed (£400).'

I remember well both the books and the 'breakdown'. 'This was a year when Margaret Thatcher's successor won an election and lost his power just as she had done. It was becoming a pattern. The Booker Prize judges were as inde- cisive as the new Prime Minister. There was a tie between Unsworth and Ondaatje. Indecision has been banned at the Booker since then.'

'My mother is mad about books', she interrupts. 'Hers are like useless antiques, like all that brown polished furniture you see in country shops that no one wants. Yours are not even all read. You must have been even madder.'

'Mine was only ever a modest mania' I protest. 'I did not see myself as abnormal, no more abnormal than is a collector of stories about politicians.'

'Yes, I kept books that I rarely read, never read. You are right about that. I kept catalogues of words and kept them dead in cabinets, their covers "mint", which means perfect, "fine", which means as perfect as any healthy eye can see, or "good", which means good enough only for reading.'

'No, it never struck me as odd. Reading is very bad for dead books. It reduces their value and risks bringing them to life. It was a while before I recognised that this might be a disease.'

'Exactly when?', she asks.

'Only around the turn of the millennium, long after the time we've been talking about. By then I was both Editor of *The Times* and seriously ill. There was a question whether one anomalous condition would die before the patient died of another. By 2001 I had survived my peculiar case of cancer but the bibliomania died and stayed dead.'

'All that is left now are some 10,000 novels divided between wherever I have shelves. I cannot pretend that I have read them all. No, that is not true. I can pretend. I have often pretended.'

Miss R picks up again her grey-black copy of *Winter Garden*.

'And look at these too. As though to please Woodrow's ghost, I have a full set of Beryl Bainbridge's novels, from two editions of *A Weekend With Claude* (1967 and 1981) to *According to Queeney* (2001) whose beginning is a picture of a corpse,

Dr Johnson's, whose corporeal legacy, I see now, includes withered kidney testicles bubbling with cysts and a varicose spermatic vein."

'I was supposed to have stopped collecting by 2001 but Beryl must have been an exception. I have even *The Girl in the Polka Dot Dress* (2011), her novel about the assassination of Robert Kennedy which she left unfinished when she died. Another thirty days for thirty pages, she said, and it would have been done.'

'And look at this one.'

She is friendly today and she does look.

'A full set of the Australian double Booker winner, Peter Carey, including the short stories (1981), published in aluminium foil, the first Faber cover, its publisher once said to me, in which you could cook a chicken. Somewhere there is Ian McEwan's *Amsterdam* (1998), about the mind of an editor of a newspaper.'

Miss R puts this one in her pile.

'See. David Storey's golden *Saville* (1976) sits six volumes away from the far superior blue-brown *Flight Into Camden* (1960), once one of my favourite of all novels. I used to think that I had, in a certain sense, flown into Camden myself, from Nottinghamshire via Essex, Oxford and Islington. But I would hate to think I liked the book for no better reason than that.'

She is patient with my collector's enthusiasm, often so irritating to others, and surveys the different sections on the shelves. Between A-for-Atwood and B-for-Bainbridge, R-for-Rushdie and S-for-Storey are assorted other relics, a balsa car and radar dish, a nineteenth century guide to Rome, a set of postcards of parrots, all examined surprisingly slowly as she puts them away, nothing that anyone else would want to keep.

'The books were a collection that I once thought might last. I afterwards ceased to think so. In the year 2000, when the doctors said that my last living months were close, I took some time to arrange each one in alphabetical order, each with an *Ex Libris* bookplate showing a seabird, a little tern, with a copy of *The Times* in its mouth.'

'From a collector's interest this was an act of lunacy, a systematic removal of "mint" status with every sticky label. Even for someone wanting to leave something behind it was a feeble gesture but, at the time, that was the only kind I could make. I still have the books. The only difference is that I have stopped adding to them. The bodily disease killed the mental obsession even as it let the body escape.'

'So, you are still a collector?', Miss R asks. 'Everything is electronic. Even my mother has stopped now.'

'No, but not because of what is electronic. It's just the absence of a sickness. Look at these. Never again since the year 2000 have I formed the words *Watership Down* (Rex Collings, 1st Edition, 1972, in paper-bag brown dust jacket; £1500) or *The Rachel Papers* (1st Edition, signed, 1973; slight tear to end papers; £350).'

'While I was a Senecan I collected like a miniature emperor, ordering for the brief thrill of the order, not always even opening the parcels. Whenever I tired of politicians and their courts (and even more with why I cared about them) I would pick out some Ben Okri or a bit of Julian Barnes.'

'I would maybe read a few pages, sometimes even finish a novel in a fierce defiance of dullness. Then suddenly the need was gone. Two years after I escaped cancer I left *The Times* too. I joined the *TLS*. My office was suddenly empty of politics and filled and refilled with what I wanted to be within it. And now it is time for a new office.'

'Have these books been worth their space?'

'See this. In his essay *On Tranquillity of the Mind*, Seneca offers to a friend his top tips for mental peace: disregard riches, control all passions and restrict one's book list to a few classic texts. Whenever Seneca begins such an argument he is about to lay himself open to some of the most damning counter-charges later made against him, excessive wealth, sexual and other hypocrisies. But on book-collecting he is right.'

7.8.14

I thought maybe that Miss R had finished with the Senecans but she has not.

'Tell me more about your mother's books', I ask, politely but clumsily, stumbling into where she does not want to go and easily keeps me at bay.

'Are David Hart's novels in the shelves?', she asks. 'Should I add them to my pile?'

She is most welcome to turn the pages of *The Colonel* (First Edition, good, 1983, £2) and *Come To The Edge* (First Edition, signed 'with love', mint, 1988, £1). She will be one of the few to have ever done so. Neither is a collector's item to collectors of books.

'In those Poll Tax months what happened to David Hart?'

'He never wavered from his position that the Thatcher era was over. Ronnie and he still disagreed, merely agreeing to differ more quietly.'

'There had been "eight good years", David said, and the rest of her time would be only wreckage. He began to live more in the country and less in town. He was already looking to the future after his "best friend" had gone.'

'But look at his books if you like. In *Come To The Edge* the owner of a great English house plots the founding of a

Great England political party. The Conservatives are deeply infiltrated by Socialists. The landed and the landless are set to rise up against the mercenary middle class. In his fiction sat the seed of what he hoped would be the truth.'

'And then as soon as Margaret Thatcher had fallen in 1990, he wanted her successor, John Major, to fall too. He had successfully predicted her end but had failed to see what would happen next.'

'Chronology, chronology, chronology. You are moving too fast.'

'There is not much dispute about Margaret Thatcher's fall. 'The riots against the Poll Tax simultaneously ruined her reputation for radicalism and for common sense. Geoffrey Howe, one of her once closest and dullest allies, condemned her in parliament. Michael Heseltine, the "Tarzan" who had been plotting against her since the Westland affair, made an open challenge. She treated none of them seriously enough.

Within two weeks she was out and on her way to Dulwich, to that Barrat Home in which she did not stay for long.'

'The victory in the race to replace her went to the plotter who seemed the least to be plotting. Ronnie's friend, Geoffrey Tucker, genial Mr G, master of the plotters' Chinese restaurant table in 1979, was the earliest to call me and predict that this would be John Major.'

'David called unhappily with the same message well before it was a universally acknowledged truth. There was nothing, bar deceptive cunning, that David admired about the bank manager who was about to take the office of his heroine. Worst of all, the new Prime Minister's advisers made clear, even before they took power, that they wanted nothing to do with David Hart, not even through back channels, not even in secret.'

'Once John Major had caused a second surprise by winning an election in his own right in 1992, David retired still further to country life, plotting hopelessly from afar. Of the other Senecans, Woodrow slipped easily from helping Margaret to helping John, from an object of his devotion to a mere source of power. Ronnie did the same but with much more difficulty, arousing jealousy and anger in his Margaret that he found hard to bear. Frank and I merely returned to our work, I now as Editor of *The Times*, watching closely as the next phase of disintegration began.'

'Every close watcher of the Conservative Party had the same problem at this time. Who was the one to follow? The answer should have been obvious. A Prime Minister has the power. But when Margaret Thatcher lost her starring part she never left the stage. Even two years on, every Tory who loved her thought her still the victim of a vicious stabbing. Every Tory who hated her found that hating their leader was still the best game they knew.'

8.8.14

Most of the books have now gone. All but a single chair has gone. Miss R has moved to the letters. She is sitting on the floor by the door and sifting through unbound paper. Her white shoes act as weights. She says she does not need me to talk. She needs to read. Some of what she is reading I know well. Other parts I do not.

The letters are all in the pile from Mr V. She holds one in which he boasted of his latest palaces of wood. She has another in which he showed his satisfaction when my father was dying. That was sixteen years ago. Mr V wrote that he was saddened but he was not a deceiving writer and he showed that he was not.

In other letters which Miss R now riffles through her hands, I learnt that he held my father responsible for his losing his job and his exile to Walton-on-the-Naze. He was not happy there. He liked to boast about Walton's new fame as the home of the world's oldest parrot, a fossil discovery from fifty million years ago, Palaeopsittacus Georgii, George's Old Parrot, with its own fossilised seeds and nuts. He described how his balsa house stood once beneath 'an avian sky, a sun-blocking mass of red, green, yellow, blue and shit'. But the glamour did not last.

One of the letters beneath Miss R's left shoe is a full denunciation of my father. The reasoning is incomprehensible but the tone is not. Another is about Mrs Thatcher's fate. In a third, from around the same time, Mr V says that he has 'given up the balsa'. All remaining relics of Rome have gone. His old house and my old house have all gone under the knife. The price of new wood is now beyond his reach.

So, in 1998, when Max Stothard was dying, and when Mr V

knew that he was dying, I was not surprised by the pleasure from Walton-on-the-Naze, well beyond the usual quiet relief of a survivor. None of what I read was new and it was all from a long time ago. It was my own response that surprised me more.

This was the first time I noticed how the dying of a person brings out memories so very different from a death. Mr V wrote abuse in my father's final months that he would not have written when my father was dead. I, too, who loved my father, sat with him in the hospice and failed to focus on all that was his best, his easy pleasures, his tolerance, even his tested tolerance of Mr V, his modesty, his mass of brain, so much of it kept in reserve.

This was not what I expected. If 'nil nisi bonum' applies to the dead, how much more should it apply to those not yet quite dead. As soon as he was gone I was able to invoke the 'nothing but good' principle with ease, recall all his many virtues but when he was going I could not. I did the opposite.

While his nurses were carefully matching morphine to his pain I was thinking of what he had wasted of himself (I shudder at it now) and how he had done too little to understand my mother. I was remembering what Mr V had too fiercely said, almost agreeing with some of it: that Max Stothard was too fond of a quiet life, too content to get by, so lacking in imagination as to be almost wilfully bound to the here and now.

My father was wholly without rage, a true virtue for Stoics. But while he was dying I remembered the only time that I had ever seen him angry, the first time he said I should never see V or her father again, the time I disobeyed him and he hit me.

At the moment of his death I was not even thinking about him at all, but of a shirt I had seen in a shop window, and whether I had time to buy it before 5.30, the time when every shop in Chelmsford closed, the time that was never quite early enough for my father who loathed all shops, the thought of them even more than the reality. So when he drew his last breath my thoughts were on shopping, which I too hate, almost as much as he did.

And so it is today at the dying of a building. Miss R has not heard memories that my friends and colleagues would expect me to have. This is not what the memoir of an Editor is supposed to be, the kind of memoir that I could have written, of meetings with great men, of awards, successes, the kind that are spread over this office floor. Instead Miss R has heard different memories, the ones that she has asked for, worse ones, flattering to no one.

If the building were dead I might not be thinking of the plots of politicians and the sins of the press. I should be thinking of virtues and pleasures, scoops and scandals exposed, the friendships that were once within those walls, the triumphs, as we defined them for ourselves, the strategies hatched to sell more copies of *The Times*, the successes by which my own success was measured long ago.

Instead the plant has been dying and I have been describing to Miss R a band of squabbling ghosts, figures reduced to an H, an L, a T and a J. This morning there is a giant pipe, newly arrived on a pile of fibreglass and seed buds, like a tooth removed by dental engineering and cushioned on cotton wool. Beneath the high cranes there are low cranes, bobbing and bowing, dancing with the fire hoses.

11.8.14
I now have a firm date for leaving. I do not have much more time by this view of memories. Miss R has been sweating over my final boxes, making notes, checking letters and files.

Damp and pink silk do not fit well. We have snapped at each other for no good reason.

Gradually she is forming her own books into labelled piles. In five shelves yet to be emptied in front of my *TLS* desk, are more than a hundred books we have not touched yet.

These are the not very literate reminders of the decades when I had only to type the letter T for the letters H.A.T.C.H.E.R to follow.

Here sit rows of memoirs by so many Tory men whom no one wants to remember now, coy titles about kitchen cabinets and Tarzan, nicknames that a man hated when he was famous but, when he entered the ghost world, was all that remained, thick books with 'blue' in their titles next to thin books, more thick than thin.

Miss R has rejected Michael Heseltine's *Life in the Jungle* (2000); First Edition, mint, 50p. She has found by luck or best interviewer's instinct probably the only one of these that is worth taking to the new office, the only one that has found a life beyond the graveyard, albeit a fictional life.

Its title is *Dancing With Dogma* (1992); First Edition, Good, £5. Its author was the late Sir Ian Gilmour, a member of Margaret Thatcher's first Cabinet, disloyal to her in every role he held. Sir Ian was one of Woodrow's least liked Conservatives, an elegant journalist, sometime owner and editor of *The Spectator*, rich, urbane, ever delighting in his role as 'wettest of the wets', bitterly disdainful of her Falklands policy except to the extent that 'it would surely do for her what Suez had done for Eden'.

His memoir's cover shows him dancing at a Tory seaside ball with a Prime Minister whom he despised – and it is this image that has made the book survive, printed throughout the pages of the novel beside it on my shelves like Brighton Pier through *Brighton Rock*. The novelist, Alan Hollinghurst, won the Booker Prize in 2004 for this finest piece of Thatcher fiction, *The Line of*

Beauty, a beautiful line that stretched through politics, cocaine, critical theory and the contours of arse and AIDS, gripping the Thatcher age in ways that Miss R and her colleagues will struggle to match. Other historians have already struggled.

For understanding the years of *The Senecans* the best fiction is often better than the best journalism. *The Line of Beauty* begins after the Falklands victory when the 'pale gilt image of the triumphant PM' is everywhere. Her recapture of Port Stanley merits an annual public holiday and a reconsideration of how we feel now about Lord Nelson's long dominance of the skyline.

A Reaganite lobbyist promotes Star Wars technology as David Hart used to do. The rich get rich and 'the poor get . . . the Conservatives', is the line that lightens a dinner party. Madam's 'genius' can move any conversation away from reality – from fine food, fetid neighbours and a *pied a terre* that is better described as a 'fuck-flat'.

There is subtle textual and sexual variance. The gay hero, an outsider at the court of 'the Lady', catches a dance with her that causes rage among those whose claim is greater but whose opportunism is less. It is one of the finest novels of our time for imitating its world.

Miss R hasn't read it yet. She places it on the pile that she has asked to take away.

12.8.14
Over the past few days the lawn down below has changed colour in the heat – from brown to bright green to an even brighter yellow around its edge. Despite the efforts of Wapping's chemical gardeners, the edge of our newspaper lawn was often nauseous yellow where it met the concrete. This will be its final season.

'It reminds me of Cyril Lawn', says Miss R.

'Don't you remember? That artificial turf of the 1960s. My grandfather still uses it. A bit yellow now.'

'Yes, I do. My father laid it in the corridor that led to our garden, plastic tufts sold to him under the slogan "THIS IS LUXURY YOU CAN AFFORD BY CYRIL LORD". To his horror and distress our Essex patch of Cyril Lord's Cyril Lawn became yellow within days.'

We talk, idly but cautiously. She does not mind incidentals about colours and carpets unless she sees the conversation hardening around places where she does not want to go. I try to ask more about her 'Thatcher project' but she is as vague as a party-going spy.

She wants only to return to the Senecans. She wants to take them beyond 1990, beyond the Thatcher fall. We start to talk about 1992 but her mood is more sceptical than before. She says that she does not accept what I'm telling her. I object. She goes back to exterior floor-coverings. I complain again.

'Listen', I insist after half an hour of politics and soft pile, 'it was definitely Woodrow who first told me about John Major's "breakdown" on Black Wednesday.'

'Black Wednesday was what September 16th,1992 was called. It was in Margaret's successor's sixth month as an elected occupant of Number Ten and my own first week as Editor of *The Times*.'

Miss R is crisp.

'I am not disputing the name of the day', she says, 'only your account of who told you what happened on it.'

My account, I know, does not fit with those of others.

'Believe me. Woodrow Wyatt was both the source of the "breakdown" story and the man who most vigorously denied the truth of his own account. He was also the man who most aggressively abused me for publishing it.'

She nods as though I am giving in to her view.

'Yes, this makes your research more difficult. It does not make my memory unreliable or my statement untrue. Denial of the truth is by no means unusual to a newspaper editor. It goes with the territory, as my father used to say, talking of territory that was somewhat different.'

I have known since April that Miss R would at some time reach this point. She has her four subjects. She still identifies them in her notebook by the letters we saw in the smoke when the building first began to fall, H for Hart, T for Millar, J for Johnson, L for Wyatt.

She has learnt a little now – more Latin than she wants to learn – about what brought the Senecans together and what did not. Today she wants to talk about their part in the most difficult day of John Major's time in office, the day, as *The Times* reported, that he disappeared from view, abandoned his desk, becoming lost to his courtiers, civil servants and to the world.

John Major himself has always denied this. His is the official story. Maybe it was never very important anyway. But what Miss R wants to know is where I first heard the opposite.

'I'm telling you again that it was Woodrow who told the story first. The other Senecans played their part but Woodrow was the first.'

She shakes her head.

'Woodrow did not mean to be my source. He did not even know that I was about to overhear him in his borrowed office, one of those that are now a black square against the sky, at a desk where he was speaking on the telephone, and where he was listening, mostly listening, to someone else.'

'So, yes, all that I am saying is that Woodrow knew about the "breakdown". He was talking to someone else about it. Woodrow would not mind my saying that. He would always want to be known for knowing. I was not meaning to over-hear. Nor did I think at first that I had overheard anything very much.'

Miss R's eyes say that she is going to have to report this explanation back to someone else, and that she too is not going to be believed.

'At the time in question', I say as though in court, 'I hardly knew even where I was. But it was somewhere in the windowless middle of that vertical chess board, the part they are blasting away now with fire hoses and cranes, the part where I never normally went, the place where the advertising sellers used to sit. I was looking for my columnist in the offices of the *News of the World*, also somewhere I had never been before.'

Miss R says nothing.

'If Woodrow had wanted to, he could have come to see me in my own office. That would have been more convenient. But he normally preferred not to come to *The Times*. He thought that my colleagues disliked him. They did.'

'He and I needed to speak only briefly, about some "crass" editing of his column, the commonest reason for us to meet face-to-face, blue-marked proofs in our fists. I circled the blue-carpeted corridors where I thought he might be. There was no chance that he would be in the restaurant or at the hairdresser. Eventually I found him behind a door beside the red rail that ran around the atrium called Adland, the rail that is now that single spot of colour in the vertical squares of dust.'

'He was talking on the telephone about the odds for a horse race. I waited and walked around the Adland corridor again, in a continuous square, back to where I had begun. He was still on the telephone.'

'What I heard then seemed nothing at first. The clearest words were coat-hanger, vacuum, television and pillow. It could have been an order from a department store or the inventory of a holiday cottage. In its more mumbling themes the conversation covered "John's terrible state", the "heroic support" he was getting from a few of his very best friends and the incompetence of the Prime Minister's office. None of this was much different from Woodrow's usual tirades.'

'Yet, as he went on, repeating, restating, turning the words around, the story was there, along with an anxiety in his voice, a slackening in his characteristic crisp twang. The Voice of Reason always spoke as he wrote, assuredly and with the aim of instilling assuredness in whoever was hearing or reading. This time there was a touch of fear.'

'So yes, I heard the story more than once. And I heard it from Woodrow and from whomever he was talking to, a woman I am fairly sure. I did not wait outside any longer. I abandoned my mission to discuss his complaints. I walked away, around the red steel rails. Later he crossed the path into the Rum Store and came to see me at *The Times*. I mentioned nothing of what I had overheard.'

'How much could you really tell from Lord Wyatt's voice?' Miss R is listening, languidly leaning against the door. Of the two of us she seems much the more at home.

She scribbles on her Seneca pad in symbols that must be some kind of shorthand. I cannot be sure, never having learnt it myself and still remembering the relief when I rose to a position on *The Times* where no one could expect it from me.

'What made you so sure what he was saying?' She picks up a book from one of her new stacks on the floor. It is the two-tone brown copy of Kingsley Amis's, *The Old Devils*, the winner of the 1986 Booker Prize, signed inside as a gift from the author 'chez Woodrow'. Miss R might be beginning her own novel collection now.

'I knew Woodrow well enough to recognise what was

important, I say. He was not a man of mysterious depth. There were difficult times between us but not in our under-standing of each other. Woodrow still affected to be a kind of father figure, helping me through treacherous shoals. He thought I was sometimes naive just as I thought him shame-less almost all of the time.'

13.8.14

'The next Senecan to give me his "wisdom, dear boy" was Ronnie, still the Prime Minister's speechwriter despite pining quietly for the previous Prime Minister. We were in the very back of The Old Rose. If he had something especially awkward to say he would always move furthest from the rumbling Highway. That was where we liked to sit, even without a Latin lesson, whenever I could not come to the West End.'

'Ronnie was pleased about the economic consequences of Black Wednesday, surely a White Wednesday, he said, for all Senecans. The further we stood from European money the better he liked it – as, of course, did She.'

'He used the word "She" with delight. Ronnie and I were still feeling our way in the new era. We were re-establishing our relationship in a system intended to be so different from what came before, kinder, gentler, warmer. Although Ronnie was a man divided now in loyalties he was on this subject happy to be back with me saying what his mistress wanted him to say.'

'He could not so easily speak for John Major, his master. To me Ronnie was still the willowy T, leaning forward like any actor playing a plotter's part, describing the blackness inside the bubble of power as the British currency fell out of the ERM, the Exchange Rate Mechanism of the European Monetary System, its acronym then as famous as NATO or a GCSE.'

Miss R picks up one of her novels, a hint perhaps that I am heading in the wrong direction. She does not want a story about economic management but she need not worry. I am not going to tell one.

'Ronnie was not an economist. None of us was. Woodrow could call odds; he held a profitable political sinecure as Chairman of the Tote. David was a property investor; he knew when to call markets. Frank and I were almost blind to numbers. Words were all we had.'

'Ronnie, in fact, was almost Roman in his disregard for economics. Like Seneca, he spoke only of the moral aspects of money. He was a playwright who wrote economic speeches when someone else had provided the charts.'

'The only time he ever talked of even meeting an economist was when recounting how John Maynard Keynes, wartime bursar of King's College, Cambridge, persuaded him to stick to his part in the University Greek play of 1940. Ronnie liked to talk about Keynes but he never told Margaret about him. The man who believed in borrowing money to spend it was always best left unmentioned.'

'At the back of The Old Rose the other chairs were empty. Ronnie still spoke in his lowest voice, as though learning lines. He was an instinctive, visual raconteur, a writer and a vivid source for other writers.'

'He was not the least surprised at what I had learnt. He recounted the Black Wednesday scenes, the fall of numbingly large numbers, the helplessness as billions of pounds disappeared. He described a centre where there was no Thatcher, no economic policy, no European policy and where, for a critical time in the middle of the day, there was no Prime Minister of any kind.'

'I listened. The line of his thought was, as often, telescoped into an impromptu play. The enforced absence of Mrs

Thatcher was his prologue. Act One showed the frailty of her successor and the falling faith in the policy of imprisoning the pound in a European cell. The new element was Act Two, the twist in the story in which John Major, at a time when Whitehall needed some sort of certainty (any sort), was communing with his bedroom pillows instead of his computer screens. Without Woodrow's corroboration it would have been hard to believe as anything other than a play.'

Miss R still looks unconvinced.

'If Ronnie were alive in this office now, he would tell you himself about this story which, as days went on, went out to other journalists too. He quickly ceased to be shy about it. Others who claimed to know talked to others who found it useful to believe. Soon there was only one story that anyone, anywhere, with any knowledge at all, was talking about.'

'No one yet had published anything. I called David on the phone. He did not like to talk when his words were "insecure". He wanted me to come to Claridge's. I preferred that he came to The Old Rose which, after some argument, he did. I was meeting Frank there later.'

'David, when he finally arrived, knew no more than I knew already. He was reluctant to believe that I was a conspirator or had made the whole story up. As a conspirator himself he did not want an amateur threatening his status. He agreed that there must be something in what I told him.'

'He had become more distant in these different days, a different man from the boaster of the Falklands War, the Miners' Strike and Wapping. I was now the Editor. His heydays were almost forgotten.'

'Not so long ago David had been as aggressive to her "enemy within" as to her "enemy without". He had led the aggressors. None of that was wanted now. Sex, ideology and agriculture were his lifelong hobbies but the second was out of fashion and the third was fun only when he had a new tractor. He was back to his position of acting out the Sixteen Pleasures in the Lanesborough Hotel.'

'The new Prime Minister was not interested in his principles but would anyone else ever be? That was his anxiety.'

Miss R scribbles notes at any mention of principles just as she closes her book at the mention of positions. One by one she turns to face the office floor the photocopies of David's Ariadnes and Messalinas, their arses above heads, hands gripping bedposts.

'Mrs Thatcher was genuinely principled', she adds with a voice raised as a question.

'Yes, indeed. The longer she had held the principles the better she liked them. When she died last year claims were made that she was a magnet for intellectuals, Friedmanites, Hayekians and the like. Ronnie would have laughed at that. His own view was that she did most of her thinking very early. She liked the clash of ideas she had already considered. She liked intellectuals but liked them less than those who dressed her own views in intellectual language.'

'David's principles were of unfettered freedom, a creed that made a mere coal strike into a life-or-death conflict. Even his enemies, of whom there were many, conceded that, with his "soul politics", his legal funds and his helicopter, he made this difference – and thus made a bit of history. He came to like Seneca because Seneca helped him both to think and to seem to be thinking.'

'David and Ronnie agreed that John Major distrusted any thinking except in a tactical sense. The new Prime Minister could undoubtedly be devious. He had staged a brilliant withdrawal to his dentist when the challenge to Margaret's leadership came and those loyal to her were asked to stand and be counted. David had admired that. Retreat was a necessary skill, a too characteristic one as now it seemed. David admired nothing else about the new Prime Minister.'

Miss R writes a large letter H on her pad.

'After a short period focused on women and agricultural machinery, David's first response to the new era was to renew his plot for a New Right party to supplant the Conservatives. He especially loved its symbol, the soaring bird, the flattened M which he said would be easy for graffiti artists to paint on walls. This time he saw the core of his new movement not in anti-union miners but in suburban mothers opposed to gay sex education. He had his "shock troops" among Conservative students. He wrote his name on the plans with a sharp-pointed dagger for a D. He had high hopes of support from Poland.'

'But hardly had these birds and enthusiasms soared when they collapsed. He cited "security reasons" and refused to mention his graffiti any more. He decided to retire to his combine harvesters, sitting out the downturn for "as long as it took", like a canny property speculator, waiting for the moment when he might best influence the next succession.'

'So, when we spoke about Black Wednesday, he was only a little bit curious about why so many dull and mostly unexcitable men should believe that the PM's mind had broken down. He was out of circulation.'

'And yet it was a strange story, he agreed, the requests for briefing that brought only silence, the revelation that in John Major's office there was not even a functioning television aerial. He described the sudden sense throughout the arteries of Whitehall that the heart of power had ceased to beat.'

'I listened to him as encouragement but his metaphor was by then not a new one. His fresh contribution was the thought that something should certainly be published. It was wrong, he said, that everyone inside knew what nobody outside did.'

'I laughed quietly at that. David lived his whole life on information known only to the very few. When Frank arrived with his Seneca's essays and a Latin grammar he laughed quietly too. We did not wish to draw attention to ourselves. The bar that was empty at 11.00 became quickly busier at 12.00.'

'Frank did not wish to be distracted from his declensions but he did have new details which he reluctantly disclosed – on condition that we then wasted no more time on gossip. The Prime Minister, he reminded us, was in temporary quarters in Admiralty House while Ten Downing Street was being "refurbished". He said the word as though John Major were personally choosing the curtains in John Lewis.'

'Communications had, indeed, been less than ideal. Requests for briefings came in and nothing went out. A wire coat-hanger from a secretary's dry cleaning had been necessary as an aerial before the television would work, only and appropriately in black and white.

When the picture appeared it showed rates of interest rising, rearing and bucking like a viper in a charmer's basket. Every lunge was ever more fatal. If the Prime Minister had taken to his bed and chewed a freshly laundered pillowcase, who, frankly, could blame him?'

'And now please, he pleaded, could we go back to *De Beneficiis*, *On Giving and Getting*, the right way and the wrong way to repay favours and receive gifts.'

14.8.14

'Next day two reporters at *The Times* began work. Would the story "stand up", as we say? Yes, it "had legs". Sources were sources. We rapidly had a story. I could have been more cautious. It is sometimes too easy to confirm a story that everyone thinks is true, that the Editor has good reason to think is true. Some who knew held back. Some who didn't know didn't care.'

Miss R is as enthused as though she were on the hunt herself, her back against the door.

'Why was something so unlikely so believed?'

'Because it did not seem unlikely. There was madness and poison everywhere. More important was the character of John Major himself, not the character that his friends saw, charming, open, attractive, especially to women, but the public man, the not-Thatcher, the not-bloody-minded man, the not invulnerable to hurt, the not anything much but not her. Into the vacuum of "nots", on top of the ordinariness that separated him from his predecessor, flowed anything comic and mundane that could fill the gaps.'

'That afternoon Woodrow called me at the office. He liked to talk to me more now that I was Editor. He could sense drama from afar. He knew that there was drama most days. That was what we both loved and it would be many years before I began to love it less.'

'He asked if he would be seeing me that night "in the Locarno Room". I had no idea what he was talking about. We were having one of our "slipper wheel" quarrels. He said that I needed him as a friend at court. I said that I did not. I did not want to be at his court. Did it even exist? One of us always put the phone down briskly on the other.'

'I did not know what I was doing that night. A newspaper editor can always say that – even dishonestly. He can always stay in his office. Normally he is safer there.'

Miss R stirs, moves to the window and changes the subject as though she has noticed a gap in her notes.

'Where exactly was your office then? She is confused by both the destruction and preservation before us, the yellow jackets in the smoke and the grey suits flitting in and out of the heritage brick.'

I point again along the wall where we first saw the Senecans run as letters, H for Hart, J for Johnson, up on to the roof, the part beneath that thin tower on top of the Rum Store, the one like a Soviet army cigarette, black-tipped, beige-bricked.

'That was where I worked, under what was a chimney once. In the days before *The Times* came to Wapping it funnelled the furnace of some forgotten industrial malpractice. That was where I most felt the thrill of the job, the sense of the centre of a web, the place where I decided what to do and what others should do, instantly and without question, most of which I forget, some that I remember more clearly now.'

'The carpet tiles smelt of sour wine. The floor was damp from leaks in the roof. The evaporation of my "new editor's" celebratory Good Ordinary Claret took weeks. Woodrow disapproved of the choice of drink, (surely something better could have been found for such an occasion) but he had come to my windowless bunker party nonetheless. He was still anxious about his column. He could not afford to lose it.'

'He had forgotten, he said, how disgusting our Rum Store was. Seneca's Rome had sewers that were more suitable than this squat brick tube. It was just as the Queen Mother had described t to him. Did I remember how we had marked her official visit by taking her on a much too exhausting walk, how her Dubonnet had too much lemonade and how some mannerless creature ad asked her over lunch whether she was keeping a diary?'

'Yes, I did remember and how we had planned to brighten he brick and concrete with roses but had balked at the cost. confessed that I had been the host without manners on the natter of the diary. He knew that already.'

'We had reached a new uneasiness. Six years after the unch with Kingsley Amis, despite the "slipper wheel" and what he saw as my dangerous naivety, I was more in control than before. Margaret Thatcher's court was gone. All courtiers were out of fashion. Woodrow was still a *Times* columnist but, in the new era, there were even more of my colleagues who thought that he should not be.'

'But at 7.00 pm, just as he had known and said that I would, I arrived at the Foreign Office and climbed the wide marble stairs to the Locarno Room. I felt tired. A man I barely knew asked if I was well. I sipped a drink and wished I had not. There were already dozens of thick necks in this grandest suite of Her Majesty's grandest department. I tried to look closely without looking at anyone in particular.'

'I knew why I had come but, even before I had taken ten steps, I knew I should have stayed beneath my chimney. Another unknown man asked after my health, politely but firmly. He looked to me like one of the men in *The Undertaking*, that Greenwich play on my first Thatcher night, a pinstriped fraud on a stage with the fantasising dead.'

'I wondered if I should leave. The neck of the man asking me questions was built of triple-layered folds from one flat ear to another, a pitted nose, heavy-lidded eyes propped beneath a bright broad forehead where wrinkles ran like waste pipes. His colleagues looked much the same and it was as hard at first to see between the pillars of neck as to tell their double-breasted owners apart. At least I was suitably suited myself.'

'The quieter places were beside the walls, an alternating pattern of panels in blue and gold. I could already see Woodrow who had chosen blue as his backdrop. His thin white hair, streaked carefully over his shining skull, absorbed the same jewel-like blue. These rooms, the invitation told us, were newly restored to their grandeur of the 1930s.'

'A junior foreign minister was showing off the work. When Woodrow had asked me whether I would be "at the

Locarno Room for the Lennox-Boyds" he made it sound as though it were a dinner. I had said not. But there was something in the Editor's office diary about the Foreign Office and this was it, fortunately as it turned out because by then there was something important that I needed to tell him.'

'Woodrow was buried in the party's first half hour by the bulk of other people. I watched him. I met an American friend whom I genuinely wanted to see. I began to feel better and a bit guilty. To compare the Locarno Room to a mortuary of the surreal was an exaggeration. I had to beware exaggeration.'

'Where I stood was more like a gallery of plaster casts, thick white shapes, eighteenth-century copies of Roman heads, Renaissance copies of Greek originals, solid ghosts, ghostly nonetheless, politicians and bureaucrats with that peculiar spirit quality that comes when avoidance of trouble is the highest art.'

'Seneca would have fitted in easily among the Locarno crowd, the Seneca of his best surviving portrait, a double bust from two centuries after his death in which he shares a block of marble and, by not very subtle implication, a mind and brain, with the face of Socrates. Woodrow was blending in with natural ease, his forehead just a little shallower than Seneca's, his chin sharper, his eyes set in false mockery.'

'My columnist's bowties were hardly classical. Nor was the unlit cigar by his belt which he wore as though it were a pistol or a whip. But he and Seneca shared much of the same space, merely a trapdoor of time between them. There was so much else that these two shared (or so it seemed as I watched and waited, waved to men I knew and drank warming white wine), a relentless insecurity, a raw nerve in every jowled crevice, a resolute desire for principle as well as power, pleasure and its resistance.'

'This was not intended to be a Senecan night. Woodrow

had anyway proved himself the least attentive, the least inventive, of the group. I had one specific piece of business, to tell Woodrow about the article that had come from his unknowing phone call, now already on *The Times* presses for the following day, a short but striking story of John Major's melancholic state of mind, maddened, said some, miserable, said all, and what that meant for what happened when his power was collapsing all around him.'

Miss R is being patient despite herself. 'Was Woodrow the only one who "knew"?' She voices the quotation marks of doubt.

'Oh no. Woodrow was one of many in the Locarno Room who "knew" about the "black dog" that bit the PM on the day that he lost his economic policy. But he did not know what was about to be said about it in *The Times* the next day. That was what he would have wanted to know the most. The Black Wednesday event was in the past, but not yet safely in the past. Woodrow knew merely what had happened, alongside others of the sharp-nosed, the thick-necked and at least one well informed woman.'

'There was a small group at the end furthest from the entrance, "where Lord Salisbury had once had his desk" a man said, "where the Locarno Treaty itself was signed" added another. This area was as though roped off by invisible red threads. No one approached too near. I recognised there one of the most powerful marble men who, in Frank's report to The Old Rose, had spoken of the hour in which the heartbeat of government had stopped.'

'Amid the rest of the throng there were two others who had done the same, with added details about pillow-biting in the purple-plumped upholstery of the prime ministerial bedroom. How did they know? They had reliably heard.'

'"Can Major take the strain?" ran the headline when I left

the office. "Did he crack up?" asked the second paragraph.
Journalists were quoted. "Friends of" were invoked. Minor
errors were still unspotted. It was not a great piece of work but
a gripping one. The first edition was already rumbling towards
the presses, soon to be on its way to Cornwall and Scotland and
to those desks in Whitehall whose occupants had the task of
seeing first what others would see soon enough.'

'I was still keen to tell Woodrow before he learnt of this from
anyone else, or still worse from the morning paper itself. I owed
him that, a debt of etiquette even though he would be horrified,
I was sure, to hear what I had done. Or maybe he would have
pulled back his shoulders like a sly bird and laughed.'

'An adviser likes an early warning whatever his view of the
news. How can he advise what others cannot advise unless
he knows what others do not know? He wants to know when
every little bomb will explode, particularly when he is one of
those who have lit its long and multi-stranded fuse. Woodrow
would never know about the fuse (I would naturally protect
my source from himself) but he was never going to know
about the explosion if he stayed inside the knot of statues
beside the blue-panelled wall.'

'I slipped out to the foot of the stairs, thinking that I
might catch him as he left. I wanted to speak to a few others
too. I wanted to speak to David and Ronnie and to Frank
but none of them was necessarily going to be there, Frank
the most likely, David almost certainly not, Ronnie, well one
could never be sure. Then suddenly, and behind the last
curve of the staircase, I saw all four of my Senecans, the last
time that I ever saw them all together.'

'This was absolutely a surprise. Events were ever more
driving us apart. Frank and I kept up a little Latin and some
plotting against some mutual enemies but he had adopted
the distance from the Senecans that he thought appropriate

for the new Deputy Editor of the *Sunday Telegraph*. Woodrow thought David now as nothing but a spiv, Ronnie as a pen-for-rent who was lukewarm to John and a fanner of Margaret's worst Queen-over-the-water fantasies.'

'David thought Woodrow a toad and Ronnie a useful idiot. Ronnie, while still happy to play Seneca with me, thought David a bit deranged, very dilatory at Latin, and he did not think of Woodrow much at all. But this time, this one and final time, they looked like life-long friends.'

'Ronnie and David stood apart but talking. Between them were two locked bicycles, not a standard Foreign Office feature and neither of the machines belonging to my conspirators. I say conspirators because on this occasion they truly did look like conspirators too, as though they intended to be seen in a conspiratorial pose or, at least, did not at all mind.'

'I was confident about the non-ownership of the bicycles because Ronnie still rode only in his elderly Rolls Royce which he could always somehow, somewhere park. David liked best to travel by helicopter, often piloting himself, dreaming of swoops against striking miners, somehow maintaining his licence even when the wasting disease had destroyed the voluntary use of his limbs. On land he was always driven – by a man in a Mercedes, not always the same man in the same Mercedes – and to have seen him on a bicycle would have been as unlikely as seeing Seneca or Socrates on one.'

'I saw them together as I watched Woodrow reach the last stone step, slipping slightly on the last of the red carpeted strips, righting himself by a straightening of his tie. I think of him now as a man of slippers. He made so many jokes, threats and quotes about the slippery slopes of power. At this point he was merely mumbling his way out, mumbling towards Frank, who was just arriving, and Ronnie and David whom he seemed not yet to have seen.'

'Ronnie and David, though talking, seemed also not quite to have met. Each was looking past the other's shoulder like parrots kissing in cages. For David a conspirator's cloak was a familiar guise, his essential nature as his enemies saw him. His distant stare that night more than usually brought to mind Lord Lucan evading capture for the murder of his children's nanny, a man backed into a corner but certain that with a moustache and a limousine he would escape.'

'Ronnie was smiling into a different empty space. He looked at that moment like the most lauded of film idols, with the kind of face that Margaret Thatcher, in so many instances, had so clear a liking for, an even, varnished gaze. David still complained that honours were her form of sexual favours. Ronnie was manifestly her type, the friend of Greer Garson and Celia Johnson, the toast of Hollywood in the years when she was still studying her chemistry books, still not yet embarked on her career as a whipper of cream.'

'Frank was running his hand across his thick black hair, looking around, already sketching the scene into his diary. Each of the Senecans looked as their undertaker or favoured biographer would want them to look, Ronnie as open and natural as an actor can easily be, as pale as David was dark, Woodrow in a worsted hue, a spotted grey, Frank in Marks & Spencer blue. Each had his position. I was sure that later they were planning to meet.'

'Ronnie seemed the most commanding. Margaret Thatcher's once favourite speechwriter knew already what was coming in *The Times* the next day. He was almost the first to know. I had phoned him from the car. The others did not. Or, at least, they did not know so from me.'

'Ronnie was also by a foot the tallest. This gave him the greatest opportunity for the avoidance of meeting eyes. He swivelled away as though to check on his bicycle while somehow at the same time grasping Woodrow's hand. All four then shook hands, not what the thick-necked men up in the Locarno Rooms would naturally do to their friends. At that moment each wanted unequivocally to be a stranger.'

'What was going on?' Miss R asks if I know now any more than I knew then.

'I know less', I answer. 'You should have found me earlier.' She purses her lips.

Maybe both of us are going to write about this time together. She said as much at the start. My own diary began as a defence against her, just as sometimes I used to write as a defence against Frank. I am wondering about her 'Thatcher project' and if she is really a writer. If she is I doubt that the books will be very much alike. She is writing history. I am writing non-fiction. There is a difference.

If I were Miss R, the historian, I would have to decide on the credibility of my sources, the reliability of each man or woman whom she has chosen to interview. I would judge the significance of all the various plots against John Major, those that were real but unimportant, those that were important but imagined. For non-fiction I just record what happens in this emptying room.

Of course, if I were a novelist of newspapers, vying for a place on Miss R's freshest pile, it would be possible to finish the story in any way I chose, finding plausibilities that might satisfy her better than anything I have said so far. If I were fully infected with fiction I could build upon an unsupported possibility a narrative in which Ronnie knows most from those closest, Woodrow hears quickly too, and Frank gleans added details from the Mandarins. Maybe Frank hopes that, by publishing them, I will prove to everyone his worst illusions about *The Times*. Motives of everyone would be mixed, a hope of pleasing and appeasing Margaret, a hope of advancing a new Tory leader, a hope of advancing themselves, a simple love of mischief.

Miss R puts her notebook on top of her fiction pile. She returns coldly to her questions. 'What happened next?'

There is a call from outside, some *TLS* problem of today. I have to leave – and ask her to leave – before I can answer.

15.8.14

'What happened next?' Miss S scrawls the words like graffiti in her second yellow SENECA notebook.

I do not answer immediately. I like to answer her quickly. She is more likely to believe me if I do.

'What happened to whom?'

'To you', she says.

'Nothing, not immediately', I reply. 'One of Seneca's most influential contributions to "self-improvement" was what he called his "Way". Every night a man should think back over his day, questioning his own intentions, wondering whether a more virtuous decision might have been substituted for every decision taken.'

'Seneca's Way is not the way of newspapers. Critics charge that editors are too able to be thoughtless and ruthless, too powerful, too little accountable and sometimes we have all been so. We take positions and change them. Each day the present so quickly obliterates the past that a thought about an old thought hardly ever happens.'

'Did nothing happen at all?'

'Officially, not very much.'

'The next time I was in Downing Street I was told by an aristocratic aide – firmly as though to a misguided child – that since John Major and I were "both from the same sort of background" we surely ought "to understand each other much better than we seemed to do". It was "in all our interests".

'The next time I met Woodrow he responded with denial and rage. There was not the slightest scintilla of truth in our story. The sooner that I slipped off the "slipper wheel" the better.'

'I repeated "not the slightest scintilla" to David. Not a spark of truth, he queried, showing off his new interest in Latin. He doubted that. Men like Woodrow always liked to use Latin words for lying. That was a good reason for learning more of their language. There surely had to be a spark of truth in the Prime Minister losing his mind as well as his temper. He would find out.'

'The next time I met Ronnie he was unusually quiet. Margaret, he said, was doubly disappointed – both that the incident took place and that *The Times* published it. "The first, I think, rather more than the second, my dear".'

'Frank laughed. He had already moved on, just as I had, just as all journalists do.'

18.8.14

'Yes, but how did you yourself feel about what you had done?' Miss R has been coming back and forth for four months and this morning, for the first time, she asks the desperate question that journalists normally ask much earlier, especially those broadcasting on TV or radio. I should respect her, I suppose, for holding back so long.

How did I feel? There is nothing I can say. I am beginning to wish that I was part of a more conventional interview, one of those where the subject can promote achievements and success, provide a 'balanced view', ideally slightly unbalanced in the interviewee's interests. I could describe my encouragement of young writers, some important 'scoops' on schools and prisons policy if I could remember them, and lunches with Social Democrats to discuss libel law reform. It is too late for that now.

Miss R and I look again together down the cobbled street to The Old Rose. I see Ronnie and Woodrow, the L and M in wary alliance. I see David and Frank, H and J, hyphenate and justify as the type-setters used to say. Together we see the plant and the spaces within the plant, red against black, black against red. Remembering Woodrow makes me remember again the roses on trellises that we thought might brighten the Queen Mother's Wapping day. The colleague who rescued me from my 'do you keep a diary, ma'am?' gaffe did so by asking our guest a question about rose-growing in Scotland.

19.8.14
'Why, if the "breakdown" story wasn't true, was it so widely believed?'

Miss R sweeps her eyes this morning across the piles she created yesterday. I look back at her in mock surprise.

'Who's saying it wasn't true?'

'Almost everyone, as far as I can see.'

'But that is because John Major is now respected. Everyone

who came after him was so much worse. The same thing happened to Roman emperors. The best route to a glorious reputation is to be followed by fools.'

'The early 1990s were such a crazy, toxic time. A "believing age" had been replaced by a different age, a brutal but mercifully short age, of believing anything at all. The "hard thinking" had become the "no thinking" and the "soft thinking" of New Labour was still ahead.'

Miss R flicks back through her notebook.

'Margaret Thatcher had been forced from office. John Major had won an election without her. But in many places, among many people, it was as though she were still in power – or still about to return to power. Nero was the same.'

'Did you keep up the Latin lessons?'

'Since Frank had now joined Lord Black at the *Sunday Telegraph*, he and I met less often. But at least three of us still met occasionally in The Old Rose, still talking, at Frank's insistence, mostly of Latin matters.'

'Ronnie was the most regular other attender, Woodrow the least. David said that there were certain times when simply no one could discern fact from fiction.'

Miss R looks blankly around us. She point to what little is left on the political shelves in a hopeful seeking of help.

'Every reader who cares can now know the official history of the 90s. There are countless books, some of them here about to be dumped into their own yellow skip. No one will rescue "the Bastards' Tales", the boasts of how John Major was harried to defeat in 1997, never recovering from that Black Wednesday of 1992 when the pound collapsed from its European restraints (certainly), the central policy of the government collapsed (certainly) and the Prime Minister himself left a vacuum at the centre of power while he found a pillow on which to bite (possibly, possibly not).'

Once upon a time I might have written a different account of those years, a traditional Editor's verdict with much 'allegedly', many cautions and caveats. This year Miss R is looking from me only for what others cannot or may not tell her. Then she will move on.

20.8.14

Each time she leaves she takes a few of the books she wants. Her mind is on the letters now. At the top of her carefully tied bundle there is one that I have had my eye on ever since she pulled it from the piles. I can tell her about if she asks. Its date is November, 1993.

Mr V barely registered John Major. Three years after the fall, the words from Walton were still of the 'assassination' of Mrs Thatcher. What was a fading term even among her friends was long a living fact for him, as for other adherents, a constant cause of scratchy italic rage. For years he wrote as though the coup against her had only just taken place, or he had only just now read about it, or that it might in good time be reversed.

Margaret had deserved a dignified departure, he wrote. He wrote this repeatedly. Instead, she was betrayed by every-one who had once relied on her (and that included me), shoved before parliament to answer some last questions, prodded into declaring how much she was enjoying herself, and sent away to live in a housing estate. Her successor looked like the man who used to collect the takings at the Odeon.

Miss R picks up this letter and holds it gently in her hand. I have read it many times. It is written in a pale brown ink, a colour barely browner than salt water over sand, readable only in parts even when I first received it, now hard to discern at all except by nib marks. It seems like the note of a failing man except for Mr V's proud boast that he has returned to balsa.

He has carved a sculpture of his heroine's final parliamentary performance inside the Palace of Westminster. He has received local acclaim for it. Photographers have visited from *The Chronicle*. He wants to know when I might come and see what I can so readily imagine, the green leather benches made cream, the rejected Prime Minister as a stooping letter P, the sculptor in aertex and white.

21.8.14

Miss R is agitated again today. She does not want to tell me why. She sounds like a writer who has lost confidence in her project. I have known enough of those – and been one sometimes myself too. Instead of more chronology she wants much more 'context'. Context is her new word. She listens less and searches more. She sifts letters from newsprint and puts poems next to grammars.

'I need more to read.'

I know now that our interview is coming to an end. I have one suggestion. Although Margaret Thatcher was never famed for encouraging the arts, this final period did inspire one too little-known novel. I can already see my copy close to where she is leaning her hand. Philip Hensher's *Kitchen Venom*, published in 1996, was – and still is – the best book about this final phase of the Thatcher era.

Today it lies sullenly on the floor, in bookish protest that no one has opened it for a long time, the blue-covered version although I think there is also somewhere a cream one and a pink. It is a highly Senecan novel, dark, epigrammatic, suffused with philosophy and revenge, narrated in part by the Iron Lady herself as a deposed but not quite departed ghost.

The Prime Minister's fall from power in 1990 is, in Hensher's fiction, a wholly random event, as random as the murder of an Italian rent-boy by a powerful House of Commons clerk. In as much as anything is intended in the story, it is impossible to say when it began to be intended. There is an ancient sense of Fortune with a capital F.

The 'leaderene' and the cog in the parliamentary machine are well matched. The greatest politician of her age lovingly fingers the silk around her neck (no one has ever better described Mrs Thatcher dressing) in the same way that the subversive clerk, anticipating the fuck that has cost him £50, feels the silk of the hired boy's skin. The mistress of politics in her prime crushes the world like a dead cigarette with every high-heeled step she takes. But the clerk crushes whichever politician is in power, concentrating most of his mental energy on remembering the name of every Trollope novel.

Venom is as ubiquitous as alcohol. Fierce intelligence is everywhere, too, most of it useless and pointless. Haunting is his theme. His heroine remains for some while as a spiritual presence in Westminster and Whitehall, passing on her power 'in a command and a request'.

'You might enjoy it. You should add it to your reading for after *The Line of Beauty*.'

But her agitation has passed.

'Are you pleased that you became a journalist?' She asks this question slowly, as though it is the one she has long most wanted to ask.

No one has asked me that for a very long time. This is an even more desperate question than 'how did I feel?' Probably the last person to ask it was the man who wrote the letters in brown ink.

'Yes, of course, I am pleased that I became a journalist, proud too most of the time.'

'What about the rest of the time?'

22.8.14

When Miss R came here first she struggled for space. Almost all of my boxes have now gone. But she has added piles of her own, personal letters and Latin plays, even borrowing some of the labels that read DO NOT MOVE TILL LAST DAY.

'For evidence', she claims with a smile, she has set aside Kingsley Amis's *The Old Devils*, the copy inscribed to me 'Chez Woodrow.'

'For atmosphere' there is now *Kitchen Venom* as well as *The Line of Beauty*.

On top of the pile is Ian McEwan's *Amsterdam*, its cover a frosty scene of French duellists, name and title in brown, winner of the Booker Prize in 1998. 'This one is a bit about you', she says as she sits down on the floor.

I try to look surprised. I am not wholly surprised. It is an identification I have heard before. 'Some said Peter Stothard, others Alan Rusbridger. But I have no idea . . .': that was how the author himself put it, writing in a presentation copy for charity last year, words extracted by the *Guardian*, edited by Alan Rusbridger.

McEwan was being mischievous maybe but I can hardly blame him for that. Mischief is what writers make. For Miss R, newly interested in my pride or lack of pride, in 'how did I feel?' or how did I ever feel, *Amsterdam* is a reasonable destination.

'Tell me about it', she says, by which she means, I think, that she genuinely wants me to tell her, not that her question is of the 'tell-me-about-it' teenage kind.

'McEwan', I try to summarise quickly, 'has two rival characters, the duellists of the cover. The musician in the foreground need not concern us, but further back there is a newspaper editor, a man in charge of *The Judge*, a paper not unlike *The Times*. Maybe I have the two men the wrong way around. How do I know? I don't. It does not matter.'

'The story need not concern us either, only the character of the editor, Vernon Halliday, who responds to a story of political scandal with bouts of confidence and hubris, self-righteousness and self-criticism, shock at the effects of his actions and reasoned doubt about whether he is doing anything at all.'

She opens the book, finds some blue-pencilled quotes and notes the passages, page numbers first. She reads aloud, not in her glass-etcher's voice but softly and slowly.

'After talking to forty people in his first two hours of work, offering "opinions that were bound to be interpreted as a command", Vernon finds himself with thirty rare uninterrupted seconds: "It seemed to him that he was infinitely diluted; he was simply the sum of all the people who had listened to him and, when he was alone, he was nothing at all." He was "finely dissolved throughout the building" and "globally disseminated like dust".'

'Did you have hours like that?'

'Not many but a few, quite enough truth for fiction.'

'*Amsterdam* is set in the mid-1990s, more or less on my own editorial watch. Halliday is both a pedant on grammar and a risk-taker in the newsroom. I recognise myself there. He dismisses a story on hepatitis as too dull even for the *TLS*. He is described as a "hard-working lieutenant for two gifted editors in succession".'

'Pedantic about Latin quotes? Happy to take a risk? Liable to invoke the *TLS*? Yes to all of those.'

'Both Harold Evans, who opposed Margaret Thatcher, and his successor, Charles Douglas-Home, who cheered the paper through the Falklands War, were "gifted" and, in different ways, seen to be so. I worked hard for them both – and for their successors too, including my friend, Charles Wilson, the Editor so disapproved of by Frank Johnson in the Senecan times.'

'Halliday is a well-observed character. He is not always sure that he is alive. Few men of power ever admit that in their memoirs. That is why novelists matter. In the brief moments of the day when the Editor of *The Judge* is alone, a light goes out. "Even the ensuing darkness encompassed or inconvenienced no one in particular. He could not say for certain that the absence was his." Most Editors would understand this Editor very well.'

25.8.14

When Miss R returns this morning a bookmark shows that she has almost finished *Amsterdam*. When I say nothing, she simply stands in the corner and reads some more until I continue my story from where it stopped.

'As the Major government decayed, his predecessor's ghost came ever more vividly back to life, the fiercest among the flittering flocks who pursued the new Prime Minister. The question was quick in coming. Who should replace this Tory leader who had failed to inspire? Even four years after her fall was there not still the possibility that the replacement might be Margaret Thatcher once again?'

'There was a Christmas party, held in her museum home of signed Ronald Reagan photographs, frosted MT paperweights and an almost all-black oil painting of the hostess with a shady Tory lady. When we spoke I was wholly unready for the blasts against her successor. Three times she said that she was not looking to come back to power. Each time she looked hard about, daring me, or anyone else, to disagree. The only way to avoid her eye was to catch a peculiarly vile blue view of the Falklands.'

'What help were her Senecans then?, asks Miss R, holding *Amsterdam* at her waist.

'Ronnie became a double man in those days. Fortunately, he was well trained for that. Every time that his heroine heard he had written a speech for Major, she banned him from her presence. Ronnie tried to please both sides. He said he did not approve of her haunting Downing Street as though a part of her had never left. Woodrow claimed that he too was against her afterlife. I doubt whether, when he was with the former Prime Minister, he defended the new Prime Minister very much.'

'In Ronnie's mind there was never a doubt that Margaret still mattered. He always believed that if Mrs Thatcher felt well (a state she regularly discussed with him) she really was well. If she was well (a truth he would always readily believe) she would speak well and that if she spoke well (which, under his direction, she usually would) she would act well. He still believed this even though it mattered less now. He wished he had done even more when it had mattered more.'

'Although Margaret had been out of power for two years, Sir Ronald Millar, in his own mind, was still a national bene-factor, keeping the ousted queen alive. This life of hers was not in his playwright's mind alone. To Woodrow Wyatt and David Hart – and to many more from the Locarno Room and beyond – Mrs Thatcher might still be needed again.'

'Ronnie often recalled in The Old Rose how long after Nero had fallen to his dagger, years after his last cry of "O what an artist dies in me", Seneca's pupil still had supporters in Greece who were sure he was coming back. No one liked to criticise his repetition. It was something of a comforter for him. Frank saw Margaret in something of the same light, her stalwarts as exiled cohorts landing at Clacton, like William of Orange at Torbay, meeting up with local worthies such as Lord Tebbit, assuring her that Essex was rallying to her side.'

'Frank mocked but he also yearned. In the traditional ways of the Conservative Party a former leader had to be either loyal or dead. But Mrs Thatcher's own bitter predecessor, Edward Heath, had rewritten the rules. There was now an ousted dictator role in British politics, just like in Argentina, he would jollily say.'

'Margaret herself had entered the House of Lords, a desperate fall, thought David, although he would have loved the humiliation for himself. There was still a range of possible uses for the newly ennobled baroness, to push her successor in the right directions, to promote a better successor if one were needed. If the idea of a Thatcher Mark Two, fresh and repolished, were wholly absurd, David might yet make the Lady think that it was not.'

'For Woodrow she was a ripe fruit that had to be kept from rotting – by flattery, by drink, by calls upon her party loyalty to stop being an angry ghost and to help John Major where she could. She always told the Voice of Reason that she was heeding his advice. She was inconsistent in keeping to that pledge.'

'Woodrow said that David was a menace, increasingly obsessed by the SAS and the Bravo Two Zero books about its heroes. Margaret was "history", that most respected state of comfort and condemnation. She must remain as history. John had to remain as Prime Minister. The Labour Party would destroy itself as it so often had before. Most importantly, Woodrow had to remain. Every adviser was fine as long as Woodrow was fine.'

'And the lessons at The Old Rose?'

'The spirit of the Latin lessons was now almost gone. We rarely tried to persuade one another. For David, Margaret was a long dying animal, ready soon to be stuffed as an icon for followers of some spiritual successor, hand-picked by himself. For Ronnie she was still the star whom he had helped to mould. For Frank and me she was a subject who, as time moved on, became less of a subject.'

'Margaret herself was mostly more pragmatic than her ghost, more realistic than the image her admirers made of her. Although she never forgave Ronnie for working for John Major she needed him to write her own speeches and gradually the two were warmer together again. He had always been much more than a speechwriter to her. She saw that more clearly now, he suggested slyly.'

'Ronnie still had the matinee-idol looks that she liked. She trusted him when he said she could wear expensive pearls without looking like a plutocrat's wife. He was tall. His hair was dark. His face was still polished enough to be her one remaining mirror when so many others had passed on. His voice was low. He made her calm and kept her calm. In exile she needed calm more than ever.'

'"We talked about Stoicism", Ronnie said. I believed him as best I could although others reported a more random pattern to her mind. She somehow felt a greater need for principles when she did not need to apply them, he explained. She felt herself to be a Stoic, he insisted. He made her an honorary member of our extinct club. No one else could ever be her Seneca. It was Ronnie who came closest to the Stoic ideal of a tutor whose pupil was the greatest power in the world.'

'Sometimes he tried to guide her to lighter reading, less philosophy more Dorothy L. Sayers. She loved the poetry of John Masefield and had more time for that too. His own ideal novels were those of his mentor, C. P. Snow, "Charles", as he called him with an accentuated long A. *The Masters,* the story of the battle for succession at a Cambridge College, was his favourite. He had dramatized it for the West End, where it had run for a decade. It was one of the foundations of his fortune, the fuel for his bronze Rolls Royce.'

'That play was deep within his mind. He had lived the plot, the moderniser vs the traditionalist, the complexities of new against old in a conservative institution. That was why it had worked so well. Plotting and plotting were the same thing, with Charles, with David and Woodrow: and Margaret could enjoy the plot too.'

'He continued to take her to the theatre. He recalled how in the old days they saw an early performance of Evita: "if a woman like Eva Peron with no ideals can get that far, think how far I can get with all the ideals that I have", she told him. Ronnie readied her well for the Falklands and in the nineties the Haymarket Theatre remained his home. He had an office there. He could arrange staff members in the audience to clap when she arrived.'

'Such applause was less easy to arrange when she was Prime Minister. But she did not care so much about the occasional boo or heckle then. In exile she cared more. Her reluctance to be retired was too often all too clear. And in her unaccustomed weakness it was easier for the cautious and cowardly to hurt her.'

'Just as theatre trips were not as easy as once they had been, nor were lunches at party conferences. The last time I had a lunch with Mrs Thatcher was in 1996, in Bournemouth.'

'Are you interested in "last times"?'

She waves her *Amsterdam* in what seems like a 'yes, possibly'.

'The sound when we entered the dining room was a hush, not quite a hiss but not what she was hoping for. I joked that a not very supportive Tory MP had just been found drunk in a seaside gutter. "A calamity, dear", she insisted. That sort of satisfaction was never a cheer to her. She was vigorously insistent that her salmon be "very well cooked".'

'Margaret's successful performances were almost all abroad. In America her status was unshaken by her fall. In Downing Street and in London newspaper offices her faraway speeches were read for signs of treachery to John Major. She always professed loyalty but often did not sound very loyal. Woodrow would sometimes admonish her for making her successor's life too difficult. Ronnie was milder in the same campaign. Both men were at different levels insincere.'

'David had no need to express a public position. He used to listen carefully to her distant words, occasionally referring me to a line of language that he claimed was one of his own. His game was the succession, the long game, not to be played for maybe four or five years. He did not have a single candidate. He had different plans for different times.'

'Every day, it seemed, John Major's leadership was about to be challenged. Every week a challenge failed to happen. He called his Tory critics "bastards" and worse. Woodrow redoubled his support for the Major government. The worse John's problems, the more strident the Voice of Reason became on his behalf.'

'Whatever Woodrow's sincerity – and David and Ronnie deeply doubted it – he was a noisy friend in hard times. He and I were arguing constantly still about his column. Increasingly he wanted to use it to abuse *The Times* for our own attacks on John Major, cheerfully misquoting us unless we were alert.'

'Maybe I should not have been so sensitive. Majorism was maybe infectious to us all. David thought that Major must go – and that one of his own protégés should take over as soon as he could engineer it. Woodrow thought this absurd. He told me that Margaret Thatcher was "100 per cent behind

John now". Ronnie said she was not. I believed Ronnie more.'

'Woodrow said again that I would lose my own job long before he lost his: I was naive, utopian and would surely soon fall off the 'slipper wheel'. The sooner the better, he announced at a party to celebrate a book by his fellow *Times* columnist, Bernard Levin, about utopias, *A World Elsewhere*.

'Newspaper editors become accustomed to hearing regularly of their own demise. Woodrow had firm views about how the Editor of *The Times* should behave. I should be a proponent only of what was practical. All else was indulgence, fine only for columnists.'

'John Major was as close to my views and background as anyone available was likely to be. So why did I not help him more, or help him at all? Did I want a Labour government? I said that I might.'

'John Major's last years of weakness in power were a spur to every worst conspiratorial urge. Woodrow spun the slippery wheel as loyally as he could. Ronnie sighed and spoke to Margaret whenever he could. David wanted the best future place that he could get. He needed the succession to go to the candidate whom he had personally helped the most, the one who would owe him the most, who would give him an office in Downing Street and the title, the knighthood, or maybe even the peerage that Thatcher had somehow failed to give.'

'That required a stream of stratagems towards rivals to his own men, most of all against a puritan political thinker, John Redwood, who alone had the will to stand against John Major in a leadership contest in 1995. David's favourite, Michael Portillo, one of the veterans of the Heartbreak House weekend, was left waiting in the wings, in useless readiness to strike if the Prime Minister emerged as a stricken beast. David installed forty phone lines in a Portillo campaign headquarters. In a last burst of Bravo-Two-Zeroing he told his man to cite the SAS slogan, Who Dares Wins. Neither decision was a good one. John Major was not stricken enough and limped on. Woodrow cheered loudly (and sometimes almost persuasively) at his champion's courage.'

'Woodrow and I found it much easier to talk about Beryl Bainbridge's novels than about Margaret Thatcher's heir. He harped on about the writer's betrayal by her publisher, praising her "wonderful books", complaining that she did not get the recognition she deserved. All publishing was politics. All things were politics. That was what I seemed never to learn.'

'He had by then come to hate David. In conversation and in his column he professed ever greater support for John Major, warning anyone who would listen of the enemies within the Tory camp. Foreign Secretary, Malcolm Rifkind, ostensibly a Major loyalist too, was "Hart's second choice if Portillo fell". That position, said Woodrow, was a very slippery position to hold, hardly a position at all. His great hope now was that some event would happen. Perhaps the Argentines could oblige for a second time and launch a noisy attack on the Falklands.'

'But then, as time moved on and a Labour victory in 1997 became absolutely certain, even David swung back towards backing Major, or telling me every day that he did, and that I should, and that everyone should. Woodrow hated David all the more for joining the sinking ship so late.'

'Ronnie was keen that Margaret Thatcher jump aboard too. And sullenly she did so. At a dinner for the US general and politician, Colin Powell, I asked her if she would really prefer the Tory ship to sink. She smiled quizzically, looked away sadly and sharply, and answered a politer question from her neighbour instead. A few weeks before the poll she told me at an anniversary dinner in honour of Charles Douglas-Home that Tony Blair "would not let Britain down".'

26.8.14

Miss R has a page of poems in her hand this morning.

'What are these?' She is playful, kicking her white shoes towards me in what may be self-parody, brandishing her electronic tablet like a table-tennis bat.

'John Major used to protect himself from the Bastards' abuse by writing every day a limerick. He showed them to no one, he told me much later, but the writing made him feel better.'

'Were you surprised?'

'Not very. Inside so many public men, Ronnie used to say, there is a secret artist trying to get out. John Major was a deliberately secret poet; secrecy was the way he wanted it. Woodrow Wyatt was a sadly secret playwright; no one wanted to put on his plays; he did not have the money to put them on himself but he went on writing. David Hart was an almost secret novelist and playwright: he could pay enough for his works to be produced but not enough for them to be seen or read.'

'In 1992, even Ronnie himself, once feted from Her Majesty's to Hollywood, was fast becoming a secret playwright. His plays were deemed old-fashioned, doomed to be forgotten. He was merely a speechwriter and even his speeches were heard more often in Kentucky or Kansas (wherever Margaret Thatcher could earn herself $25,000 for making them) than in Brighton or Blackpool where her Tories too had cruelly moved on.'

'Maybe Ronnie was right, that it was art that kept them all going, Major, Millar, Wyatt, Hart. Add Jeffrey Archer, whom Woodrow despised for his bumptious insecurity but envied for his powers of storytelling. Add Norman Tebbit's man, Michael Dobbs, Lord Dobbs of Wylye and his *House of Cards*.'

She taps in the names.

'Add my fellow book-collector, Kenneth Baker, anthologist, former Booker Prize chairman, loyalist to both Thatcher and to Major, senior architect of the poll-tax policy that produced the change from the one to the other. Add Douglas Hurd too, thin, languid, kind, Etonian, a man who thrilled (well, a little bit) with his hardback thrillers, a holder of the highest offices of state and a candidate in his own mind to succeed to the premiership. Fiction is its own empire. The courtiers are characters and the author can never be wrong.'

Miss R looks again at the poems which she has removed from their place on a dusty shelf between Messalina's favourite position and my copy (her copy now, she seems to think) of *Amsterdam*. She reads a few lines to herself, smiles and asks if these are John Major's finest.

'No', I say. 'He said he would never let his own be published in his lifetime. After his death they will go to Churchill College, Cambridge, with the rest of his papers. They will sit beside the Thatcher archive of which, in one sense, they are part.'

These ones are Ronnie's and mine. One lunchtime at The Old Rose, we just imagined what they might be like.

'Should I read them out aloud?'

She does, with an Essex accent and youthful vigour. My co-author, if he were still alive, would have tried to coach away some of her vowels but would otherwise have been pleased. Each poem is on a separate page and there is a rustling and crackling between them.

Sir Ronald wrote most of her speeches.
He was one of the stickiest leeches,
Who anyone saw
In her underwear drawer,
As cool as a boy stealing peaches.

Woodrow Wyatt is all of a flatter,
He'll natter and natter and natter,
He doesn't much like me,
He'd happily spike me.
I'd rather be friends with a ratter.

The best of those bastards was Frank.
He said I'd be good in a bank. A bank?
And he in a college,
With people of knowledge,
Where people like me stank and sank.

Mr Hart says he'd like his new name,
The one Margaret promised (that Dame!)
But a Baron or Knight does not sound quite right
For a smooth, oily bastard who smears me in spite
And an ally whom no one will claim.

On the Wednesday which some call a black one
And others refer to as white,
They say that a ghost speaking Sechuan
Would have out-performed me in the fright,
That I went back to bed
And chewed pillows instead,
As the pound shrank away in the night.

'Do you have any more?', she asks, standing up on her shoes as though she is about to dance.

28.8.14

This is a day of deep noise and dust from the cranes and wrecking balls. Down the cobbled street where H, T, L and J once walked are the new pink and blue doors of small businesses, Baguette Kitchen, Fake Sea Recordings and High Heels Low Life. Past these and then around the corner to the tables where the Senecans used to meet, the scene is of contrasting quiet.

Far away beyond the chemical lawn and the chess board in the sky there is only a dusty neglect. No fire hoses play on the barricaded facade of The Old Rose this morning. There is no longer even a trace of the nearby night club whose name I forget, nor the fish-and-chip shop I never visited. The wreckers and removers have already paid their visit, leaving nothing but dandelions and a brown field of grass, discarded traffic cones and white plastic chairs.

'Brownfield' is in part a technical term here, a developer's word for land that has been built upon before and can be built upon again without agitating defenders of 'green fields'. During the construction of a new supermarket, the fish-and-chip shop, nightclub, pub and a Babe Ruth's baseball restaurant were found to have sat above much that had been 'built on before'. Not only were there previous 'restaurants and associated leisure facilities' from the 1890s and 1980s but also from around two thousand years ago. To take a flight of fancy, Petronius himself might have arbitrated the elegance of the decor and deemed it charmingly provincial. Seneca could have taken lunch here.

Although none of us knew this in 1987, around the site of our impromptu Latin school there was all the time a Roman sports bar, for bathing, eating, drinking and swapping philosophies. Beneath the frying pans for fish and chicken nuggets the diggers found a site dating from the first to the fourth centuries, ovens and geysers, possibly a tower for observing unwanted guests, more remains of these earlier eateries than ours had left, amphorae for wine, broken glasses, hairpins, combs, earrings, a place for patching up one's make-up, leather shorts, nail clippings, wheat, bones of pork, lamb, and chicken (mostly chicken), not quite what Trimalchio would have offered but good evidence of good times.

I must not be too fanciful, tempted by the shock of this though I am. Seneca would not have visited there himself. The leader of our club was an asthmatic. North was his wrong direction. Phlegm fell heavy on his lungs. In his youth he swam in cold waters as cold as the Thames. There was a medical fashion for that but in most of his life he abhorred all fashion, perfume, bath oils and foreign fashions in particular.

Seneca would also have been nervous for his safety in London, reasonably so, even more than in Rome. His personal reputation around these parts was poor, a result of some allegedly ruthless banking practices, a sudden decision to call in his British loans, maybe through inside knowledge of Nero's plans to abandon our unprofitable island. This was one of the causes, his enemies claimed, of Boadicea's revolt. His first attempt to resign from the court followed quickly afterwards.

Then, maybe, Seneca was the saviour of Roman Britain. Once London had been reduced by the Iceni queen to a layer of blood and ash there was no prospect of withdrawal. Honour would not have allowed it. So, while Seneca survived in a weakened state, the life of occupation continued here more strongly, northwards as far as Hadrian's Wall, with soldiers and sellers of goods from far afield, reading Latin (more poetry than prose), eating, drinking and taking the waters.

Probably some of Seneca's books, at least, were read where we used to discuss them, papyrus rolls and pamphlet bestsellers of their time. Many olive oil jars came from his home fields of Cordoba. Some of them survived to be discovered, slumped beside the coins that paid the bills and much graffiti of abuse, complaint and praise, everything that is now neatly set out in a report entitled 'A Roman Settlement and Bath House at Shadwell. Excavations at Tobacco Dock and Babe Ruth Restaurant, the Highway, London, by Pre-Construct Archaeology Ltd (2011)'.

29. 8.14

'We began with David Hart. You wrote most in your letters about David Hart. Let's end with him too. Let's end when he ended.'

Miss R is sitting on my empty desk. Next week I am going at last to Cordoba.

'David was the last Senecan to die, in 2012, some fifteen years after Ronnie and Woodrow, six years after Frank. He died well by any Stoic standard. He died by changing in ways that put politics and plots into proper proportion, gradually losing the uses of his limbs, one by one, piece by piece, progressively, as his doctors told him.'

'I particularly remember that P-word. It would always raise a smile – at least for as long as he was able to smile. David smiled at anything suggesting that any bit of him was "progressive". He was sceptical of all progress, cheerfully calling Seneca to his support.'

'Motor Neurone Disease?' Miss R gives a look of questioning distaste.

'It does not destroy everything, only voluntary muscles, fingers and thumbs the first, the tongue the worst. His sexual drive, he insisted, being involuntary, was undimmed. He flew his helicopter much longer that he was safe to fly it. He drank claret through a straw and employed an attentive nurse.'

'In dying he did become a rather different man. With a disease challenging his every certainty about what he was, what any man is, he did become more progressive, certainly more of an optimist – about ideas and cures and even, to his and my surprise, about the new Labour Party. In his final years he became part of a new story, one that was lighter, more comic, less Senecan, not Senecan at all.'

'This move had been looming for some time. Even back in 1997, when Ronnie and Woodrow were still alive and grumbling and grousing against New Labour, David decided that Margaret Thatcher was right about Britain being "safe with Blair". He was delighted, before the election, when I first told him of her whispered message to me at that Reform Club dinner for his old friend, Charles Douglas-Home.'

'He was thrilled at the polling day headline in the *Sun*, WHO BLAIRS WINS, a reminder that not everyone mocked his obsession with the SAS. He boasted that Seneca had adapted the line from Virgil. The slogan may not have worked for Michael Portillo but it was perfect for the man whom Margaret Thatcher had endorsed as her true successor.'

'Britain, David suddenly declared, was assuredly safe in Tony's hands. Saddam Hussein and other threats to Western interests were the ones who would soon not be safe. All was well. It began to matter to him rather less now who was leader of the Conservative Party.'

Miss R seems unsure whether this is part of her research period or not. 'When did he first feel his disease, first see it? When did his disease begin?'

I am keen to be gone. I am thinking of Seneca now. In a wasted life, death begins sooner. In a fulfilled and virtuous life, death begins closer to the grave.

'I don't know precisely', I reply.

She shakes her head.

'The last occasion that I clearly remember David holding a knife and fork was outside The Red Lion on Whitehall on July 30, 1997. I have that date in my diary. For a year or two afterwards I hardly saw him at all.'

She writes down the words 'knife and fork' and scowls when I read them back to her.

'Yes, the cutlery was stainless steel, dishwasher-approved, common stuff, recorded in my diary alongside the date, written down at the time even before I knew about the start of his long dying. David did not normally eat outside public houses, nor even in them, not even in our Old Rose or in those close to the centre of power – and none in London is closer than The Red Lion.'

'He was on that night holding gingerly the tools with which other people ate. He was forcing the knife blade into the prongs, looking quizzically at a glass of pale wine. Perhaps he already sensed he had a problem. Perhaps he did not.'

'More important then, he was there in the right place to mark the end of the Tory courts of Downing Street and the ascendancy of New Labour. Farewell to Seneca, farewell to the classics. Hail the New Romantics. If any event signalled that shift it was the one he had come to The Red Lion to observe. He could only observe it through me but that was fine.'

'David would once have mocked what he was waiting then to witness, what he was prepared to wait outside a Whitehall pub to witness at one remove from the reality. But David was adapting enthusiastically to the new political age.'

'Earlier in the afternoon he had confirmed that I was going to the "Cool Britannia" party and asked when I thought I would leave. He had placed himself with his knife and fork so that he saw me as soon as I emerged from the Downing Street gates and could usher me into his illegally attendant

Tony Blair and Noel Gallagher, the author in centre

car. He was waiting because he said he had news. But he wanted to be the first to know the news from me.'

'The party given by Tony Blair to mark the difference between his own premiership and that of John Major, was not a small event but neither was it one to which David was invited, or could have expected to be. I was still Editor of *The Times* and would be there for another five years. He was only beginning to work on his links to New Labour, identifying a confidant with close access to the Prime Minister and a keen interest in arms trading and Machiavelli. If he was to learn what happened when Tony Blair and the rock stars closed the chapter on "thirteen years of Tory misrule", he had to put up with second best.'

His questioning that night was peculiarly insistent. I wondered why he needed to know so much gossip so quickly. He was impatient that there were so many stars whose names I hardly knew. He recalled sourly an election party at his London flat when I had sat next to Eric Clapton, an enthusiastic Thatcherite then, without immediately recognising "the guitar god" on his couch.'

'It is possible that he already sensed the waste within his limbs that would come to make cutlery useless and wine accessible only through a tube. More likely he needed to pretend to someone else, some paymaster or client, that he still stood on the inside track of power, that whatsoever king might reign he was still the same wise courtier.'

'I did everything that I could. I started for him at the beginning.'

Miss R smiles approval.

'The first three letters that I heard at the party were an explosive P, a hissing S and an F, which sounded as though several more Fs might soon follow it. This was not the kind of missing letter game that Ronnie used to play with Margaret. These were no quotes from Alexander Pope, no questions about which courtiers' names could be written without a P, an S and an F.'

'These letters were simpler than that. My Downing Street welcome was "piss off". Since Noel Gallagher, the then famed profaner from Oasis was at least ten yards away, and talking to the Prime Minister, the words could only have come from the then not-yet-famed new chief of Downing Street, Alastair Campbell.'

Miss R looks surprised at the idea that there was ever a time when Alastair Campbell was 'not yet famed'. His story is better entrenched in her personal history than anything bar the Poll Tax.

'David laughed. He tried hard not to look surprised. He never wanted to show any shock at a fact. It was central to his sense of himself that he knew the facts. In 2014 it is a TV cliché that the new wise men of New Labour communicated by pisses, fucks and cuntings but in the summer of 1997 this was a glamorous secret. Alastair Campbell himself, soon to be the senior courtier in Tony Blair's court, was still best known, even affectionately, as a mere former journalist, reformed alcoholic and one-time contributor to the erotic positions of *Forum* magazine.'

'The Campbell anger – and the language that came from it – had not yet transformed its owner's reputation. Rule by rage was rare in the Tory era. Senecan standards applied even where Seneca was unknown. Wobbly Thursday was an exception. That was why it brought such grief.'

'When John Major described Michael Portillo and other Tory rivals as "bastards" he was speaking when he thought that no one else could hear. When a drink-fuelled Tory patrician called a rebel from his own side "a cunt" he was at least talking to me and not to the man himself. Ronnie and Woodrow did not agree on much but both disapproved of Major's very private threat to "fucking crucify the Right", Ronnie because he thought he should not say it, Woodrow because he knew he could not do it.'

'Campbell, however, was different. Anyone whom he told to piss off was grateful not to have been cunted instead. And he did not care who knew. This was the sort of detail that David very much wanted to know.'

'I was not too shocked myself. This choice of welcome was already almost familiar. Relations between Campbell and *The Times* were poor. Most of my first meetings with Tony Blair at Number Ten were taken up with the new leader putting the best possible gloss on his spin-doctoring spokesman. Protector and protected reversed their roles. Each time, just as Blair reassured me that some Campbellite abuse had been mere "over-excitement at the wonderful new challenges ahead of us", Campbell himself would storm into the room with some new printed outrage in *The Times*. "I'm trying to defend you", said Blair, "and shouldn't it be the other way round and aren't you rather undermining my case?"'

'David asked if Alastair wasn't "just a bit over-excited", making a slow note on a pad with a gold pencil and, as almost always, trying to give a fellow courtier the benefit of any doubt.

I replied that he was calm as milk. On this Cool Britannia night, when the Blairs had asked every fashionable guitarist and fashion icon over for a thank you drink in their new home, it was the Prime Minister who was over-excited. All that Campbell was doing was dealing a little light abuse to an editor who had used the words "obscene" and "photo-opportunity" too closely together.'

'David now looked disbelieving: "You didn't say that?" No, it was a learned friend who was standing beside me. He was saying that only Lord Byron could have described properly such a crazy scene.'

'Lord Byron? What did bloody Byron have to do with it? David disliked what he knew of the author of *Don Juan*'.

'What scene? Who was there? Who was talking to whom? Was Gordon Brown there? The questions came tumbling from his tongue. I don't recall any slurring then but David was never a good interrogator. He was fascinated by tags and other tradecraft. He admired the rougher ends of the security services. He would not have been much use to them.'

'He made me impatient too. I was the journalist. He said he had news for me. He was supposed to be my source. I was not supposed to be his source and yet, at certain moments, that was exactly what he wanted me to be, an exchanger of gifts and services in the oldest way honoured by time. I suddenly could not even remember if Gordon Brown had been there. I was not going to go back to find out.'

'As my learned fellow guest predicted, the Cool Britannia celebration was an eloquent mixture of sycophancy, sleaze and celebs. There was indeed a Byronic cast of every "Jack Jargon", "Miss Bombazeen" and "Dick Dubious". Where were Byron's "sophists, bards, statesmen, all unquiet things"? In short supply. At the mention of statesmen David looked at me fiercely. He liked to appear as a man of literature but he needed to choose territory that he had traversed before.'

'Byron was not his territory. He had not prepared for Byron. He had not asked a friendly tutor. Nor did poetry interest his clients. The volume of the car radio rose as though to mask my coming (and much hoped for) indiscretions from anyone listening in.'

'Sad to say, I repeated, there were not many statesmen in the room at all, unless we counted the oil paintings (Addington and Peel, meet Mr Adman and Miss Pullstringer). From wall to wall there were challengers only to be Byron's "young bard, Rockrhyme, who had newly come out and glimmered as a six week's star".'

'There were also contenders for other parts, "Lord Pyrrho too, the great freethinker; and Sir John Pottledeep, the mighty drinker'. Drinks for lesser guests were less lavishly supplied.'

'David sighed. Did you speak to Blair himself? What did he say? He spoke about the party, I replied. No, not the Labour Party. "These people who are big in the rock world, they really understand what's going on in this country": that was the first thing that the new Prime Minister said to me. "Take Mick Hucknall of Simply Red, he has an amazingly sharp mind. And Mick Jagger. I went to talk to him the other night about Brown Sugar and there he was, asking me about Monetary Union".'

'"Blair wasn't talking to Noel Gallagher about Monetary Union?", David asked with as blank a face as he could make. Oh no, I said. Blair said only that "he's very switched on to everything, if you know what I mean".'

'David closed his notebook and turned down the radio. I

quickly told him the rest of what I could remember, how, once the Prime Minister had left the Oasis star, no one else wanted to take up the celebrity challenge. The more house-trained half of Oasis was on his own, abandoned to look at the carpet and the curtains. "My mum is going to ask me what it's like inside", he growled as a group of political reporters passed by, "and it'll be terrible if I don't know the answers".'

'This neglect seemed odd. Noel Gallagher was charming, much less liable to cunt a man than was Alastair Campbell. New Labour theorists admired him. He wore the Union Jack on stage, reclaiming a symbol that in the Thatcher era had been hijacked by the fringes of the Right, some of them David's friends, all of them unhealthily attached to the Red, White and Blue. Blair's men wanted the flag back.'

'Someone eventually brought over the young-looking, blondish but not very Oasis-like chief executive of Barclays Bank, who was being wooed to help Gordon Brown remodel the social security system. "I'm with the Nat West", said Gallagher rather more brightly, "but, hey Meg", he turned to his wife, "you're with Barclays or is that your mum?" Before we could find the answer, or watch a rocker's introduction to a closely hovering Bishop of London, Campbell came by and whisked off his trophy for a Downing Street tour.'

'Even in those early New Labour days the non-celebrity discussion was about how Gordon Brown of Number Eleven would get along with the Blairites of Number Ten who already saw him as an invasive disease. The two top men in New Labour were already like student flatmates who had planned to go on sharing accommodation while working in London but were minute-by-minute having second thoughts.

'That was what David wanted to know about most. Did Campbell seem frightened of Brown? Was everyone frightened of Campbell? Did the Downing Street tour include what had been the bedroom of John Major? Were there jokes about chewed pillows? Were the curtains still purple?'

'I had seen the bedroom. I did not remember any jokes. Everything seemed quite imperial, I said, uncertain about what the precise colour had been, a bit like the columns of The Old Rose. David looked pleased. He liked things imperial. He just needed to be inside the court if he could.'

I said I had spoken to my sometime friend, the Labour lobbyist Jenny Jeger, the J in the GJW partnership, a reminder of my first years as a newspaper reporter. We had not spoken for a decade at least. What had happened to G, the Scottish Liberal? He was fine: his wife, she thought, preferred his gillie, some kind of aquatic gamekeeper, "very D. H. Lawrence". And to W, the Heathman Tory? He was fine too, still collecting art and lost causes.'

I did not ask J how she was herself. She was too obviously not well, half the weight of when we first spoke of party finance scandals in 1981. I was just about to take her aside, past a gaggle of Brownites, when we were interrupted by two gangster-like men who said they were shoe-designers.'

'We looked down at their shoes, each in an identical pair, black, boat-like with raised seams that reminded me of the limits of what was allowed at school. "Not ours", they said in unison, as though the question needed no posing; "Gucci". Jenny, weakened by cancer though she was, had a stick and pushed off rapidly, with more speed than I could match, into a throng of Pet Shop Boys, TV chefs and an especially thick crowd around the man who plays the Blackadder fool at the Tudor court.

David was not interested in Jenny Jeger, nor in her aunt, the sometime Labour MP for Camden. J did not have long to live and was already part of that most distant recent past. David's boredom reminded him that he had left his tweed cap in The Red Lion and he ordered the car back to where we had begun.

David Hart

The cap was inside on a ledge, set up like a dinner plate, with a knife and fork on either side, by a drinker making a joke.'

Miss R asks if she can take a break. She does not normally ask. We walk together around the rest of the disintegrating office. She seems as though she wants to speak. Instead she sweats. She visits the bathroom. When she returns she is less comfortable still. I wait, take a deep breath, and wait again. She waves me to go on. I am not sure what to say.

30.8.14
Almost everyone around me, it seems, has reached some sort of end. We are over sixty, those of us who started work

when Old Labour was dying, who survived (and even prospered) with Mrs Thatcher and who welcomed (briefly) Tony Blair as the next generation's choice. We have been lucky in life, many of us very lucky.

Mr V, who must be in his late eighties now, repeats that theme often in his notes. He has never known anyone more fortunate than the boy whom he introduced to the retirement of Seneca. He often asks about Margaret – also if 'Josephine is still in her cage', reminding me in bold italics that I once wrote an article about a parrot that was 'the oldest bird in the zoo'. It was one of my 'better pieces'. He has an inexhaustible interest in old parrots.

Josephine was, in fact, not a parrot. She was an Indian hornbill, more than fifty years in captivity, whom I used to visit for encouragement (mine) from time to time. She died in 1998 which was when I wrote about her life, the only obituary of a bird ever to appear in *The Times*. Mr V's multiple congratulations on my gracious treatment of Josephine came with the implicit criticism that for Margaret I could have done better.

V herself only rarely contacts me – and solely to direct criticism at my work, my way of life, and, yes, at least once, my luck. I have tried to reply more often to Mr V but his daughter just comes and goes, mostly goes. When I saw her last she said she had an ex-husband and an adult daughter of her own, very like her but not to look at. She gave little other idea of how lucky she had been herself.

31.8.14

How did Seneca die? Miss R asks her question like an interrogator who is certain she is going to be lied to.

Cordoba is close ahead. I try to look as harshly back.

THE SENECANS

The death of Seneca is not something I can lie about. The story is too famous for its truth to be easily changed. His suicide by suffocation may not be as well known in 2014 AD as it was in 114 AD or 1014 or 1614 or at the beginning of the First World War. But it is still the best known incident in his life. That is what he would have wanted, what every Stoic wanted.

'The call to kill himself was inevitable from the moment he failed to persuade Nero to let him retire. An emperor might demand suicide at any time, deeming it a favour to his friend that he not be strangled by a gaoler's noose, or racked to paraplegia.'

'Imagining all the many ways of death was for a Stoic a way of making none of them matter and banishing the fear of death that was so destructive to life. This was not the sole key to happiness, as some of Seneca's teachers had taught him in his youth. But it was significant for virtue.'

'The purpose of life for a good man was that he should work for the common good, focus on what is present, what is possible; he should grab life but not be surprised when life eludes him; he should always be prepared to leave life.'

'There is no mention in that on my SENECA notebook'. Miss R flicks through her now full book of notes to check that she is not mistaken.

'No, death is not what the self-help industry of today finds helpful.'

'So why did he die?'

'He was caught in a plot to assassinate Nero and replace him with a man called Lucius Calpurnius Piso. Few today remember Piso's name. It hardly matters now. It hardly mattered then, the name of a vain senator who sang popular songs and was hardly better than a mad emperor who performed his own poetry. Every Julio-Claudian was threatened by one or other old buffer called Piso.'

'It was a very poor plot. Piso delayed too long. The assassin's knife did eventually come for Nero, but too late, too predictably, and it was easily brushed aside. Piso delayed because he preferred to be an emperor than a murderer – and thought that he could not be both.'

'The plot was betrayed by its own frailest plotters. Seneca's friend, Epicharis, a woman who was only a minor conspirator, survived the rack, said nothing and hanged herself, an example to the men in that slippery court, wrote Tacitus, and Seneca would have agreed. His nephew Lucan the poet betrayed everyone. Who ever knew whom his brother, Novatus, betrayed? Novatus helped to save St Paul from the Jews but he could not save himself, or anyone else, from Nero.'

'When the time came for the assassination, hardly anyone even noticed. The Emperor was screwing his little eyes to watch the games in the Circus at the time. He barely blinked. The news became known only when the revenge began, widening circles in a pool of blood which ended only when there was no one left to kill.'

'Seneca was at the very edges of this pool. That was enough. Some of his friends believed that Seneca would have made a better ruler of the Roman world than Piso or any other replacement. He did not disagree with them. That in itself was more than enough to have him dead.'

'When Seneca first tried to retire from court, the scene that Mr V showed me in the Walton balsa house, Nero preferred to keep his former tutor close. But that was then. Seneca was undeniably a candidate for the throne. Even the guard who brought him his suicide sentence thought so. So the former tutor could hardly blame the former pupil for ordering his death.'

'Seneca's wife was condemned too. She was inevitably a suspect. In the terror of this time a person's innocence was the least of defences. Seneca's difficulty was the simple difficulty of dying, his fleshless wrists from which no blood flowed, his scrawny ankles, his stomach that could not absorb the hemlock of Socrates, the death that his reputation demanded – and would eventually bring him to their shared portrait bust.'

'It seemed that his wife would die more easily, more quickly. She would share his eternal glory. He was pleased. He was also wrong. He died thinking that he and his wife were dying together. Nero's guards were watching them both as they slit their wrists and lay back for death to take them away. But his wife did not die. Nero changed his orders. He tempted Pompeia Paulina with life. The guards tied tourniquets. The Emperor's reputation might be improved if he allowed a few more years to the loyal spouse of his tutor.'

'Pompeia retires and becomes a celebrity widow. The historian, Tacitus, disapproved. Pompeia became for him a possessor of mere fame who might, like her husband, have had a greater glory. Tacitus was Seneca's supporter. Like the writer for Foyles, he saw Seneca as a good man who tried to make the worst a little better. There was another more hostile historian, Cassius Dio, who took the modern view that a man's death as a martyr cannot expunge a life of flattery and collaboration.'

'It was three more years before a new plot succeeded where Piso's (if you could really call it his) had failed. The Spanish legions led the revolt. Some of the revolution came from Cordoba. Nero died deploring the death of so great an artist as himself. In 69 AD there were four different emperors. Throughout the east Nero remained long a ghost in power over the superstitious, just as Ronnie so often reminded me. Was he really dead? Many were unsure.'

'That is the story of how Seneca died.'

There is suddenly a coldness in this emptying office. Miss

R's gaze reminds me now of the day she first arrived. She has listened enough. But she is still waiting for the answer that she wants. She says her mother told her a different story.

'How did you first see him die?'

I pause. She asks again. I remember how in interviews we used to seek the 'killer question'. Miss R looks like a reporter who has found it.

'Do you remember your very last visit to Walton-on-the-Naze?'

She twists her fingers. She arches her back against the empty bookcases. She does not say that I should show her a different kind of remembering but that is what she means. Five months ago it would have been hard to make the jump in time but now it is easier. Seneca and the Senecans are now almost as one, layer upon layers in these last dying Wapping days.

'Yes', I say.

I answer easily, much more easily than I would have expected. I know what she wants. I don't know how she knows.

'It was on the fourth visit that V and I made to her father. To each of these trips I always gave a number; and the number has stuck. Mr V looked even paler than he had been on visits one, two and three, barely separate from the balsa model landscape around him. In my peppered-grey eleven-year-old's uniform (my story for my mother was that I had Sunday work at school) I felt almost flamboyant.'

'V, as before, left me alone with her father almost as soon as we arrived. She had things to buy, food for our lunch, a gift from her mother. Mr V did not mind. He set off on a tour of balsa Rome in full tutorial flow: Seneca was a hero, a man who tried to order his world: ageing Prime Minister Harold Macmillan was a villain, a man of disintegration; the old Tory way was collapsing from within; socialism was coming like effluent on the tide; trade unions were worse than guitarists. Mr V shouted out the case for his balsa philosopher, that human excesses were the only enemy, virtue the only good, self-restraint the route to freedom, anger against the powerful a dangerous necessity.'

'Of course, I knew nothing of any of this then. I recognised rage but not mania. I grasped none of Seneca's influence on my balsa-carver. I learnt that only later from his letters, from that pile of them now tumbling onto this floor, from their favourite themes of how poverty is as potent as wealth, death as life, and that most of the things that men prize, freedom, food, property, sex and drink are secondary things.'

'This favourite villa, he said, pointing with a knife at the edge of the pale table, was always kept in perfect order. It was where Seneca wanted to go when he knew that Nero was tired of his teacher, tired of philosophy, tired of being ordered, maybe worse than tired.'

'And then Mr V recited the retirement scene, just as he had done before, just as if he were reading a playscript. Perhaps there was a chance that his hero might be safe. The crumpled Seneca was an owner of at least five villas, places where he might hide.'

'I must have looked ever more uncomprehending. At this time I had merely unfulfilled ambitions to learn Latin and Roman history. I had my *Incipe* school cap but nothing much more. "Begin", said my badge but I had not yet begun.'

'Then, suddenly, outside in the porch, there was the sound of a falling flowerpot, a crack and the clumping of earth. A key grated in the lock. V was back.'

'I turned for a second towards the door, paused, smiled and swung back to see Mr V, white-eyed, white-dressed, pointing his wood knife into the middle of his balsa model. There was no warning – unless his lecture had been a warning',

'He began with the palace, slicing the columns, cutting the chest in two, picking out the book boxes as though they were food between teeth, slashing at the roof, pushing his fist through five walls at a time, bathrooms, bedrooms, book rooms, stamping on the miniature Emperor and leaving his miniature tutor alone and intact, as though after an earthquake.'

'From central Rome to suburban villa, from 62 to 65 AD, from attempted retirement to attempting death, was a journey of seconds. He pointed to the bath house, to the balsa philosopher and soldiers, the supervisors of suicide thick set and erect, the victim bent, his wife lying on a narrow bed. He slashed and sliced. There was no blood of his or mine (he was skilled with his knife) but it felt as though there was everywhere blood.'

'V seemed barely even surprised. She quietly took my hand (the first time she ever took my hand) and led me away. As we walked out towards the bus stop, she realised that she was still carrying the present to Mr V from her mother. She stopped, turned and took it back to the porch where she left it like an offering at a plague house.'

'I know', says Miss R.

'You know what?' I want to go on but she stops me.

'I knew the answer before you began. It's the one question I've asked you whose answer I already knew. My mother did not tell me much of your childhood but she did tell me that. She is like you in one way, only one way really. She remembers detail well.'

'In fact', she makes a thin-lipped smile, 'I know more than you've told me. I know that a bus arrived quickly that day, that for the first hour of the journey home you sat together in silence, and that, after an hour, when you were almost back on the Rothmans estate, she apologised about the knife.'

Miss R has lost all her smile. She is breathing hard.

'I would like to have heard that apology myself', she says. 'I have never heard my mother say sorry for anything.'

'When you arrived, before you went to your separate houses, V then told you why her father stayed inside with his models and his parrot. He was afraid of what he might do with his knife if he were out.'

'He was right to be afraid but he was lucky too. He never hurt anyone. He stayed with history. Seneca's was the first of many death scenes in that house by the sea. Nero would be one day followed by Thatcher. I don't think my grandfather will be there much longer.'

She puts a finger to her lips. 'Yes, now you know.'

She watches for a reaction but does not wait for one.

'Listen.'

She makes the word a single syllable.

'I'm listening.'

'So, yes. My own first sight of what we call politics was the same as yours. When I was young Seneca was almost a member of the family, malign for my mother and me, magic in so many ways to the man you call Mr V.'

'Yes, I could have told you that in my first letter. But we had never met. It was hard to make a man and his Seneca sound serious, although they certainly were serious. You know that.'

'I could have explained more about why I wanted to come. Your four men for Margaret Thatcher was a subject waiting at work to be chosen, an opportunity to understand our past as you had done. Thanks to some of Sir Ronald's friends and a few of Mr Hart's, I already knew a bit about the Latin lessons.'

'I could have written much more in my letter about what happened back in Essex since you left, what was still happening to all the Vs as you have always called us. I could have asked for a family favour, some help for me in my job. Many people do that. But I wasn't sure you would want to do a favour for V or her daughter.'

'You might have done a favour for Mr V. I've thought about that while we have been talking, or rather why you have been talking. Yes, I did find you at a good time. And listening was all that I wanted to do until just now.'

'You and your Mr V are on the same side. It sounds strange but you are. You don't have the rage. My mother says she has never seen or heard of you being angry. But there is much you seriously share. My grandfather built frail models of the past in balsa. You do what he did but in words. There is less difference than you think.'

I want to protest, or at least to suggest or qualify, but my mouth is dry and she continues before I can say anything.

'You and I are on different sides. My mother says that you first learnt about Left and Right at her house, that you and she used to talk about that in our box-room of books.

'Left and Right are not as clear words as once they were. They are not the only words to divide the world. I know that. They are not the only ways to define how we think but they are still very useful words. My mother and I look one way; you and our Mr V look the other. You always knew that about her. Now you know the same about me.'

'You have spent most of your life just looking, not doing. Lucky for you, I think, now that I know a bit more about where you've been. I've learnt a lot from the Senecans but I don't want a new breed of them. Do you?'

She rises, smooths her skirt, carefully avoids the paper piles, repeats the movements of her very first arrival and heads for the door. 'Not much has changed between us and you in fifty years. We are where we were.'

With a swing of white plastic she is gone.

September

Quintus Metellus Pius was so anxious for his deeds to be praised that he consulted poets from Cordoba – even though their Latin came with a foreign accent

—CICERO *In defence of Archias,* 62 BC

Puente Romano, Cordoba

26.9.14

After three weeks beside the bridge over the Guadalquivir it is time now to go back to the Thames, to colder sky and a plant that will be no longer dying but dead, its power to make memory gone. My last sight through my window was of new machines arriving to replace the wrecking cranes, mobile cement factories, corkscrews two-storeys high. That will be someone else's sight when I return.

Here in Seneca's birthplace the destruction of brick and stone goes more slowly. The Cordobans ground grand marble into lime for centuries after the Romans left. Much of the very finest art in a city of fine arts was lost. The better the statue the better the cement it made, or so the builders believed, and modern builders say that they were right.

The evening air is warm. The light is grey and golden. I have watched with tourist eyes. I know the skyline better than I knew my old view back home. I can name the minarets. The walls of mosques and monasteries crumble into soft low clouds over this slow, beery river that the Romans called the Baetis, its banks today silver with the sheen of birch.

Out in the flat stream there are flat-bottomed barges like the one that two thousand years ago brought olive oil and elephant bones to the baths beside The Old Rose. In a modest contribution to progress workmen spread steaming tarmac over cobbled stones.

After five months of 'first times', it is time for a few now of 'the last'.

Mr V is dead. His daughter wrote a note to the *TLS* that arrived here yesterday. She asked if I had enjoyed my last months at Wapping. She thanked me for helping her daughter. She was pleased to hear that I was so well. She hoped that the youngest V had been well behaved and had not dressed too strangely.

The letter described how a white-dressed body was found by a man delivering a parrot. The owner of the petshop was the only holder of Mr V's keys. There was a half-completed balsa wood castle in the house, maybe the Tower of London, a large cage and a letter saying that the new bird should be 'ideally white like Old George'. All of that should be buried with their owner but probably will not be.

Her daughter was not a deceiver. V was anxious that I should not think that. She was a good daughter, better than her mother, similar in views, smarter at work, inclined to easy assumptions but then she was still young. Even her grandfather became proud of her by the time he died, despairing of her politics, proud of her job, just as he had been proud of his birds and balsa.

Perhaps he was. I somehow doubt it but *nil nisi bonum de mortuis*. Whatever Mr V thought of Miss R, I am as grateful to them both as to the tumbling walls of Wapping. There is much that I would not have remembered and written on my own.

Finally, the last of the 'last times'.

I am pleased that none of the Senecans was at Margaret Thatcher's 'ceremonial' funeral, that none of them saw her devourers cry 'the Witch is Dead' and her devotees win the war of noise. Little that was said on that soldiers' day recalled the courtiers, the writers, the plotters. On her death certificate she was a Stateswoman Retired.

Woodrow was already long dead by then – though not to the angry subjects of his posthumously published *Journals*.

After surviving barely six months of the Blair era he lived on in a livelier art than he had ever shown in life itself. I think of him as dead in the morgue but still dictating. He kept his racecourse pass at the Tote because Margaret Thatcher renewed his chairmanship as one of her final acts in office. He kept his column in *The Times* almost to the end.

Remembering him has made me think more about Beryl Bainbridge. She died in 2010. I will read *Winter Garden* again. Colin Haycraft died before her in 1994, leaving rumours of their relationship that confirmed Woodrow's worst suspicions. When I get home I will see whether Duckworth, now owned by the no less legendary Peter Mayer, might be publisher of *The Senecans*.

I am also going to buy one of Beryl's oil paintings from the 1960s. I have seen it in a gallery, a picture of two children on a broken, sloping sofa in a yellow room, a peculiar reminder of the house in Walton-on-the-Naze where I first saw Seneca fifty years ago. Perhaps we could use it in the book.

Wapping said goodbye last week with rumbling and the wreckers' roar. Cordoba has been whispering its welcome. Welcome, or so I hear this city say, to the man in the pink cotton jacket, welcome from the birds of the abandoned water mill, the pigeons in the niches cut for saints, Cordoba's clouds of inland gulls, its canaries in cages, its parakeets, too small for the taste of Mr V, in multi-coloured packs in its autumn trees.

The most popular attraction here is a great mosque of columns and gardens, the Mezquita, a forest within walls, a survivor from the ninth century when this city was the most prosperous in Europe, an Islamic university reviving Aristotle and Cicero, Seneca and Plato, passing the best of antiquity to modern minds. Its most peculiar attraction is inside it, an opulent Catholic Cathedral: the two together would have made a perfect balsa subject for Mr V.

We said goodbye to Ronnie in June 1998, only six months after Woodrow. Margaret Thatcher and John Major, both by then former prime ministers, each avoiding the other's eyes, listened to a young boy reading John Masefield's *Sea Fever* in the actors' church in Covent Garden. Sir Ronald Millar had only a short naval career between Seneca at King's and Hollywood with the stars but he was proud of his ships. 'I must go down to the sea again' he would recite sometimes when his Tory masters were madder than he could bear.

A photographer asked for a picture of the two together. John Major readily agreed but it took only the most direct request from me for her to join him, her eyes staring skywards as though seeking redemption. Afterwards at the Savoy, Ronnie's spirit flittered disapprovingly while his two clients avoided each other, both of them staying on for hours, Sir John chatting to the theatrical antiquities, Lady Thatcher to survivors of her court. 'I'm piling up my cannonballs', she said with a narrowing of her eyes and a pause: 'for when they are needed, really needed'.

Against whom? Her successor was by then as much a part of history as she. Against New Labour? It did not yet seem so. We could only guess. And then she too began to recite *Sea Fever*, 'and all I need is a tall ship and a star to steer her by', warmly, gently, just as Ronnie always tried to see her.

Frank never published his diary. His cancer crept up before he could. We said goodbye to him at the RAF church in the Strand. No one ever suggested that this was for reasons of military yearnings, merely that it was close to where he was born and showed something of how far he had come. In death David gave him the name 'Franco', a designation that he would never have dared while Frank was alive.

Our very last argument was, like all our best arguments, about journalism not politics, about who did what to whom at *The Times*, perversely and specifically about that England football manager, Glenn Hoddle, who in an interview said that those who were disabled were paying for sins committed in their past lives. To Tony Blair (who called successfully for Hoddle's dismissal) and the spirit of the Blair age this was an affront to decency and reason. To Frank it was merely an expression of a belief, freely expressed and held for centuries.

The behaviour of *The Times* in helping Hoddle out of his job, he said, was as bad as in the Parkinson Affair and in so many others since. In fact, I replied, in those two words that always annoyed him, the Hoddle story would have been 'out' whether and however I had published it. Editors do have powers but not all the powers that Frank liked to think.

And so we went on, petulant, pushing and shoving to the end. So much so that, while I was with his admirers in the RAF pews, I was thinking not of his mind or wit but of the transmigration of footballers' souls, his support of an unfashionable strand of ancient philosophy. There were writers, classicists and historians in the pews as well as politicians. Seneca would have felt fully at home as a Senecan departed. A famous opera singer sang.

The Old Rose still stands on the Highway, its bar closed, its columns bleached violet and pink, its windows boarded, its cellars awaiting the further attention of archaeologists. In Cordoba too there are minor Roman remains and more being found. Some of the Mezquita's lower stones were cut in the lives of Claudius and Nero; so too some of those in the arches of the Puente Romano, the Roman bridge that stands here over dry stones and shallow pools, waiting for the rainy season.

Eleven columns survive from a temple to the imperial family. There are stones from the Forum beneath the floor of the Bar Council. There are no traces of the foreign-sounding flatterers who Cicero tells us once worked here, the poets who make Cordoba the oldest city of letters west of Italy.

I missed David's death after his long time dying. I was in Alexandria at the time. He had hoped to be buried in a mausoleum on his Suffolk estate. There was a planning row which I read about in the *East Anglian Times*. Inside he should have had his D. H. Lawrence, his Petronius, his best set of *The Positions*. I doubt that he was allowed them.

The last time that I saw David at the theatre he was not watching the actors but being acted. He was a character in the play about the Miners' strike that Miss R had heard about in her researches. This 'David Hart' of *Wonderland* was theatrically 'camp', which he would not have liked, and wore a sheepskin flying jacket, which he never did. David would still have been pleased to be remembered.

Up the hill from the bridge there is a modern Roman bath beside the mosaic floor of an ancient Roman house. That is where I have been spending each afternoon. Between paragraphs I have waded, swam and slid from one end of these underground waters to the other, from the hottest spring lit by a low green light, through the warm mist, along the ledges of cold stone, then round and back. The walls are dark. There are small piles of small clothes. Giggles grow from the shadows as though ghosts are laughing and loving their own laughter. There is the rhythmic slap of wave upon wall, the same sound as in the still parts of the Baetis by night.

A hundred yards away Seneca has his own cobbled square close to the temple. Black stones mark the pattern of two trees, one taller than the other, an ancient headless statue and a fountain which he shares with his nephew, Lucan. An inscription salutes their glorious fame, their *incluta fama*. It is popular with writers of graffiti marking the thirty years since the Falklands War. So far it has avoided the tarmac of improvement.

John Major came to Spain last year to open the Avenida de John Major in Candeleda, not too far away, where the plaque is blue and white on a yellow background next to a tobacco fermentation centre and a sports hall. The Spaniards love him because he spent holidays here and because he is not Margaret Thatcher and, even better, not Tony Blair, a 'war criminal' on the walls of Cordoba.

Everywhere John Major's reputation has risen and continues to rise. Journalists love him now. At a public inquiry into bad behaviour by the press he only very gently complained at the deeds done against him in office, several of them done by me. He looked like a pale moon beaming from inner space. Unlike so many others he was not looking for trouble. He did not name names. He looked far fitter than most of the politicians gone by.

Unlike his predecessor he has avoided the House of Lords. By leaving parliament (and accepting a Knighthood of the Garter) Sir John need not any longer see the enemies he called 'the bastards' or the flattering bastards who were his greater enemies. There might be pleasure for him in watching them all decay, but greater pleasure in being free of them, free, not least, to earn as much money as he can without having to justify his business to the scrutiny of peers.

He could be forgiven for laughing all the way to the finance house, as Frank used to say. He began there. He can go back there – and to his poems, maybe some about the Senecans, verses that, until he dies, I can merely, with Ronnie's help, imagine.

By the southwestern gate of the city wall Cordoba's greatest son has a statue in hollow bronze. This one is barely a hundred years old, a study of a strong man, more imperial than philosophical, carrying a text, possibly a play or a poem but more likely a speech. He is standing above a cascade of icy water. He looks down towards the river, to evaporating ancient walls on his left, some sturdy trinket-stores on his right, down over the banks of birches and planes into islands of birds, a sanctuary for herons and sluggish ducks, parrots who have escaped from zoos, geese who have invaded from the olive fields.

Acknowledgements

To Mary Beard, Peter Brookes, Sally Emerson, the estate of Beryl Bainbridge, Jo Evans, Sue Foll, Toby Lichtig, Hazel O'Leary, Ruth Scurr, Sally Soames, Ed Victor, Paul Webb.